ENHANCED GRIEF PEER SUPPORT TRAINING

INTERNATIONAL GRIEF INSTITUTE, LLC
WWW.INTERNATIONALGRIEFINSTITUTE.COM

TEMPLATES

Icarelibrary.com/specialists

PASSWORD: Templates

Certified iCare Specialist Manual – 1st ed.
International Grief Institute, LLC
www.InternationalGriefInstitute.com

Cover Design by AlyBlue Media, LLC
Interior Design by AlyBlue Media LLC
Published by AlyBlue Media, LLC

ISBN: 978-1-950712-41-0
AlyBlue Media, LLC
Ferndale, WA 98248
www.AlyBlueMedia.com

PRINTED IN THE UNITED STATES OF AMERICA

CONTENTS

SECTION ONE
Grief 101

IN THIS SECTION

1. Grief 101
2. Immediate needs of the client
3. Year 1, 2 & beyond
4. Working from a trauma informed perspective
5. Psychological crisis & stress

iCare

CHAPTER 1

GRIEF 101

Grieving doesn't stop when funeral services end.

SHERRY DEE MOBLEY

IN THIS CHAPTER

- ✓ **Grief reactions**
- ✓ **Red flags**
- ✓ **Grief types**
- ✓ **Grief models**

Birth, school, driver license, and college. Many of life's milestones come with preparation and education. Grief, as a whole, is not included. As one of life's most natural events, death and grief have been around since the beginning of mankind, yet many cultures find the topic too uncomfortable to talk about, leaving society ill equipped to help someone in their time of need. This can create a wide rift between mourners and those who want to help but don't know what to say or do.

Because every loss is unique as a fingerprint, this manual is created for educators and advocates who desire to be part of a societal change dedicated to both supporting mourners, and providing future generations with a better understanding of how to help during one of life's most natural events.

A HISTORICAL SNAPSHOT

Prior to the era of funeral homes, families tended to their own losses. The deceased was often laid on the parlor table for visitations followed by a procession to the church and cemetery. Some communities had a small group of women who came in to help with the "laying of the dead."

Funeral homes began operating in the U.S. in the mid-1800s, when funeral directors began to care for the dead. This was a result of the need for embalming practices during the civil war. Men were dying far from home; embalming allowed for their bodies to make the long journey back to be buried near family. Early funeral directors were called undertakers and morticians. The first mortuary school was established in 1882.

A SHIFT IN CARE

By the 1900s, funeral homes became a place for loved ones to be taken care of by morticians. Although families no longer took care of the deceased in their own homes, funeral directors still visited people in their homes and shared a cup of coffee and stories about the loved one. Communities were close-knit and most families used the same funeral home for generations.

Today, when families find themselves sitting at a funeral home's conference table, they look to the funeral home to guide them not just on how to lay their loved one to rest, but to take the first steps forward in the aftermath. Yet many funeral homes provide little aftercare, leaving an opportunity for you as a Certified iCare Specialist to provide families and communities with support and direction.

A CURRENT SNAPSHOT

Grief is a normal reaction to loss, yet complex in that it impacts many areas of one's life in unpredictable ways. Further, because each loss is unique, they're not comparable. There are commonalities between losses, such as two mothers both losing a teenage daughter. But the similarities might end there, for each individual has a unique set of filters. Their childhood experiences, personalities, religious beliefs, cultural differences, and diverse socioeconomic backgrounds all affect one's inner resilience and ability to journey toward reconciliation of the loss. Further, profound, traumatic deaths can create a psychological crisis with long-lasting effects on one's ability to cope and function.

In order to meet the needs of mourners, specialists must have a solid knowledge of how death of a loved one impacts us, and be equipped with tools to execute a program or service that has a positive impact on those served.

Grief reactions

Understanding what constitutes normal reactions is necessary to understand how to provide support. Though the nature and scope of grief differs, common reactions occur in 6 distinct categories.

- ☑ Cognitive
- ☑ Emotional
- ☑ Behavioral
- ☑ Physical
- ☑ Social
- ☑ Spiritual

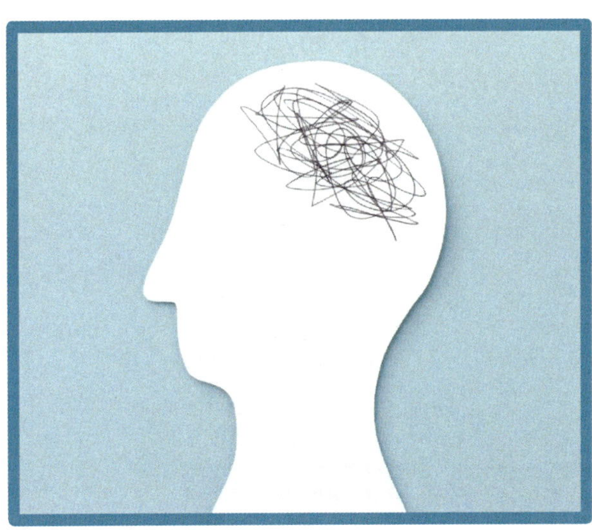

Cognitive affects

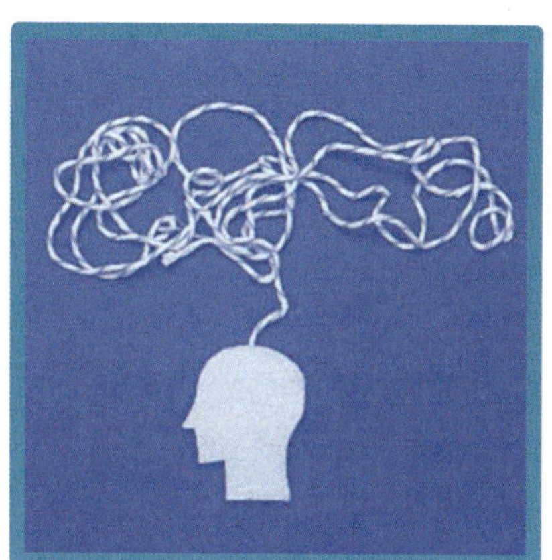

Psychologically, every event is interpreted through a number of filters unique to each person including:

- Physical proximity to the event
- Relational proximity to the event
- History of prior trauma
- Support system
- Personality

Cognitively, grief is a highly distracting process that diverts our emotional bandwidth and creates fears both rational and irrational. During the acute stage of grief, people are in emotional shock and actively trying to process what happened. Lack of sufficient support from the very beginning can overwhelm a person's ability to cope and may result in distress, impairment and dysfunction. Influencing factors also include:

- the extent of exposure to the event
- the amount of support during the loss event and its aftermath
- the amount of personal loss and social disruption

COGNITIVE REACTIONS

NORMAL REACTIONS

- Forgetfulness
- Poor concentration
- Low productivity
- Negative attitude
- Confusion
- Guilt
- Preoccupation with loss event

ABNORMAL REACTIONS

- Suicidal/homicidal ideation
- Paranoid ideation
- Dissociation
- Disabling guilt
- Hallucinations
- Delusions
- Persistent helplessness

Behavioral affects

Humans are naturally social and often have strong familial bonds, which is why most have strong mourning reactions. Raw emotions coupled with cognitive affects often lead to behavioral reactions that can be uncharacteristic for the mourner, yet fall within the range of what's considered normal mourning behavior.

BEHAVIORAL REACTIONS

NORMAL REACTIONS

- 1000-yard stare
- Hyper-startle
- Sleep disturbance
- Crying spells
- Isolation
- Resentment
- Lashing out
- Increased risk-taking
- Distrust
- Withdrawal
- Impulsiveness
- Change in eating

ABNORMAL REACTIONS

- Violence
- Antisocial acts
- Abuse of others
- Long-term diminished personal hygiene
- Self-harm
- Immobility
- Self-medication

Emotional affects

Not all people respond the same way to death of a loved one. The emotional impact depends on a number of factors including inner resilience, personality, childhood experiences, and availability of support through family, friends, and coworkers. Some have more severe, longer lasting reactions.

EMOTIONAL REACTIONS

NORMAL REACTIONS

- Anxiety
- Frustration and/or irritability
- Mood swings
- Temper outbursts
- Nightmares
- Crying spells

ABNORMAL REACTIONS

- Panic attacks
- Immobilizing depression
- PTSD
- Depression
- Impaired functioning
- Infantile emotions

Physical affects

Although societal thinking considers grief an emotional experience, the brain's stress hormones including cortisol, adrenaline and norepinephrine affect the body, too. Short bursts of those hormones are designed to help us survive imminent danger. Ongoing bursts, such as when one is grieving, are hard on the body, and can lead to comorbidities such as compromised immunotherapy, adrenal fatigue, hypertension, and even takotsubo syndrome, also known as stress cardiomyopathy or broken heart syndrome.

It's important for mourners to notify his/her doctor of the death, and engage in medical supervision and care as appropriate.

PHYSICAL REACTIONS

NORMAL REACTIONS

- Change in appetite
- Headaches
- Fatigue
- Insomnia
- Weight change
- Restlessness
- Upset stomach

ABNORMAL REACTIONS

- Chest pain
- Irregular heartbeats
- Recurrent dizziness
- Recurrent headaches
- Collapse/loss of consciousness
- Numbness

IMPORTANT

All evidence of physical dysfunction should be taken seriously and referred to a physician, even if it seems ambiguous.

IMPORTANT

Physical complaints such as chest pain and breathing difficulty require immediate medical attention.

Spiritual affects

Few things can shake one's faith like death of a loved one. For some, faith can deepen as it becomes a safe haven for the sorrow. For others, it can be a source of disappointment when a church isn't equipped to minister in the way the mourner needs. Some mourners feel let down or even find themselves angry at their deity, wondering why their loved one wasn't spared death. Some may even quit attending services. These reactions are not uncommon.

The best way to help a mourner cope with a crisis of faith is to avoid getting caught up in the mourner's anger. Simply hold the space with compassion, and practice attentive listening so the mourner can work through it in their own way and time. More often than not, their faith will come full circle.

SPIRITUAL REACTIONS

NORMAL REACTIONS

- Emptiness
- Loss of meaning
- Doubt
- Unforgiving
- Praying for a magical resurrection
- Loss of direction
- Cynicism
- Extreme or sudden religiosity
- Cessation from practice of faith

ABNORMAL REACTIONS

- Religious hallucinations
- Religious delusions

Social affects

Following death of a loved one, many mourners face an unexpected shift in their social life. Because everyone processes loss in his or her own way, the journey through the aftermath can strain even the closest relationships. Some bonds remain steady, while others falter and even fall away. As the mourner seeks support through grief groups and other outlets, they often form new friendships with those who speak their loss language.

SOCIAL REACTIONS

NORMAL REACTIONS

- Altered friendships
- Changes in workplace
- Altered status
- Role redefinitions
- Loss of motivation
- Loss of perspective
- Goal reorientation

ABNORMAL REACTIONS

- Withdrawal from all social contacts
- Quitting employment
- Total reassociation with antisocial groups
- Running away, disappearing

Red flags

Beyond intense physical complaints, there are 3 reactions that are red flags for immediate evaluation:

- Suicidal thoughts with plan and intent
- Homicidal thoughts with plan and intent
- Hallucinations and/or delusions

It isn't uncommon for vague and fleeting suicidal thoughts to occur following death of a close loved one, but a formal mental health evaluation will help determine the danger level.

IMPORTANT

Any sign or symptom of abnormal reactions warrant referral to the next level of care. Refer whenever in doubt.

Grief types

Just as the grief journey is unique to each of us, there are also numerous types of grief. Below are the most common types you'll encounter as a specialist.

NORMAL GRIEF

A normal reaction to a loss event.

ANTICIPATORY GRIEF

Grieving an anticipated death before it occurs, common when a loved one is dying from a terminal illness.

TRAUMATIC GRIEF

Experiencing a sudden and unexpected loss; common when one has witnessed the actual death event.

CUMULATIVE GRIEF

Experiencing a second loss while still grieving a prior loss. Also known as grief overload.

COMPLICATED GRIEF

An ongoing, heightened state of mourning that is debilitating, and incapacitates on a long-term basis. It's a grief reaction that occurs continually while experiencing extreme distress with no progress towards feeling better and no improvement in day-to-day functioning.

DELAYED GRIEF

Reacting much later to a death due to initial avoidance of the loss and emotional pain.

MASKED GRIEF

A reaction that impairs normal functioning without the individual recognizing that the behaviors are related to the loss. Symptoms are often masked as either physical symptoms or other maladaptive behaviors.

DISENFRANCHISED GRIEF

A rejection of one's mourning by their culture, family, social or work environment. The grief and suffering are disqualified by those around the mourner.

ABSENT GRIEF

Reacting to a major loss by blocking one's feelings as though it never happened. The individual shows no reaction at all and fails to give it importance in his or her life.

Grief models

Over the years, researchers have attempted to create various grief model theories in an effort to help clinicians and practitioners better understand what cognitive, social and emotional challenges their clients commonly experience. Although each model has its own parameters based on theories, it's important to remember that theories are concepts only, and grief remains as unique as a fingerprint.

Below are some of those models and the prongs of their theory.

DUAL PROCESS

DR. MARGARET STROEBE & DR. HENK SCHUT

- Loss orientation
- Restoration orientation

FOUR TASKS OF MOURNING

DR. J. WILLIAM WORDEN

- To accept the reality of the loss
- To work through the pain of grief
- To adjust to life without the deceased
- To maintain a connection to the deceased while moving on with life

FIVE STAGES OF GRIEF

DR. ELISABETH KÜBLER-ROSS

- Denial
- Anger
- Bargaining
- Depression
- Acceptance

SIX R PROCESSES OF MOURNING

DR. THERESE RANDO

- Recognize
- React
- Recollect
- Relinquish
- Readjust
- Reinvest

Summary

- **Grief is a process that can't be immediately fixed.**
  It's natural to want to fix things that are broken, but grief is a process of reconciliation between the head and the heart. Don't feel guilty that you can't ease someone's pain. Holding the space and offering tools from your toolbox is the very best way to provide support and hope that one day it won't always feel this raw.

- **Grief is an emotional wound.**
  The brain can't tell the difference between physical and emotional pain, and the body reacts the same. It takes time to heal from any injury, and some wounds are so deep, they'll leave a lifelong scar. In the early months, it's helpful to think of the mourner as a patient in the ICU of Grief United General, and treat them as you would any other hospital patient: with love, compassion and kindness.

- **Crying is normal.**
  Crying is a healthy response to emotional pain. Suppressed grief leads to complications. As talking and crying go hand in hand, the bereaved need the gift of listening in the coming months.

- **The rollercoaster effect**
  Grief is often compared to a rollercoaster because it contains many emotional twists and blind turns at varying speeds. It is very unpredictable, and can feel very scary. Reassure the mourner that eventually it will slow down and stabilize.

- **Isolation is common.**
  Like a wounded animal in the wild, many mourners find comfort by hibernating away from social interaction. If it is safe to leave him or her alone, it's okay to allow them the space and time to adjust as long as you see s/he is not harming themselves or anyone else.

- **The façade.**
  Many hide grief due to societal or familial pressures to be strong. Appearances can be deceiving, and superficial conversations are not an accurate gage of how a mourner is doing.

- **Grief creates fear.**
  Grief exacerbates or heightens many fears, both irrational and rational. The mourner often fears the future without his/her loved one, fears feeling sad forever, fears losing another loved one, and more. These fears are normal. When the mourner is given a safe space to verbalize his/her fears, they usually lessen with time.

- **Don't take it personally.**
  Reactions often mirror our emotions, and emotional overloads can lead to reactive meltdowns. As an emotional wound, grief is also exhausting, and exhaustion naturally makes us cranky which, in turn, can escalate otherwise small issues. Patience and compassion are key.

- **Timelines don't apply.**
  The bereavement process and timeline are unique to every individual, and some may grieve in subtle ways for the rest of his/her life.

CHAPTER 2

IMMEDIATE NEEDS OF THE CLIENT

We should not waste another day in doing things we'd rather. Instead, we should reach out once more because our families matter.

MARTHA ANDERSON

KEYNOTE

PEER SUPPORT GOAL: Help the mourner feel safe, understood, and empowered to help themselves.

Psychological first aid

Supporting a mourner begins with psychological first aid designed to establish a sense of safety, determine social support, and foster hope. Resilience is our business; our goal is to help mourners stabilize and learn to move forward with their deceased loved one in their heart instead of their arms. This requires clear expectations to help minimize the potential for frustration and clarify roles and boundaries.

- Our role is not to be a therapist. It is to provide support.
- Use an intake questionnaire to help you understand the mourner's living situation and social support.

Power of questions

Listening is a primary goal that allows the mourner to articulate and express emotions, which helps them process their experience. Questions are a powerful way to invite the mourner to express themselves and guide them toward finding their own solutions.

There are multiple types of questions that can help you support the mourner by giving them an opportunity to verbalize their thoughts and emotions. Questions also help you find out the person's opinions, and what his/her needs might be.

- Ask questions that probe, "What if . . . ."
- Ask positive what-if questions that allow for a positive outcome.

BASIC COMMUNICATION TECHNIQUES

Use the following communication techniques when working with a mourner (International Critical Incident Stress Foundation).

TECHNIQUE	PURPOSE	NOTE
SILENCE	To encourage continued uninterrupted speech.	Be careful you don't inadvertently communicate lack of interest.
NONVERBAL CUES	To probe and show interest.	Example: Nodding of the head and facial expressions.
RESTATEMENT	To show you're listening, check for accuracy, to clarify, and to probe.	Be careful you don't inadvertently sound like a mindless parrot. Use restatement to clarify semantic ambiguities.
PARAPHRASING	To show interest, empathy, and probe for further conversation.	Use this instead of restatement.
REFLECTION OF EMOTION	To identify the mourner's feelings based on verbal and/or nonverbal cues.	This helps to express feelings so they don't block problem-solving.
OPEN-END QUESTIONS	To provide maximal response options.	Good to use when you get stuck.
CLOSED-END QUESTIONS	To direct or focus response, and provide structure.	You only learn what you know to ask, so this is a good technique when pursuing a specific target.

QUESTION DOS

KEYNOTE

Maintain confidentiality at all times unless the mourner is in danger. If in danger, we are ethically obligated to report it.

- Start with closed questions to gather facts, then ask open questions to gather understanding.
- Paraphrase what you hear to summarize and avoid confusion.
- Use reframing questions.
  "What can you learn from this?"
- Use focusing questions.
  "What is the first thing you can do?"
- Use expanding questions.
  "What would you do?" This is very useful if a mourner says something is impossible.
- Use open-ended questions.
  "How do you feel about this?"
- Use reflective questions to probe deeper.
  "Why did you say this?"
- Probing questions reveal true motivations or what the mourner truly means, and allows you to go deeper into the conversation. "How does this person make you feel mad?"
  - Use comparisons to help probe. "That's too hard for you, compared to what?"
  - Do question generalizations such as "always" and "never."
  - Assume possibilities. If the mourner says something is impossible, don't let them shut themselves down by asking, "What would happen if you did?"
- Use exploratory questions.
  - "What's the first thing on your mind?"
  - "What worked before?"
  - "What are you leaning toward?"
- Use action questions.
  - "What immediate action can you take?"
  - "What's the next step? When will you do it?"
  - "What are ways to prepare for obstacles?"
  - "What information do you need to achieve this?"

QUESTION DON'TS

- Avoid leading questions.
- Avoid asking questions that imply. "Does that make you frustrated?" Instead say, "How does this make you feel?" Let the mourner come to his/her own conclusion.
- Avoid closed yes/no questions.
- Avoid "why" questions because they have an element of judgement, and imply you're challenging them in a negative way. Instead ask when, how, who, where, or "What makes you think that?"
- Don't argue with the mourner, as they need validation, not judgment.
- Don't minimize what the mourner expresses, even if it isn't the same as what you experienced.

ADDITIONAL QUESTIONS

- It is very normal for people to experience a lot of emotional and physical changes when they are grieving. It takes a lot of energy to adapt to all the changes. Have you notified your doctor that you've lost a loved one?
- How are you feeling physically?
- How are you sleeping?
- How is your appetite?
- What kind of support do you have from friends and family?
- Are there any strong feelings that have been difficult or persistent?
- Have you had thoughts of self harm or suicide?
- Have you been able to resume a schedule for yourself?
- What time of the day or week is hardest for you?
- Are you a member of a church or congregation? If so, have you attended since the death? How was that for you? [This is often either a very difficult or a very comforting experience.]
- What is hardest for you?
- How are the other family members coping? Is there anyone you are particularly concerned about?
- Is anyone pushing you to do things you don't feel ready for? How are you handling this?

RESPONSES

Use paraphrases to reflect what they've said. For example, "Sounds like things feel overwhelming to you right now." Below are suggestions.

- Staying in touch with your doctor is an important part of your care. I encourage you to make an appointment if you haven't already done so.
- Some days can be harder than others. I want you to know that this is very normal. Eventually the rawness will soften.
- Grief is unique as a fingerprint. We find that even within families, different people grieve differently.
- Often times the days leading up to significant dates can be trying, and sometimes harder than the day itself.
- Tell me more about that . . . .
- If you're having trouble with low appetite, try eating smaller meals more frequently and limit processed foods to be sure you're getting quality nutrients.
- It's not uncommon for your sleep pattern to be impacted after losing a loved one. If you're having trouble practicing good sleep hygiene, here are some tips from the National Sleep Foundation to try:
    - Limit daytime naps to 30 minutes.
    - Avoid stimulants such as caffeine and nicotine close to bedtime. And when it comes to alcohol, moderation is key. While alcohol is well-known to help you fall asleep faster, too much close to bedtime can disrupt sleep as the body begins to process the alcohol.
    - As little as 10 minutes of exercise, such as walking, can improve sleep quality. For the best night's sleep, avoid strenuous workouts close to bedtime.
    - Steer clear of food that's known to be disruptive to sleep, such as heavy or rich foods, fatty or fried meals, spicy dishes, citrus fruits, and carbonated drinks.
    - Adequate exposure to natural light is particularly important for individuals who may not get outside frequently. Exposure to sunlight during the day helps to maintain a healthy sleep-wake cycle.
    - Establish a regular bedtime routine to help the body recognize that it is bedtime. Try taking a warm shower or bath, read a book, or do light stretches. When possible, try to avoid emotionally upsetting conversations and activities before attempting to sleep.
    - Make sure that your sleep environment is pleasant. A comfortable mattress and pillow, and a room temp between 60 and 67 degrees are ideal.

RED FLAGS

Certified iCare Specialists™ should be attentive to any of the following red flags. Refer for additional assessment and support if:

- He or she always seems irritable, annoyed, intolerant, or angry.
- He or she is experiencing an ongoing sense of numbness and/or isolation.
- He or she feels as though they have no one to talk to about their loss.
- He or she feels highly anxious most of the time, either about their own eventual death or the death of someone they love.
- His or her behavior is interfering with relationships or day-to-day functioning.
- He or she is afraid of getting close to people for fear of experiencing another loss.
- He or she has experienced a trigger of addiction struggles.
- He or she has experienced a trigger of compulsive behaviors.
- He or she is engaging in unsafe or unhealthy coping behaviors such as:
    - inappropriate use of prescription drugs
    - inappropriate use of nonprescription drugs
    - use of illegal drugs
    - excessive alcohol
    - engaging in unsafe sexual activities
    - behaving in a reckless manner
    - driving in an unsafe or reckless manner

Tell the person, "Given what you've been telling me, I would like to recommend . . . "

1. local resources
2. a counselor
3. local support groups
4. local hospice organization
5. faith-based organizations
6. national hotlines

IMPORTANT

Call 911 immediately if the mourner expresses suicidal or homicidal ideation.

Nonverbal communication

Nonverbal communication holds as much opportunity as verbal communication. Below are nonverbal tips to help defuse anger and encourage ventilation of emotions.

- Stand at an angle so it's not so threatening.
- Place a gentle but firm hand on his/her shoulder.
- Offer a soft pillow or stuffed animal.
- Show interest. Active listening conveys understanding, fosters trust, and increases likelihood of compliance.
- Make eye contact.
- Be relaxed but attentive.
- Mirror the person's stance, when needed, to break emotional escalation or redirect the flow of conversation.

Helping vs Dependency

Supporting someone in grief comes with important caveats and responsibilities that are critical to help preserve boundaries. Peer support empowers the mourner to find their own solutions and gives them ownership of doing things for themselves. Having these checks in place minimizes the potential for iCare Specialists to interfere with the mourner's own resilience.

EMPATHY VS PROJECTION

Empathy is a connection without judgment. It's putting yourself in the mourner's shoes without projecting your biases.

- Stay aware of your own emotions.
- Make statements that show you understand without directing or telling the mourner what to do. "From what I'm hearing, you feel this way . . . ."
- Give the mourner ownership over their own problems and solutions.
- Help the mourner do things for themselves by giving them tools to find solutions.
- If something isn't working for the mourner, try something else. Peer support helps mourners identify what works for them.

VOCABULARY

What is empathy?

An emotional gift of accepting someone without judgment.

What is bias?

Beliefs that are reinforced by our surroundings and the people we associate with.

Triggers

Grief triggers are anything that brings up memories related to the loss, and spark anxiety and/or emotional outbursts. They are little reminders that throw mourners back in time and ambush emotions. They can happen anytime, anywhere, and be severe enough to induce a panic attack. If someone is struggling with severe triggers and panic attacks, encourage them to seek the care of their primary medical provider.

KEYNOTE

Triggers are a normal component of the grief process.

TRIGGER EXAMPLES

- Spotting someone in the crowd who looks like a deceased loved one.
- The first flush of a deceased loved one's favorite flower.
- Scene of an accident.
- Sight of a hospital or favorite restaurant chain.
- Scent of loved one's cologne, perfume, flowers, food, etc.
- Sound of a song, train whistle, baby crying, horn honking, certain TV commercial, etc.
- A certain moment in time such as 11:30 p.m. when the original call came or the death occurred.
- Holidays, birthdays, anniversaries.

HOW YOU CAN HELP

Grief triggers are not preventable, yet education about triggers coupled with gentle reassurance can help the mourner learn to expect them, and work through them when they do occur.

- Reassure them that triggers are normal and will lessen with time.
- Avoid minimizing the trigger's significance, even if you don't understand it.
- Hold the space for the mourner to work through it on their own. Reassure them that they're safe and remind them to breathe through the wave of emotional pain. Comfort and support at the height of the moment can help tremendously.

WHAT TO KNOW

- ✓ **People experiencing the same loss may not have the same triggers.**
- ✓ **Triggers can be subtle or surprising.**
- ✓ **Triggers may or may not lessen with time.**

Helpful checklist

Following death of a loved one, there is lots to do besides planning the funeral or memorial service. Some funeral homes provide helpful checklists, others don't. Use the checklist below, or print it from the templates page at **icarelibrary.com/specialists** and give to your families to help them manage and track common post-death action items.

ACTION ITEMS FOR NEXT OF KIN

- ❒ Obtain a certified death certificate from the county's Vital Records office, often found at the local health department. Consider purchasing more than one certificate if money allows, because some banks and other offices require an official certificate, not a copy.
- ❒ Make copies of the death certificate as needed.
- ❒ File life insurance claims, if applicable.
- ❒ Notify bank(s) and/or credit union(s), if applicable.
- ❒ Notify credit card companies, if applicable.
- ❒ Notify financial portfolio manager, if applicable.
- ❒ If the deceased used a post office box for mail, notify the post office and have the mail forwarded to next of kin.
- ❒ For any vehicle, boat, RV, or motorcycle titles, file an Affidavit of Inheritance with the Department of Licensing as needed. Refer to will for allocations, if applicable.
- ❒ Consider opening a probate with the local court to help manage any debt.
- ❒ Contact Social Security Administration to change benefits and file for death benefits, if applicable.
- ❒ Contact the Veteran's Administration, if applicable.
- ❒ Contact place of employment or union about possible benefits.

PROBATE

Although not required, setting up a probate is helpful when the deceased fails to leave a will or name an executor of his/her estate. The probate court helps next of kin decide how to pay debt and distribute assets. Call the local probate court number to begin this process.

SOCIAL SECURITY

The number for the Social Security Administration office is (800) 772-1213. Benefits include a one-time benefit to the surviving spouse or dependent children. If applying for benefits other than death, the mourner may need a birth certificate and/or marriage license.

BANKING INFORMATION

The mourner should make a prompt request for release from each bank or financial institution in which the deceased and the mourner held any joint accounts. This is necessary before s/he can withdraw funds from that account to help pay expenses. The bank will instruct the mourner on what forms are required.

TITLES, DEEDS, AND REGISTRATIONS

Before the mourner removes the deceased's name from any property deeds, check with local officials where the property is located. The mourner will need a copy of the death certificate for this process. The same is true for changing vehicle titles and registrations.

BILLS AND CREDIT OBLIGATION

Thoroughly gather outstanding bills and credit obligations such as loans and credit cards. Some installment loans and credit cards may be covered by credit life insurance which will pay off the account balances in the event of death.

INSURANCE NEEDS

Insurance needs often change with the passing of a spouse or other loved one. The mourner should talk to a trusted advisor about what is appropriate and make the necessary adjustments to prevent being over-insured or underinsured.

M02/LETTER 1 INSERT

More ways to help

There are many opportunities to support mourners after the funeral, the only limitation is your imagination. The following gestures are suggestions compiled from *Grief Diaries: How to Help the Newly Bereaved*. Because funeral expenses are often unexpected, many mourners greatly appreciate gift cards and nonperishable items such as toilet paper and bottled water to accommodate visitors who stop by.

KEYNOTE

Avoid assumptions about how a mourner is doing based on appearance.

Many well-meaning people say, “Call me if you need any-thing.” Yet, mourners often fear being a burden, or aren’t comfortable asking for help. Both situations hinder the mourner from reaching out. Further, the fog of grief clouds most everything, including memory and judgment. For this reason, it’s important to remember to offer only the help you can provide, and without expectation for being entertained when you do. Finally, no matter how small you perceive an act of kindness to be, chances are it will bring more comfort than you know.

SUGGESTIONS:

- Provide nourishment. Most mourners have little appetite, but family and friends who call in will appreciate a sandwiches or piece of fruit, especially if they stay long enough to help tackle tasks. Non-returnable food containers will help minimize the need to remember who owns which pan.

- Coordinate childcare or carpooling so mourners can accomplish what needs to be done or take a much-needed nap.
- In lieu of flowers, consider giving store gift cards to help ease the financial burden of needing to buy unexpected supplies.
- Donate stamps for the thank-you cards.
- Coordinate chores. Because the mourner's brain is operating under duress, sometimes even simple tasks are too much. Consider the mail, laundry, dishes, feeding and/or walking the pets, mowing the lawn, picking up prescriptions, etc.

KEYNOTE

Mourners are often sensitive about the deceased loved one's belongings.

When in doubt, please ask before touching or moving belongings or keepsakes.

- Care packages are much appreciated from those who live out of state. For those who are local, consider leaving an anonymous care package on the doorstep so the mourner doesn't have to write a thank-you card.
- Sharing memories of the deceased loved one is like music to a mourner's ears.
- Drop and run. Deliver supplies without expectations of being entertained.
- Many mourners appreciate comfort items such as chocolate, body wash or a scented candle (see Resilience Rx sensorial therapy handout).
- Help write out thank you cards, seal them shut, apply postage and mail.
- Help return any medical equipment no longer needed in the home.

SUPPLIES:

- Milk, juice, coffee
- Bread
- Eggs
- Toilet paper
- Bottled water
- Disposable plates, cups and utensils
- Food storage bags, plastic wrap, aluminum foil
- Pet food
- Dish soap
- Laundry soap
- **NOTES:**
- Bar soap
- Paper towels and napkins
- Frozen meals in disposable containers
- Gift cards to chain stores
- Gift cards to restaurants
- Postal stamps
- Thank-you cards
- Devotionals
- Scented candles
- Soothing music
- Comfort books

NOTES:

CHAPTER 3

YEAR 1, 2 & beyond

The life of the dead is placed in the memory of the living.

MARCUS TILLIUS CICERO

IN THIS CHAPTER

- ✓ Year 1
- ✓ Year 2 & beyond
- ✓ Inflammatory comments

Year One

The first year after loss is often spent in a fog, thanks in large part to the influence of stress hormones that continue to anesthetize parts of the brain. Many describe the first months as feeling like s/he is operating on autopilot, feeling numb, or even describe it as an out-of-body experience. Coupled with all the disruptions brought on by the death of the loved one, the mourner is processing the loss and learning how to survive.

A total disruption

The first year after loss brings major adjustments in nearly every area of life, including daily routine, social interactions, physical health, and more. The mourner no longer has their deceased loved one to talk to, care for, or share activities with. It can mean an unwelcome drop in the grocery bill or less laundry.

ROUTINE DISRUPTION

- The daily schedule has changed. The mourner no longer has their deceased loved one to care for or share activities with, such as watching a favorite show or evening news together.
- Sleep is disrupted due to grief stress. Also, widow/ers face returning to the marital bed alone, often for the first time in his or her marriage.
- Activities of daily living are disrupted, such as less grocery shopping, less laundry, less meal prep, and less errands that were required by the deceased loved one.
- Meals are disrupted. The deceased loved one's place at the table now sits empty, and favorite meals can trigger a wave of pain.

YEAR 1 GOALS

Maintain function of care

- ✓ Safe from harm
- ✓ Basic needs are met
- ✓ Responsibilities are covered
- ✓ Is provided with info and support
- ✓ Is cared for in light of vulnerabilities

SOCIAL DISRUPTION

- Many mourners face loss of social invitations from friends who feel uncomfortable, don't understand, or feel threatened by a new widow or widower's single status.
- As friends lessen, the mourner becomes disconnected and then often feels isolated from the world.
- Some feel pressured to date after losing a spouse, or have another child after losing a child.
- Mourners often feel like a square peg in a round world.

SNAPSHOT

- ✓ **Grief is a normal reaction to death of a loved one.**
- ✓ **Grief is unique to each individual.**
- ✓ **The brain can't tell the difference between physical pain and emotional pain.**

EMOTIONAL DISRUPTION

- Mourners often feel as though they're in a fog.
- Mourners often experience a heightened sense of fear and anxiety, and feel vulnerable.
- Mourners are often faced with sorting through loved one's personal belongings in the first year.
- Mourners face the deceased loved one's birthday, holidays, anniversary, etc. for the first time since his or her passing.
- Mourners are faced with emotional triggers when they least expect it.

PHYSICAL DISRUPTION

- Change in appetite and sleeping pattern due to stress.
- Mourners often develop comorbidities after loss.
- Adrenal fatigue leads to compromised immunity and frequent illnesses.

HELPFUL TIPS

- Avoid trying to distract the mourner by keeping him/her busy. This can reduce their emotional bandwidth for coping and can lead to feeling overwhelmed.
- Grief is unique. Different backgrounds and experiences mean we view things differently. Refrain from giving advice out of respect for different cultures and filters.
- Avoid judgment. Grief timelines are unique to each individual.
- Avoid trying to rationalize fears. Fears are a normal part of the process.
- Grief is complex and unpredictable. Don't try to match losses. Comparing journeys may inflame emotions and reactions, and heighten conflict.
- Trust that with solid social support, compassion, and patience, the mourner will eventually make steps toward reconciliation.

Year two

The second year after loss is often harder than the first, thanks in part to the shock wearing off. The brain is no longer anesthetized by the cortisol and adrenaline, grief triggers are in full force, and the reality of the loss becomes painfully acute.

YEAR 2 GOALS

Continued function of care

- ✓ **Working on self care**
- ✓ **Learning to reorganize life patterns and relationships**
- ✓ **Learning coping strategies**

Adaption

With every facet of their life disrupted, mourners now face the long process of reorganizing life patterns and learning to adapt to living with their loved one in their heart instead of their arms.

ROUTINE ADAPTATION

- Creating new daily schedule.
- Finding ways to fill time.
- Adapting to changes in activities of daily living, such as chores and grocery shopping.

SOCIAL ADAPTATION

- Adapting to shift in friends.
- Continued isolation from the world.
- Resigning to societal views on grief.
- Still feeling like a square peg in a round world.

EMOTIONAL ADAPTATION

- Facing a year of seconds (anniversary, birthday, etc).
- Dealing with triggers.
- Loss of self and sense of who they were.

PHYSICAL ADAPTATION

- Seeking comfort through healthy or unhealthy behaviors.
- Trying to manage comorbidities that develop in response to acute grief.

Beyond

After year 2, the mourner continues to learn to adapt without their loved one and begins reconciliation, the process of coming to terms with the loss. The pace of this process largely depends upon support, internal resilience, personality, childhood experiences, and other factors. If many of these factors are absent, it can leave the mourner struggling through life.

Inflammatory comments

It's hard seeing people in emotional pain, and our natural tendency is to try to fix what appears broken. Yet, well intended statements can backfire in the emotional volatility of the moment. Listed below is a compilation of what not to say from the book, *Grief Diaries: How to Help the Newly Bereaved*, and what to say instead.

"HOW ARE YOU? ARE YOU OKAY?

This statement ignores the obvious and demands an answer. Suggestion: "I've been thinking of you, how are you feeling today?" This invites the mourner to open up.

"I UNDERSTAND HOW YOU FEEL."

This statement tends to dismiss the intense emotions. Suggestion: "I have absolutely no idea how you feel, but I do have a good ear for listening."

"TIME HEALS ALL WOUNDS."

Time doesn't heal the pain. Instead, over the years coping skills become stronger. Suggestion: "I've been thinking of you and am always available for hugs."

"IT WILL GET BETTER EVERY DAY."

Grief isn't a chronological process. One day can be good, but the next two might be very hard. Suggestion: "Some days will be better than others. When you're having a rough day, I'll bring you coffee."

"CALL IF YOU NEED ANYTHING."

The brain's stress hormones cloud logical thinking. The bereaved also fear being a burden. Suggestion: "I'm going to the grocery store for toilet paper. Are you getting low?" Be specific, but not pushy.

"AT LEAST S/HE ISN'T SUFFERING."

One's suffering snuffs out all logic as to why the mourner should be glad their loved one can't feel pain. Suggestion: "S/he was a wonderful person and will be greatly missed."

"GOD MUST HAVE NEEDED HIM/HER."

No matter how steadfast one is in his or her beliefs, a profound loss often triggers an examination of why our faith didn't protect our loved one. Suggestion: "Just know that I'm praying for you."

THINGS TO SAY

From the book *Grief Diaries: How to Help the Newly Bereaved* (2016)

- ✓ **"S/he was a wonderful person and will be greatly missed."**
- ✓ **"S/he was very special."**
- ✓ **I'm so very sorry."**
- ✓ **"When you need to talk, I'm a good listener."**
- ✓ **"What was your loved one's favorite color/food/movie?"**
- ✓ **"I can't imagine what you're feeling."**
- ✓ **Ask him or her to share a story about their loved one.**
- ✓ **Offer comforting song lyrics, poems, quotes, or scriptures.**
- ✓ **"My heart hurts for you."**
- ✓ **"I'm going to the grocery store. Do you need milk?"**
- ✓ **"I'll take the kids to soccer practice."**

CHAPTER 4

PSYCHOLOGICAL CRISIS & STRESS

It's not stress that kills us. It's our reaction to it.

HANS SELYE

IN THIS CHAPTER

- ✓ Types of stress
- ✓ Psychological crisis
- ✓ Adverse childhood experiences

Stress is the body's reaction to any change that requires an adjustment or response. Stress reactions can be either positive or negative, and the brain responds accordingly by secreting the necessary hormones.

Positive stress

Positive stress, also known as beneficial stress, is called **eustress**, and its goal is to keep us alert and motivated. It has a beneficial effect on our health and well-being by triggering the brain to release happy hormones called endorphins. Without eustress, one's well-being can suffer.

EUSTRESS
Positive stress

- ✓ Keeps us alert
- ✓ Keeps us safe
- ✓ Keeps us motivated

Negative stress

Negative stress, also known as **distress**, can be either short- or long-term. Negative stress triggers the brain to respond to danger, either real or imagined, by releasing stress hormones that prepare our body to fight, flight or freeze. Because these hormones can impact our memory and performance, the Occupational Safety and Health Administration (OSHA) declared stress a hazard of the workplace that costs Corporate America more than $300 billion annually.

DISTRESS
Negative stress

- ✓ Continuous challenges
- ✓ No breaks or relief

EXAMPLES OF EUSTRESS:

- Marriage
- Promotion
- new baby
- winning money
- making a new friend
- graduation, etc.

EXAMPLES OF DISTRESS

- Divorce
- Punishment
- Injury
- Demotion
- Ill loved one
- Financial debt

Stressors are not always limited to external situations. Internal events such as feelings and thoughts (such as fear of flying) and habitual behaviors (such as chronic overscheduling or procrastination) can also cause negative stress.

TYPES OF NEGATIVE STRESS

According to the American Psychological Association, there are three types of negative stress, each with its own duration, characteristics, symptoms, and treatment approaches.

The three types of negative stress include:

- Acute stress
- Episodic stress
- Chronic stress

Short-term stress can wear on our mental reserves, while long-term distress wears down both physical and mental reserves.

ACUTE STRESS	EPISODIC STRESS	CHRONIC STRESS
✓ Most common ✓ Brief ✓ Caused by reactive thinking	✓ Frequent episodes of acute stress ✓ Person takes on more than they can handle ✓ They become rushed and pressured ✓ Relationships can become affected	✓ Ongoing extreme stress ✓ Behavioral and emotional reactions can become ingrained patterns in the brain's wiring

Acute stress

Acute stress, the most common type of negative stress, is usually brief and caused by reactive thinking. Because the stress event itself is usually limited in duration, stress hormones such as cortisol, adrenaline and norepinephrine generally don't cause significant damage to the brain or body.

EXAMPLES OF ACUTE STRESS:

- An argument
- Work or school deadline
- Upcoming situations you dread
- Being stuck in traffic

KEYNOTE

Acute stress does not cause significant damage to the brain or body.

When the situation resolves, so does the stress.

NORMAL REACTIONS TO ACUTE STRESS

COGNITIVE	EMOTIONAL	PHYSICAL
✓ Difficulty with concentration	✓ Anger	✓ Headache
✓ Sleep disruption	✓ Irritability	✓ Stomach ache
✓ Triggering of addiction	✓ Anxiety	✓ Muscle tension
	✓ Depression	✓ Elevated blood pressure
		✓ Sweaty palms
		✓ Rapid pulse
		✓ Jaw clenching

The way the mind will lean under stress is strongly influenced by training.

FRANK HERBERT

Episodic stress

Episodic stress is when someone experiences frequent episodes of acute stress. Often, the person takes on more than they can handle, and find themselves rushed and pressured, and interpersonal relationships can start to become affected.

EXAMPLES OF EPISODIC STRESS:

- Relationship problems
- Unsatisfactory job
- Recurring illness
- Type A personality
- "The Worrier" personality

KEYNOTE

Episodic acute stress can lead to more pronounced health issues, such as high blood pressure and irritable bowel.

NORMAL REACTIONS TO EPISODIC STRESS

COGNITIVE	EMOTIONAL	PHYSICAL
✓ Difficulty with concentration	✓ Anger	✓ Headache
✓ Triggering of addiction	✓ Irritability	✓ Stomach ache
✓ Trouble making decisions	✓ Anxiety	✓ Muscle tension
✓ Insomnia	✓ Depression	✓ Elevated blood pressure
✓ Compromised processing speed	✓ Impatient	✓ Sweaty palms
✓ Memory difficulties	✓ Tense	✓ Rapid pulse
✓ Mental fatigue		✓ Jaw clenching
		✓ Grinding teeth in sleep
		✓ Over or under eating
		✓ Alcohol or substance abuse

Chronic stress

Chronic stress is living with continued extreme stress, and can cause behavioral and emotional reactions to become ingrained.

EXAMPLES OF CHRONIC STRESS:

- Extreme poverty
- Violence
- Abuse
- War
- Family dysfunction
- Trauma

KEYNOTE

The brain's wiring can change in response to constant stress, making the brain constantly prone to hazardous stress effects regardless of the scenario.

NORMAL REACTIONS TO CHRONIC STRESS

COGNITIVE

- ✓ Difficulty with concentration
- ✓ Triggering of addiction
- ✓ Trouble making decisions
- ✓ Insomnia
- ✓ Compromised processing speed
- ✓ Memory difficulties
- ✓ Mental fatigue
- ✓ Suicidal ideation
- ✓ Violent thoughts
- ✓ Psychosis

EMOTIONAL

- ✓ Anger
- ✓ Irritability
- ✓ Anxiety
- ✓ Depression
- ✓ Impatient
- ✓ Tense
- ✓ Apathetic
- ✓ Does not see an escape
- ✓ Hopelessness
- ✓ Gives up

PHYSICAL

- ✓ Headache
- ✓ Nausea
- ✓ Fatigue
- ✓ Muscle tension
- ✓ Elevated blood pressure
- ✓ Sweaty palms
- ✓ Rapid pulse
- ✓ Jaw clenching
- ✓ Grinding teeth in sleep
- ✓ Over or under eating
- ✓ Alcohol or substance abuse
- ✓ Chronic health issues and co-morbidities

Distress, impairment, dysfunction

Distress is excessive stress that is distracting and difficult to manage, whereas dysfunction is impairment such that the mourner becomes ineffective at coping. Any incident that overwhelms a person's ability to cope constitutes a crisis/traumatic event, and their ability to overcome and prevent impairment depends on a variety of factors.

Distress is a **normal reaction** to an abnormal event. Dysfunction is an **abnormal reaction** to an abnormal event.

NORMAL COGNITIVE DISTRESS

- ✓ Inability to concentrate
- ✓ Sensory distortion
- ✓ Difficulty with decision making
- ✓ Confusion

ABNORMAL COGNITIVE DYSFUNCTION

- ✓ Delusions
- ✓ Hallucinations
- ✓ Disabling guilt
- ✓ Paranoid ideation
- ✓ Suicidal ideation
- ✓ Homicidal ideation

NORMAL EMOTIONAL DISTRESS

- ✓ Grief
- ✓ Anxiety
- ✓ Fear
- ✓ Anger
- ✓ Mood Swings
- ✓ Irritability

ABNORMAL EMOTIONAL DYSFUNCTION

- ✓ Panic attacks
- ✓ Infantile emotions
- ✓ Immobilizing depression
- ✓ PTSD

NORMAL BEHAVIORAL DISTRESS

- ✓ Risk taking
- ✓ Eating
- ✓ Alcohol
- ✓ Sleep disturbance
- ✓ Hypervigilant
- ✓ 1000-yard stare

ABNORMAL BEHAVIORAL DYSFUNCTION

- ✓ Violence
- ✓ Antisocial
- ✓ Abuse
- ✓ Poor hygiene
- ✓ Self medication
- ✓ Immobility

Psychological crisis

Trauma is another term for psychological crisis. An event is considered traumatic if the person experienced, witnessed, or was confronted with an event(s) that involved actual or threatened death or serious injury, or a threat to the physical integrity of self or others. The person's response must have also involved intense fear, helplessness, or horror (American Psychiatric Association, 1994). In their lifetime, nearly 90% of Americans report having experienced a traumatic event (Breslau et al., 1998).

Traumatic experiences fall into 4 general categories:

HUMAN-CAUSED THREATS

- Domestic violence and abuse
- Fire
- Active shooters
- Gang violence
- Bomb threats
- Cyberbullying and attacks
- Dangerous animals
- Suicide
- Kidnapping, missing student
- Bus accident

NATURAL HAZARDS

- Earthquake
- Tornadoes
- Hurricanes
- Floods
- Wildfires
- Landslides or mudslides
- Tsunamis
- Volcanic eruptions

TECHNOLOGICAL HAZARDS

- Explosions or accidental release of toxins from industrial plants
- Accidental release of hazardous materials from within the school, such as gas leaks or laboratory spills
- Hazardous materials releases from major highways or railroads
- Radiological releases from nuclear power stations
- Dam failure
- Power failure
- Water failure

BIOLOGICAL HAZARDS

- Infectious diseases (COVID, pandemic influenza, Staphylococcus aureus, meningitis, etc.)
- Contaminated food outbreaks: (Salmonella, botulism, E. coli, etc.)
- Toxic materials present in school laboratories

TRAUMATIC RESPONSE

People who have experienced a traumatic event may experience strong emotional and physical stress reactions known as aftershocks. They may appear a few hours, a few days, or even weeks or months later. A traumatic event does not imply mental instability or weakness, it simply indicates that the event is just too powerful for the individual to manage by him or herself. The understanding and support given to an individual can help reduce the longevity of the reaction.

Adverse childhood experiences

ACE—adverse childhood experiences—are extremely stressful events that happen during childhood. Some ACEs are so stressful, they can alter brain development and the immune system, increasing the risk of lifelong health and social problems.

KEYNOTE

The more ACEs a person has, the greater the risk for poor outcomes.

ACE EXAMPLES:

- ✓ Sexual abuse
- ✓ Physical abuse
- ✓ Mental abuse
- ✓ Mental illness in the household
- ✓ Addiction in the household
- ✓ Traumatic death of a first-degree relative

ASSIST

ASSIST stands for assurance, security, structure, information, and support. The goal is to help the mourner regain control, reestablish resilience, and reconcile the experience.

HOW YOU CAN ASSIST

ASSURANCE	SECURITY	STRUCTURE
✓ Reassure them they are important. ✓ Reassure them that they're having a normal reaction, and aren't crazy. ✓ They are not alone in their experience.	✓ Reassure them that they are safe. ✓ Reassure them that they are secure within their families. ✓ Reassure them that loved ones will look out for them.	✓ An antidote to chaos and confusion. ✓ Structure helps them maintain strength and stamina. ✓ Help them maintain routines.
INFORMATION	**SUPPORT**	**TRUTH**
✓ Counter rumors with facts. ✓ It reassures, guides, and assists with decisions. ✓ The fastest way to kill morale is to withhold information. ✓ Information helps reduce anxiety, but avoid overwhelming with too much.	✓ Provide nonintrusive support, not psychotherapy. ✓ Be gentle but direct. ✓ Listen carefully. ✓ Have resources ready. ✓ Help with tasks when possible and indicated.	✓ Always be truthful. ✓ Don't make promises you can't keep. ✓ Trust can be maintained only when truth is at the core of communication. ✓ Limit exposure to media coverage of the event.

HELPFUL TIPS

KEYNOTE

Talk is the most healing medicine.

Following are tips to help the mourner with aftershocks and to help ease or moderate some stress reactions (International Critical Incident Stress Foundation, 2015).

- Periods of appropriate physical exercise alternating with relaxation will help alleviate some of the physical reactions to stress.
- Structure time. Maintain as normal a schedule as possible but pace yourself. Wearing yourself out will reduce your emotional threshold and ability to cope.
- Spend time with people who support you, and talk to them. Talk is the most healing medicine.
- Be aware of numbing the pain with excessive use of drugs, alcohol, or risk taking.
- Give permission to feel rotten.
- Write in a journal through sleepless hours.
- Do things that feel good to you.
- Don't make any big life changes.
- Do make as many daily decisions as possible that will give you a feeling of control over your life.
- Don't fight recurring thoughts or flashbacks. They are normal and will become less painful with time.

ACTIVITY

A RELAXATION EXERCISE

One basic mechanism for stress reduction involves deep breathing. The following exercise may be a valuable tool for reducing excessive arousal quickly and effectively during upsetting moments (adapted from the book by G.S. Everly, Jr. *A Clinical Guide to the Treatment of the Human Stress Response*, 1989).

1. Assume a comfortable position. Rest your left hand (palm down) on top of your navel. Now place your right hand so that it comfortably rests over your left. Your eyes should remain open.
2. Imagine a hollow pouch lying internally beneath your hands. Begin to inhale, imagine that the air is entering through your nose and descending to fill that internal pouch. Your hands will rise as you fill the pouch with air. As you continue to inhale, imagine the pouch being filled to the top. Your ribcage and upper chest will continue the wavelike rise that was begun at your navel. The total length of your inhalation should be 3 seconds for the first week or so, then lengthen to 4 to 5 seconds as you progress in skill development.
3. Slowly begin to exhale to empty the pouch. As you do, repeat the phrase, "My body is calm." As you exhale, you will feel your raised abdomen and chest recede.

Repeat this exercise two times in succession. Then continue to breathe normally for 5 to 10 successive breath cycles but be sure to emphasize the expiration of each breath as the point of relaxation. Then you may repeat the entire process again—2 deep breaths followed by 5 to 10 normal breaths during which you concentrate on releasing any stored tension on the expiration.

Should you begin to feel lightheaded or should you experience any discomfort, stop at that point. You may wish to shorten the length of the inhalation to avoid lightheadedness.

After about one week of practicing, omit STEP 1, start with STEP 2. If you have any health concerns, consult your physician prior to using this exercise. NEVER use this exercise while driving.

CHAPTER 5

WORKING FROM A TRAUMA INFORMED PERSPECTIVE

Just as the body goes into shock after a physical trauma, so does the human psyche go into shock after the impact of a major loss.

ANNE GRANT

IN THIS CHAPTER

- ✓ Grief vs trauma
- ✓ Learning vs survival brain
- ✓ SAFER-R model

Grief vs Trauma

Grief and trauma often go hand in hand. Although not all grief has trauma associated with it, all trauma has grief associated with it. One main difference between the two is that grief creates sadness, while trauma creates fear.

Grief produces a neurocognitive pain that causes significant disruption in the brain's cognitive processes, and impacts the physiological, sociological, spiritual and psychological self in unpredictable ways. Trauma is a psychological crisis in response to a highly stressful event. It's important to note the following:

- Profound, traumatic losses such as the unexpected death of a loved one, creates a psychological crisis with long-lasting effects on one's ability to cope and function.
- Grief's biological response is predictable but the emotional response based upon one's own inner resilience, adverse childhood experiences, personality type, and more—is unique to each of us.

TRAUMA IS . . .

A psychological crisis in response to a highly stressful event.

Trauma creates FEAR.

GRIEF IS . . .

A neurocognitive pain that causes significant disruption in the brain's cognitive processes.

Grief create SADNESS.

KEYNOTE:

While you might know the person, you might not know their state of mind.

BIOLOGICAL RESPONSES

When emotional trauma occurs, it floods the brain with adrenaline, a response known as fight-or-flight syndrome. It's designed to feed the muscles energy for increased strength and speed in anticipation of fighting or running. In response, other parts of the brain are anesthetized. This causes time warp, tunnel vision, and memory loss. This is why we recall trauma events like a strobe light rather than a story.

KEYNOTE

Grief's biological response is predictable, but the emotional response is unique to each of us.

Biologically, the brain responds in a predictable pattern:

- **Brain stem** (the physical brain): Following a crisis, the brain stem is activated and the sympathetic nervous system sends the body into the fight, flight or freeze response involving over 120 chemicals.
- **Limbic system** (the emotional brain): Second, the hippocampus, amygdala, and thalamus are stimulated. They regulate emotions, the storage of memories, and the interpretation of input from the senses. We remember the feelings associated with an event much more vividly than the details.
- **Cerebral cortex** (the thinking brain): The cerebral cortex is the least active part of the brain after a crisis. Complex thinking such as problem-solving and decision-making are somewhat impaired, and explains why people become confused and have a difficult time identifying options when in crisis.

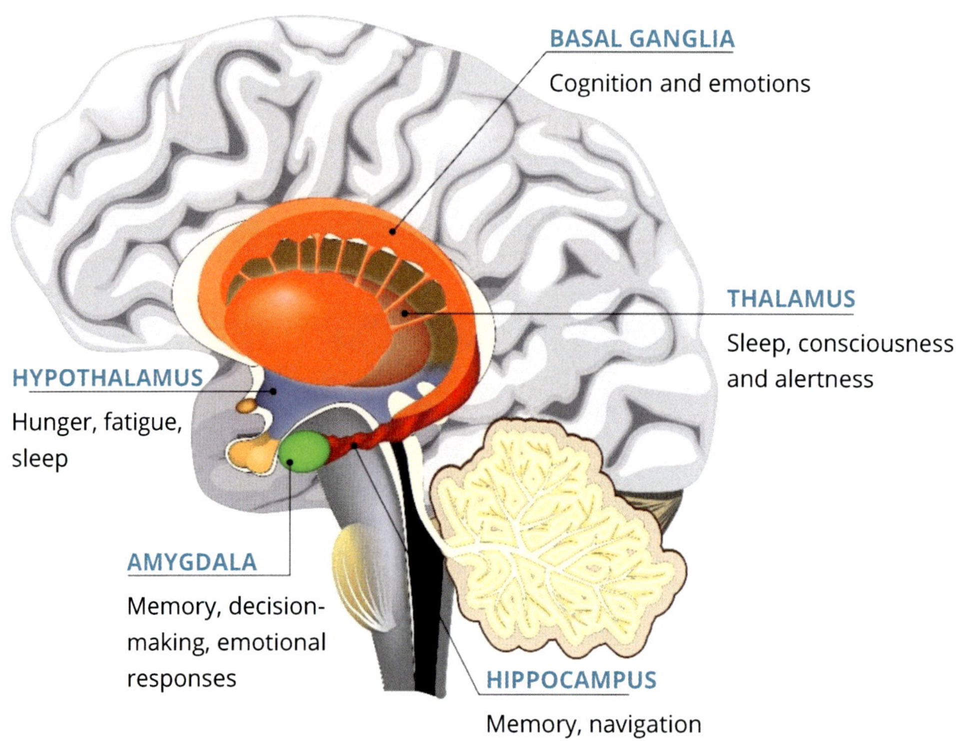

COGNITIVE AFFECTS

As mentioned in chapter one, psychologically, every event is interpreted through a number of filters unique to each person including:

- Physical proximity to the event
- Relational proximity to the event
- History of prior trauma
- Support system
- Personality

Cognitively, grief is a highly distracting process that diverts our emotional bandwidth and creates fears both rational and irrational. During the acute stage of grief, people are actively processing what happened. Healing begins in subsequent stages rather than right away.

As mentioned, not all people respond the same way to death of a loved one. The emotional impact depends on a number of factors such as inner resilience, personality, childhood experiences, and availability of support through family, friends, and coworkers. Some have more severe, longer lasting reactions.

Lack of sufficient support can overwhelm a person's ability to cope and result in distress, impairment and dysfunction.

Working from a trauma informed perspective allows you to better understand the wide range of grief reactions. It takes into account adverse childhood experiences, one's proximity to the death of their loved one, and other factors. It's an outcome driven continuum of care that enhances resiliency and assists return to function by being there for them and with them.

Studies show that understanding the trauma perspective and providing peer support is superior to psychotherapy post disaster, making it the standard of care, yet it's important to always remember that peer support is only one stop on the overall continuum of care.

IMPORTANT

Peer support is only one stop on the overall continuum of care.

Learning vs Survival brain

In normal conditions, the brain is in learning mode. It is calm, peaceful, curious, feeling playful and not afraid to make mistakes because it sees mistakes as part of the learning process. A learning brain is:

- Open to new information
- Comfortable with vagueness and ambiguity
- Sees the big picture

KEYNOTE

The survival brain can shut down other parts of the brain. This is known as emotional hijacking.

Survival brain, on the other hand, feels panicky, obsessive, and afraid of doing the wrong thing, doesn't feel calm nor open to learning new things. The survival brain just wants to get things over with. It's afraid of making mistakes, doesn't want to look stupid, and fears being picked on. It's filled with doubt about its own ability to learn and afraid other people will see how stupid it really is. A survival brain is:

- Hyperfocused on threat
- Doesn't like ambiguity—needs hard, clear facts
- Thinks in black/white terms
- Can't see beyond the small picture

Peritraumatic warning signs of posttraumatic distress

Post-traumatic stress disorder (PTSD) is a mental health condition that's triggered by a terrifying event—either experiencing it or witnessing it. Symptoms may include flashbacks, nightmares and severe anxiety, as well as uncontrollable thoughts about the event. Warning signs include:

1. Neuromuscular immobility (freezing)
2. Severe time distortion
3. Psychogenic analgesia (a feeling of distress, suffering or agony)
4. Traumatic psychogenic amnesia (when a person blocks out certain traumatic information)
5. Dissociation, depersonalization, derealization (a sense of detachment from oneself)
6. Sympathetic nervous system dysfunction (panic attacks)
7. Dysfunctional parasympathetic nervous system arousal
8. Guilt reactions (survivor guilt)
9. Giving up (helplessness, hopelessness
10. Self destructive ideation (suicidal or homicidal ideation)

SAFER-R MODEL

The SAFER-R model is a step-by-step model for working with individuals in crisis (Everly, 1995), and is considered one form of psychological first aid.

STABILIZE

Stabilize the situation for the mourner:

- Introduce yourself and establish rapport.
- Meet basic needs.
- Mitigate acute stressors, if applicable.

ACKNOWLEDGE

- Let people tell their story.
- Acknowledge the event and the mourner's reaction(s).

FACILITATE

- Facilitate understanding (normalization) by providing reassurance.

ENCOURAGE

- Encourage effective coping. Mechanisms of action include:
  - ✓ Meeting basic needs
  - ✓ Liaison or advocacy
  - ✓ Cathartic ventilation
  - ✓ Social support
  - ✓ Information
  - ✓ Stress management
  - ✓ Problem solving
  - ✓ Conflict resolution
  - ✓ Cognitive reframing
  - ✓ Spiritual
  - ✓ Financial
  - ✓ Reassurance
  - ✓ Hope

EXAMPLE:

1. **Introduce yourself**
2. **Meet basic needs, stabilize, liaison**
3. **Listen to the story**
4. **Reflect emotion**
5. **Paraphrase content**
6. **Normalize**
7. **Attribute reactions to situation, not personal weakness**
8. **Identify personal stress management tools to empower**
9. **Identify external support and coping resources**
10. **Use problem-solving or cognitive reframing, if applicable**
11. **Assess mourner's ability to safely function**

RECOVERY OR REFERRAL

- Refer to the next level of care when there is evidence that the mourner is unable to successfully attend to essential activities of daily living.

Peer support goals

The goal of peer support is to:

- Provide an empathetic listening ear
- Provide low level intervention
- Identify mourners who may be at risk to themselves or others
- Facilitate pathways to professional help when indicated

KEYNOTE

Psychological first aid can be harmful when it crosses the line between augmenting resiliency and interfering with resiliency.

Warnings

Providing peer support is an honor, yet we're all human. When helping others, it's important to know when you are over your head or getting too close and wanting to fix it instead of providing support and empowering the mourner to find his/her own solutions.

SECTION TWO
Toolbox 101

IN THIS SECTION

IN THIS CHAPTER

- ✓ Overview
- ✓ Facilitator responsibilities
- ✓ How to facilitate a support group

CHAPTER 6

SUPPORT GROUPS FACILITATION

You are there to empathize and facilitate.

VIV ALBERTINE

Starting a grief support group is a rewarding experience. They offer mourners a safe and supportive environment in which to work through their emotions. Support groups also introduce people to others who are going through a similar experience, which helps to normalize the grief experience.

Groups offer participants opportunities to learn new roles, new ways of problem-solving or coping with situations by hearing about and discussing these with the group facilitator, and from listening to the experiences of other members.

Support groups offer a cost-effective way of providing services to people by giving them a place to tell their story and talk about their loved one. It creates a safe place to express emotions and try new ideas or new ways of coping.

Groups also offer mourners a chance to chat and laugh, and learn that their hearts can hold joy and sorrow at the same time.

Overview

Facilitating a support group comes with responsibilities for planning, preparing, and leading. This chapter outlines those responsibilities along with tips to set you up for success.

International Grief Institute's iCare branch offers two programs, a faith-based and a community-based support group. Both are designed for 8 group sessions which can be easily modified to fit your schedule. The eighth session also includes a closing candlelight ceremony.

Each session includes the following:

- ✓ One grief topic for discussion
- ✓ Helpful handouts
- ✓ Caring plan

KEYNOTE

While it can be therapeutic, a support group is not a therapy group.

TOPICS

The topics cover pertinent areas that most people experience after losing someone they love. Not every topic will be applicable to everyone. Nonetheless, use the topics as a conversation starter. If that session's topic doesn't apply to many in the group, use the list of **Common Feelings** on page 75 to generate conversation. Have each participant choose one of the expressions of grief that stands out to them, and then explain why that expression is standing out. Allow the group to go in a different direction if needed for that session. The handouts will cover that session's topic at home.

HANDOUTS

iCare offers two support group programs: a faith-based program and a community-based program. Both use the same handouts. The faith-based program also incorporates scripture assignments. Facilitator manuals are designed to be used over again, while each participant should have their own workbook. You can also print the handouts from icarelibrary.com/Templates or order the workbooks from the links below.

iCare's faith-based program:	**iCare's community-based program:**
icaregriefsupport.com/church	icaregriefsupport.com/chapters

CARING PLAN

Self-care is important when grieving. We can't always predict loss and other stressors, but practicing self-help techniques that tend to our physical, mental, emotional, and spiritual needs can help us cope.

Each iCare Grief Support session includes a Resilience Rx™ tip. The goal is to offer self-help strategies that trigger positive hormones—dopamine, serotonin, and oxytocin—to help support mourners as they learn to move forward with their loved one in their heart. Encourage your participants to try the Resilience Rx™ strategies as they create their own caring plan.

TIP

Peer support is only part of the continuum of care. Encourage participants to engage in other forms of support outside the group setting.

Facilitator responsibilities

> **KEYNOTE**
>
> Monitor yourself from getting too close and wanting to fix people (interfering with their resilience).
>
> It's also important to know when you're over your head.

- Allow everyone to participate. One of the values of a support group is that participants have a chance to verbalize their loss in a safe environment. Make sure everyone has the chance to share or pass.
- Manage the group. Keep the discussion moving around the circle. Re-center the group's focus when needed.
- A grief support group is an important healing modality after loss. Help participants feel good about their contribution to the meeting.
- Practice good listening skills and maintain supportive neutrality. Don't criticize anyone for what they've said, even if you don't agree. It's important to not invalidate their experience.
- Stay alert for emotional and physical red flags, and handle appropriately.
- Maintain an active presence. Silence your cell phone so you can give 100%.
- Speak using simple words. So everyone can understand what is said, avoid using professional or academic verbiage.
- When a participant is talking, they should be the center of attention. Side conversations are not allowed during circle time.
- Bring a notebook and keep notes. You don't need to keep detailed notes, just pertinent details about your participants so you can avoid saying, "Now, who did you lose again?" You can also use the **My Participants** sheet on page 57. Also, use your notebook to summarize important moments during the session, so you can circle back to it at the next session if needed.

CLIMATE AND ENVIRONMENT

There are many factors that impact how safe and comfortable people feel about interacting with each other. The environment and general climate of a meeting sets an important tone for participation.

- Place chairs in circle if possible.
- Ensure that you have a completed registration for each participant so you have their information should you need to contact them for any reason. They need to complete the registration only once.
- Ensure that every participant signs in at the beginning of each session. We recommend you keep both the registration and sign-in forms for at least three years.
- Mic and audio/visual equipment generally aren't needed except during the closing candlelight ceremony, if desired.
- Refreshments aren't required but nice to have on hand. Most support groups have bottled water, coffee, tea, and a snack available.

SNAPSHOT

1. Make sure you have a completed registration for each participant.
2. Make sure each participant signs in at the beginning of each session so you have record of who was and wasn't there.
3. Use nametags to help personalize the experience.
4. Start the meeting on time.
5. Welcome everyone.
6. Make introductions (first meeting only).
7. Review the agenda, objectives and ground rules for the meeting (first meeting only).
8. Encourage participation. Remind the group that each participant will have an opportunity to share or pass during the discussion.
9. Stick to the agenda but be flexible when needed.
10. Seek commitment from everyone. Attending all the sessions will be of great benefit to their own well-being. For those who are in doubt, encourage them to attend at least 3 sessions.
11. Summarize the end of each meeting to bring closure where needed.
12. Thank the participants for being here and tending to their own grief.
13. Close the meeting.

TIP

- ✓ **Create a comfortable environment, and an open and trusting atmosphere.**
- ✓ **Treat participants equally and with respect.**
- ✓ **Maintain confidentiality.**
- ✓ **Deal with obstacles.**
- ✓ **Start and end on time.**

ESTABLISH GROUND RULES

Review **Ground Rules** on page 67 with the group and reiterate the following:

- ✓ Stay in the circle unless you need to use the restroom.
- ✓ Raise your hand if you have something to say.
- ✓ Listen to what other people are saying.
- ✓ No mocking, judging, or interrupting.
- ✓ Be on time coming back from breaks.
- ✓ Respect each other.
- ✓ No profanity or offensive language.
- ✓ Silence your cell phones.

COMMUNITY RESOURCES

Use the list below to identify the resources in your community, and keep a list with current contact information to give to participants.

- Other groups being held in the community
- Local bereavement organizations (if any)
- Hospice center
- Library resource center
- Senior center
- Crisis hotline number
- Funeral homes

Dealing with disrupters

When encountering a participant who is disruptive, the facilitator can maintain control of the group through assertive compassion. Assertive compassion allows the facilitator to directly address the problem without offending or singling out participants. This will help the group stay focused on the disruption itself, instead of the participant causing it. Use the tips and interventions below to help.

- ☑ Give everyone a chance to say their piece, and then review the ground rules with the group.
- ☑ Listen to both sides carefully.
- ☑ Show respect for experience.
- ☑ Find out the group's expectations for dealing with disruption.
- ☑ Stay in your facilitator role.
- ☑ Don't be defensive.

VOCABULARY

What is assertive compassion?

It is a balanced combination of control, kindness and compassion.

POSSIBLE INTERVENTIONS

- Confront the discussion and allow the group to decide how to intervene.
- Use the agenda and ground rules.
- Be honest. Say what's going on.
- Use humor if appropriate. This will help break the tension.
- Accept or legitimize the point or deal.
- Use body language to deescalate the situation.
- Have the group take a break.

NOTES:

Ready, set, go!

Now that you have a solid understand of grief, the responsibilities and ground rules of leading a support group, you're ready to plan, prepare, and lead. Following are the instructions and content to lead an 8-week support group. The format can easily be modified to a shorter or longer length of time. For an open-ended and/or drop-in support groups, use any of the topics and handouts to facilitate a single session.

PLAN

- ❑ We recommend two facilitators per support group. If one participant has a problem and leaves the room, the co-facilitator should follow to ensure his or her welfare while the lead facilitator continues leading the support group.
- ❑ Decide on maximum number of participants. If you have more than 15, consider splitting into two groups if you have the space, with two facilitators per group.
- ❑ Choose dates and meeting time.
- ❑ Secure meeting space that has ample, well-lit parking, easy access, and adequate bathroom facilities.
- ❑ Decide group type: community-based or Christ-centered. Facilitator manuals and participant workbooks for both groups can be purchased at icarelibrary.com/specialists.
- ❑ Decide format.
  - ♦ Closed 8-week sessions (participants must register) or monthly drop-in. The sessions in this manual can be used for both formats.
  - ♦ Group type: general loss, suicide, spouse loss, child loss, overdose, etc.
- ❑ Recommend 90-minute sessions.
- ❑ Provide directions beforehand, and then use sandwich board signage out front, so the meeting place is easily visible.
- ❑ Create registration process. Preregister participants using registration form in this manual.
- ❑ Decide on refreshments. Bottled water, coffee, tea, and a snack are common.
- ❑ Send out invitations to families and post flyers. Notify local newspapers, radio and TV stations if desired.
- ❑ Notify local organizations, churches, hospice groups, hospitals and other healthcare agencies, counseling agencies, etc.

PREPARE

- ❑ Prepare and print extra handouts to have on hand for those who show up without a workbook.
- ❑ Prepare registrations. For closed 8-week program, have participants register ahead of time so you have their information and know how many to expect. Keep completed registration forms on file. Printable forms are available at icarelibrary.com/specialists.
- ❑ Prepare weekly sign-in sheets. Use a new sheet for each session, and keep on file.
- ❑ Prepare nametags.
- ❑ List local and online resources. Keep list current and up to date. Give to participants at first meeting.

DON'T FORGET

- ✓ **Tissue**
- ✓ **Notebook and pen for your own use**
- ✓ **Notecards and pens for phone tree.**
- ✓ **Nametags**

LEAD

1. Arrive 30 minutes prior, and plan to stay 30 minutes after closing.
2. Set up room.
   a. Circle of chairs
   b. Side table for sign-in, registrations, handouts, and refreshments.
   c. Adjust room lighting. Keep it sufficiently light but not bright.
3. Greet participants.
   a. Have each participant fill out a registration form if they haven't already done so.
   b. Have each participant sign in on sign-in sheet.
   c. Ask participants to wear a nametag.
4. Start on time.
5. Introduce facilitators and share the facilitator's role (first session only).
   a. Facilitators sit on opposite ends of the circle.
   b. Emphasize that group support isn't counseling (each session).
6. Share any housekeeping information, such as where the bathrooms and garbage cans are located.
7. Review support group **Ground Rules** (first session only).
8. See sessions instructions for that night's topic.
9. End on time. Make this mandatory.
10. Session evaluation. Have participants complete at the end of week #8.

Support Group Registration

NAME		HOME PHONE:	
ADDRESS:		CELL PHONE:	
CITY/STATE/ZIP		AGE:	

PLEASE DESCRIBE YOUR LOSS:	
NAME:	
RELATIONSHIP TO YOU:	
DATE OF DEATH:	
AGE AT TIME OF DEATH:	
CAUSE OF DEATH:	

Name and relationship of others currently living in your home:
What are your present needs, and what do you hope to get by being here?
What else would you like the support group facilitators to know about you?

F01/SUPPORT GROUP REGISTRATION

Support Group Sign-in Sheet

GROUP NAME		MEETING DATE:	
FACILITATOR 1:		PHONE:	
FACILITATOR 2:		PHONE:	
PARTICIPANT NAME:		PARTICIPANT PHONE:	

F02/SUPPORT GROUP SIGN IN

My Participants

PARTICIPANT NAME:	LOSS TYPE	LOVED ONE'S NAME	YEAR OF LOSS
EXAMPLE: Judy Smith	Husband	Harold	2019

F03/PARTICIPANT LIST

Support Group Evaluation

GROUP NAME:		DATE:	
FACILITATORS:			
PLEASE HELP US EVALUATE OUR SUPPORT GROUP			
NAME (optional):			
YOUR LOSS:			
DATE OF LOSS:			
Do you feel you have a better understanding of your grief journey?			
Was the facilitator clear, easily heard, informative, and interactive with the group?			
What did you learn that you were not aware of before attending this group?			

Did you feel free to ask questions? ❐ Yes ❐ No

COMMENTS:

Were your questions answered to your satisfaction? ❐ Yes ❐ No

COMMENTS:

How would you rate this group? ❐ Poor ❐ Fair ❐ Good ❐ Very good ❐ Excellent

COMMENTS:

F04/SUPPORT GROUP EVALUATION

List of Handouts & Assignments

SESSION 1: GROUP PROCESS, GRIEF, MOURNING AND RECONCILIATION

- ❑ Ground Rules
- ❑ Reconciliation of grief
- ❑ Spiritual journaling
- ❑ You & I
- ❑ Common feelings
- ❑ Self-care assignment: Creating a care plan

SESSION 2: COMMUNICATING WITH FAMILY & FRIENDS

- ❑ Please listen
- ❑ Empowerment
- ❑ Please see me through my tears
- ❑ Companion
- ❑ Self-care assignment: Sensorial therapy

SESSION 3: CONFRONTATION VS ESCAPING GRIEF

- ❑ The photo album of my mind
- ❑ Self-care assignment: Sleep well

SESSION 4: CARING FOR YOURSELF

- ❑ Life quality inventory check
- ❑ Controlling stress with your calm scene
- ❑ Self-care assignment: Chromotherapy

SESSION 5: ANGER

- ❑ Hidden anger
- ❑ Anger quotes
- ❑ How to safely process anger
- ❑ Self-care assignment: Forest therapy

SESSION 6: GUILT

- ❑ Guilt
- ❑ Regret & guilt
- ❑ Self-care assignment: Dance/movement therapy

SESSION 7: RECONCILIATION

- ❑ What I need
- ❑ Griefwork & boundaries
- ❑ Reconciliation
- ❑ Grief & medication
- ❑ Self-care assignment: Laugh therapy

SESSION 8: TURNING PAIN INTO PURPOSE

- ❑ Give joy
- ❑ Turning pain into purpose
- ❑ From despair to hope
- ❑ As we close
- ❑ What now?
- ❑ The holidays
- ❑ God's script
- ❑ Self-care assignment: Hug therapy

108/LIST OF HANDOUTS

FOR FACILITATORS ONLY

SUICIDE

Every so often, a group participant will talk in language suggestive of suicide.

> "I feel so depressed. I wish I would just go away and be with him."
>
> "My wife and I were together always. I can't go on without her. When I go home at night, I feel like ending it all."

What do you do or say? How do you know whether this is a grief talk, depression, or whether your participant is really going to act? The simple fact is that **you don't know**, but you can get a little better idea whether that participant is likely to act upon his/her feelings.

In most cases, you will find that these are natural valid expressions with scant likelihood for execution, but we can never take it completely for granted.

SUGGESTIONS:

Statements such as "John, you know you don't really mean that," or "Mary, think about it. You have everything to live for," frequently cause the participant to suppress his or her feelings, and right now you want to have those feelings elicited and expressed, or you will never get further information as to how serious his or her intent is.

- Acknowledge the validity of the participant's feelings. One approach might be to say, "Many people seem to have these feelings, John. Tell me, how long have you felt this way?"
- Address the group to see if others feel this way. Attempt to steer group comments with regard to these feelings.
- Get John to talk a bit more in the group, if it is appropriate and you feel comfortable handling it. Otherwise, tell John that these are common feelings and you would like to talk with him after the group. But then, you **must** follow up with him immediately after the session. You are doing this to find answers to the following questions:
    - Is there a definite plan for dying by suicide, such as time, place and/or method?
    - How intense are the impulses?
    - How long has the person had these ideas?
    - Are others involved in the plan? If so, how?
    - Was there a precipitating event? Why is suicide being considered now?
    - Is there a history of suicidality in the past?

ACTION TO TAKE

Unless you are professionally trained and certified to handle suicide interventions, do not under any circumstances attempt an intervention.

Your role at this point is to:

- acknowledge the feelings
- elicit information
- pass this information along to a skilled professional

It is important that each incidence of suicidal feelings be passed along to the social worker or clinical supervisor who is trained in handling such matters.

H24/SUICIDE

FOR FACILITATORS ONLY

SUICIDE PROTOCOL

Suicidal ideation—thoughts about suicide—may be as detailed as a formulated plan without the suicidal act itself. The range of suicidal ideation varies greatly from detailed planning, role playing, self-harm and attempts, which may be deliberately constructed to be discovered, or where death may be fully intended.

Sometimes threats are vague or ambiguous, and/or may be aimed at a future event or time. These threats should also be taken seriously. If you are concerned about a participant being a threat to him or herself, follow the guidelines below.

If you do not have the training or knowledge to conduct a suicide risk assessment and determine the safety of a participant, call 911.

GUIDELINES

Ask the following questions in order to gain a better understanding of the scope of imminent danger:

- ❑ Does the participant want to attempt suicide?
- ❑ Does the participant have a plan to attempt suicide?
- ❑ Does the participant have the means to carry out that plan?
- ❑ Has the participant ever attempted suicide in the past?
- ❑ If so, what methods of attempt have been used in the past?

The answers to these questions will help emergency services determine the depth of the situation. If the participant has a plan and access to a lethal means, is planning to make an attempt very soon, or is currently in the process of making an attempt, this person is in imminent danger and should not be left alone. Call 911 immediately.

RESOURCES

- ❑ **Emergency:** 911
- ❑ **National Suicide Prevention Lifeline:** 1-800-273-TALK (8255)
- ❑ **Crisis Text Line:** text TALK to 741741

MORE STEPS

- ☑ Contract with the person not to act on this decision. "Will you promise to wait and not act on your feeling for the next 24 hours? Can you promise me this?"
- ☑ Tell the person that when they are a danger to themselves, you cannot maintain professional confidentiality.

- ☑ Inform a family member or friend who can go to the person's home to remove potentially harmful objects such as sharps, glass, drugs, belts and electrical cords.
- ☑ Promote hope by listening to the participant. Try not to interrupt them and be willing to sit with them as they talk about the reasons why they want to die. Let them get all those reasons out, and then listen as they come up with their own reasons to live. Do not tell the participant what you think their reasons for living should be, as what you think are reasons to live may be stressors to the participant. While listening, do not rush to judgment. Let them know they are not alone, and that help is available.
- ☑ Share referrals. Have your resources on hand. While arranging for help, stay with the participant. Do not leave them alone. Form a safety net. Ask the participant if there is anyone else they feel comfortable talking to (parents, siblings, aunts, uncles, grandparents, cousins, friends, priests, professors, mentors or coaches).

H25/SUICIDE

IMPORTANT

When a person's life is in danger, safety takes priority over privacy.

SESSION 1

TOPIC: GROUP PROCESS, GRIEF, MOURNING & RECONCILIATION

INTRO

This session focuses on the group process, ground rules, and introduces the concept of grief as a process of reconciliation.

SCRIPT

1. **Thanks for being here**—you are taking care of yourself.
2. **Housekeeping**.
   - ✓ Location of restrooms and garbage cans
   - ✓ Location of tables and chairs when not in use
   - ✓ Any facility rules
3. **Leader introduction**.
   - ✓ Say your name and where you're from
   - ✓ Share personal experience(s) with grief
4. **Group time.** Group time will focus on discussion topics and externalizing feelings in the safety of the group. Some of the workbook handouts will be used during group time, the rest are for home reading.
5. **Home time.** The following tasks are also for home time. If participants have questions or want to share self-care
   strategies, they'll have time at the next meeting.
   - ✓ Self-care plan
   - ✓ Spiritual journaling
6. **Introduce caring plan**. Explain the importance of self-care, especially when grieving. Encourage participants to create a self-care plan and explore one new addition each week using the Resilience Rx™ strategies in the workbook. The topic of self-care will be covered in more depth in session 4.

REMEMBER

- ✓ **Start and end on time.**
- ✓ **Keep conversation moving and productive.**
- ✓ **Ensure every participant has an opportunity to share or pass during the discussion.**
- ✓ **Protect the conversation from being monopolized.**
- ✓ **Stay supportive yet neutral.**

MATERIALS

- ❑ **Notebook & pen**
- ❑ **Index cards & pens**
- ❑ **Refreshments**
- ❑ **Nametags**
- ❑ **Tissue**

HOMEWORK

- ❑ **Spiritual journaling**
- ❑ **You & I**
- ❑ **Common feelings**

DISCUSSION

1. **Discuss ground rules and commitment** to the group as outlined in **Ground Rules** (handout 1).

    - ✓ Advice
    - ✓ Crying
    - ✓ Externalizing emotion
    - ✓ Comfort
    - ✓ Tolerance
    - ✓ Confidentiality
    - ✓ Rescuing

2. **Ask each participant to introduce themselves by answering the following questions**.

    - ❑ What's your name?
    - ❑ Where are you from?
    - ❑ What's the loss you've experienced?
    - ❑ When did it happen?
    - ❑ What do you expect to get by being a member of this group?
    - ❑ What are your feelings at this very moment?

3. **Introduce tonight's topic**: Group process, grief, mourning & reconciliation. Discuss that grief is a process of reconciliation between our head and our heart. Use **Reconciliation of Grief** (handout 2) as a discussion point.

    - ❑ Distinction between grief and mourning.
    - ❑ What's it like for you?
    - ❑ Reconciliation is a process, and part of the grief journey.

4. **Weekly phone calls:** Discuss how we help one another prevent isolation through phone calls.

    - ❑ Hand out index cards and pens.
    - ❑ Ask participants to write down their name and phone number on one index card.
    - ❑ Instruct them to pass their card two people to the right.
    - ❑ Each person is then asked to phone the individual whose card they have to check in to see how they're doing and help them feel less isolated.
    - ❑ This is an important beginning to continued networking. Some of these participants may become lifelong friends.

CONCLUSION

1. **Don't expect to feel better tonight**. Much like starting a new exercise routine, you may go home and feel worse before feeling stronger. By doing griefwork, you **will** eventually feel stronger. We ask that you attend at least 3 sessions before deciding that this group is not helpful for you.

2. **Review this session**. Encourage participants to read handouts, journal their thoughts, create self-care plan, and call the participant on their index card.

SESSION 1 | HANDOUT 1

GROUND RULES

Being part of a group is very therapeutic and rewarding work. What you get from being here is directly related to what you put into it. By being here and actively participating in this safe environment, you'll significantly enhance your personal growth after losing your loved one.

Holding up 4 fingers is our sign for a hug, a kind word, a gentle touch on the arm.

Like many others, you will soon begin to develop a strong commitment to our group process. As you become more comfortable here, you will find the following guidelines are an essential part of that process, serving to make this experience both useful and safe.

ADVICE

We are not here to offer advice. We are here to share experiences and feelings. If you have had similar feelings or experiences, let someone know what worked for you.

Refrain from saying, "You know, if I were you I would . . . "

CRYING

Crying is both natural and healthy. Kleenex was invented for a reason.

In this group, give yourself permission to cry without embarrassment. Here, it is okay for big folks to cry.

RESCUING

When you are visibly into feelings, a RESCUER tries to help you stop crying and to feel better through unsolicited hugs and touching.

A well-intentioned rescuer may relieve their own feelings, but you'll have been cheated out of a rare opportunity to fully experience and externalize your own. We can be far more caring by being attentive listeners.

COMFORT

As you talk through your pain, you may not want comfort forced upon you. However, it's appropriate at any time for you to seek comfort.

TOLERANCE

We often find the experiences, feelings and expressions of others to be completely foreign to our own. Here, we lovingly accept what is expressed as fully legitimate for the person expressing it. We are not here to judge each other, but to listen and offer understanding.

CONFIDENTIALITY

The only way we can feel safe and completely comfortable sharing with you is to be certain that all that is said here stays here. That means we **don't** discuss what happens in this room to anyone outside this room for any reason—even without mentioning names. Really, we don't.

H01/GROUND RULES

DOODLES, THOUGHTS, NOTES & OTHER STUFF:

RECONCILIATION OF GRIEF

GRIEF VS MOURNING

Grief is an internal experience. For some, it is an inside fear, emptiness, panic, loneliness, anger, guilt, longing, or even depression. It's often expressed as, "Grief is love with no place to go."

Mourning is a bit different. It is the process where we work through our grief by outwardly expressing our internal feelings.

VOCABULARY

Mourning is grief which is expressed to the outside world.

Grief without mourning is dangerous and destructive to the human system. By coming to this group, you are beginning or continuing a healthy mourning process.

What are you experiencing now? What is it like for you?

WHEN GROWING UP, WHO TAUGHT US HOW TO MOURN?

All our lives, most of us have been taught how to acquire, not how to lose. Children and young adults aren't offered a course in LOSS 101. No wonder it is strange and painful. Many mourn their grief as they witnessed a parent, movie or societal personality handle his or her grief.

As young people, we may have heard these messages:

- **"Don't feel bad, don't cry."**
  MESSAGE: Bury your feelings.
- **"You lost your toy! Well, just be good and Santa will bring another."**
  MESSAGE: Everything is replaceable.
- **"Now, you just keep your feelings to yourself."**
  MESSAGE: It isn't safe to share your feelings.

Who taught you how to experience loss and appropriately express feelings?

GRIEF RECONCILIATION

Intellectually, you know you really don't recover from your grief in the sense that everything is restored to the way it was before. You know it's unlikely that life will ever be the same, yet at the beginning of our loss, this is difficult to accept.

You are beginning a process—a journey toward reconciliation—where you learn to adapt to living with your loved one in your heart.

TASKS OF RECONCILIATION

There are a number of tasks ahead as you proceed with your own process of grief reconciliation.

- ✓ You learn to effectively experience and express outside of yourself the reality of the death.
- ✓ You allow yourself to fully embrace the pain of the loss, while learning how to assure that you are nurtured, physically, emotionally and spiritually.
- ✓ You learn to convert your relationship with the person who died from one of interactive presence to one of appropriate memory.
- ✓ You learn to develop a new self-identity based on a life without the person who died.
- ✓ You begin to relate the experience of the death to a context of new meaning in your life.
- ✓ You develop a lasting network of support to help you through the process.

In these next few weeks, you will learn safe ways to experience and express your grief.

- ✓ You will learn how to mourn while still taking care of yourself.
- ✓ You will begin to develop a new perspective about your loss and begin to clarify your self-identity.
- ✓ You will begin to discover a new sense of meaning in life while finding a network of supportive relationships to help you along the way.
- ✓ You are at an early stage of this process. Be patient and take it one moment at a time.
- ✓ Trust that it does get better. Because it does.

Learning to find the path for your personal reconciliation journey is what these support group sessions are all about.

H02/GRIEF RECONCILIATION

SESSION 1 | HANDOUT 3

SPIRITUAL JOURNALING

KEEPING A SPIRITUAL JOURNAL

For the weeks ahead, you'll learn to keep a spiritual journal. Whether or not you choose to continue spiritual journaling once the group sessions are done, the writing you do in the coming weeks will be rewarding in ways you are unable to fully imagine now.

- ✓ Writing is a simple yet powerful way to help process your loss and work through your grief. It helps release some of the physical, emotional and spiritual pain that grieving folks experience.
- ✓ It will help you work through many of the issues that are difficult to communicate in other ways.
- ✓ It's very personal and confidential. Nobody needs to share in your journal writing unless you specifically choose to permit it. It is simple to do spontaneously.
- ✓ It does not require making complicated plans and can be accomplished right when your feelings and needs are strongest, even at 3 a.m.

WRITE FOR YOURSELF

Even though we intellectually know that our own journal writing is for our eyes only, most of us have been conditioned differently. During school, we always wrote for others to see and usually judge, correct, and grade. At some point most of us have written a letter or two for someone else to read. Nearly all our prior writing has been to communicate with others.

FOR YOUR EYES ONLY

While this sounds like an obvious thought, it can be difficult to grant ourselves permission to write freely without editorial judgement. As you progress in your writing, you will find that you are able to overcome the mindset that you are writing for others, and will concentrate on fully serving your own need for expression.

HELPFUL HINTS

- ✓ Give yourself permission to write without perfection. God isn't looking for perfection.
- ✓ Use the pages of this book, a wide-lined school notebook, or one of those expensive designer journals. Give yourself permission to be as sloppy or as neat as you wish.
- ✓ Forget erasers. It is easier, quicker and more spontaneous to cross out words.
- ✓ There are no errors when writing for yourself, merely thoughts you wish to reread and those you want to skip. Rather than erasing or tearing out pages in order to obliterate, try putting a big X through a page or crossing out a phrase.
- ✓ Pay attention to those thoughts you are inclined to obliterate. Quite often they are a rich source of issues you need to work through in order to complete your griefwork.
- ✓ When staring at a blank page and unable to think of anything to say, write from your stream of consciousness.

- ✓ Set a time limit. Start with maybe 5 to 10 minutes.
- ✓ Write everything that comes into your mind, no matter how unconnected, scattered or inane it may seem.
- ✓ Since we aren't judging ourselves and no one else will read it, it doesn't matter that it isn't a well composed sentence or paragraph. Capture whatever thought or image comes to mind.
- ✓ Don't try to write a story. Merely begin to document your internal images, feelings, and internal dialogue.

Not having the pressure of composing something which makes sense, you just have to be able to write fast enough to keep up with your internal activity. If your thoughts lead to a particular issue, elaborate on it. When the allotted time has passed, you can choose to continue or allow yourself to stop for the day, and start fresh the next day.

You will surprise yourself at how quickly you have developed a new tool for making progress with your griefwork. With the mechanics of writing now a comfortable routine, you can become more focused.

In griefwork, we are frequently writing for one or more of the following reasons:

- ✓ To capture our experience or progress.
- ✓ To confront an issue.
- ✓ To vent, explore or express a feeling or emotion.
- ✓ To connect.
- ✓ To atone.
- ✓ To preserve a thought.
- ✓ To memorialize our loss.

BENEFITS OF SHARING

While few people feel they want to share everything they've written, there is often therapeutic value in sharing some of it.

Some, in their writings, have discovered parts of themselves which they want to share. You are under no obligation to share, however, should you wish to, there'll be an opportunity to share during each support session.

A TOOL FOR YOUR TOOLBOX

If writing has always been comfortable and easy, please continue to do it. If this is new to you, please ask for help and encouragement, as this is a useful tool that will serve you well even after you've done the largest portion of your griefwork.

YOU & I

WHAT'S DIFFERENT ABOUT THESE TWO STATEMENTS?

STATEMENT 1

"When you ask someone for help time and time again, they are going to resent you. You feel real funny and you don't want to ask again. You get depressed after you try this a number of times and get no real help. What are you supposed to do? You just go on and on, and hope it will go away."

STATEMENT 2

"I find when I ask someone for help time and time again, they seem to resent me. I feel funny and I don't want to ask again. I get depressed after I try this a number of times, and I get no real help. What am I supposed to do? I just go on and on, and hope it will go away."

BOTH STATEMENTS ARE TRYING TO SAY THE SAME THING, EXCEPT . . .

In the first statement, we hear someone else telling us by implication how we should feel. If we don't feel that way, it can feel as though we're being told that we're strange and different, and may find ourselves inwardly resenting being grouped with that person's feelings.

The second statement is a direct report of someone else's experience, and leaves it up to us to choose whether or not we associate with it. It gives us permission to listen to it, and choose how we feel:

1. "Yes, I feel the same way. This is also my experience."
2. "No. I can understand how you may feel the way you do, but what you say does not relate to me and my experience."

In groups, it is important that members relate their direct experience and take full ownership and responsibility for their statements. This is best done through the use of **I** statements.

- I have no right to tell someone, "When so and so happens, you feel this way."
- I have every right to say, "When so and so happens, I feel this way."

In the normal conversational vernacular, the **you** means of expression is frequently used. However, in self-help groups where reports of direct individual experience are frequently so helpful, the use of **I** statements becomes more and more important.

We realize how difficult it is for some to reorient their habitual form of expression. Please don't get upset if you're interrupted with a gentle request to change your expression from a **you** statement into an **I** statement.

DOODLES, THOUGHTS, NOTES & OTHER STUFF:

COMMON FEELINGS

You have undoubtedly heard the term **grief work**. You may also have heard that the only way **out** is **through**. This means that avoidance of griefwork and the bereavement process only postpones your reconciliation. During the coming weeks you have an opportunity to learn new ways of working through your grief, getting a better understanding of yourself and how to dissipate the strong feelings in healthy ways.

Many people come to support groups thinking there is something wrong with them. They are experiencing thoughts and emotions with an intensity they never thought possible.

For some, the intensity causes them to feel as though they're going crazy, are out of control, and wonder whether the rollercoaster will ever stop. It will.

YOU ARE NOT CRAZY

Following is a list of feelings and conditions which are common and normal during grief. You might experience many of these, or just a few. Much of our group time will be spent on how to recognize and deal with these feelings, their frequency and their intensity. Although normal, these feelings are still painful. These support sessions are not going to take the pain away. Because you're concentrating on your griefwork, you may even find that the pain intensifies—that, too, is normal. But you will be rewarded by your griefwork as the tunnel forward becomes brighter.

- Anniversary obsessions
- Anxiety
- Confusion
- Crying and sobbing
- Denial
- Depression
- Disbelief
- Disorganization
- Dreams
- Drugs and/or alcohol
- Emptiness
- Anger and/or rage
- Fear
- Grief attacks
- Guilt
- Helplessness
- Holiday obsessions
- Physical illness
- Joy and guilt
- Loss of intimacy
- Loss feelings
- Mystical experiences
- Numbness
- Obsession with personal objects
- Panic
- Powerlessness
- Psychological changes
- Regrets
- Release
- Relief
- Rumination
- Sadness
- Search for meaning
- Searching
- Self-focus
- Shock
- Sudden mood changes
- Suicide thoughts
- Survivor's guilt
- Time distortion
- Yearning

DOODLES, THOUGHTS, NOTES & OTHER STUFF:

SELF CARE TIP #1

Create a Care Plan

Losing someone we love changes how we live and who we are. The first step is to take good care of yourself. Self-care refers to healthy habits and activities that reduce stress by doing things that activate our positive hormones—dopamine, oxytocin, and serotonin—to counteract stress hormones.

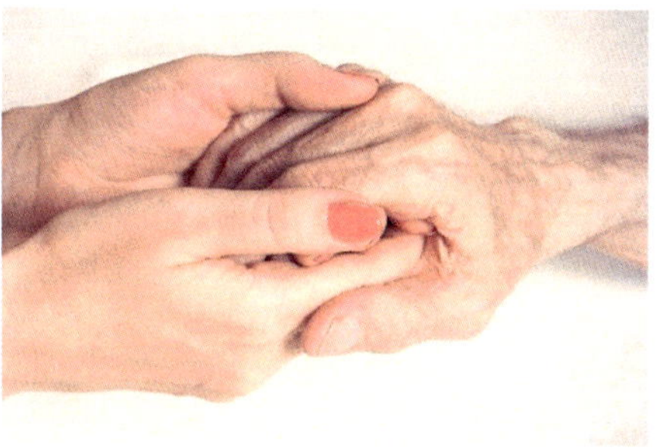

The love in the world begins with the love within ourselves. DEEPAK CHOPRA

WHY IT MATTERS

Grief is a significant stressor that impacts our emotional, mental and physical health. Self-care can improve our well-being, minimize stress, reduce the damaging effects of grief, and help us adjust as we learn to live with our loved one in our heart instead of our arms.

Creating a self-care plan that tends to your physical, emotional, social, and spiritual needs will help strengthen your inner resilience when juggling the demands of life while grieving, and can help anchor your ability to weather times of upheaval. By identify things you enjoy, you'll be able to create a unique and helpful self-care plan you'll stick with.

AIMS OF SELF CARE

- To help manage stress.
- To prevent physical illness.
- To help maintain equilibrium and honor one's own needs.

CREATE YOUR PLAN

STEP 1:
Identify your emotional, physical, social and spiritual needs.

STEP 2:
Create your self-care plan and fill it with activities you enjoy. Use Resilience Rx™ tips in this manual to help.

STEP 3:
Put it into action and stick to it.

STEP 4:
Reassess it every 3 months and adjust as needed.

PHYSICAL NEEDS

Nourishing your body will help you feel better. When you feel better, you cope better.

- ✓ Practice good sleep hygiene.
- ✓ Engage in light exercise, housekeeping or dancing to keep the body moving.
- ✓ Stay hydrated and eat for health.
- ✓ Make time for restorative relaxation.
- ✓ Enjoy a good belly laugh each day.

SOCIAL NEEDS

Fulfilling engagements and interactions help guard against depression and isolation.

- ✓ Volunteer in the community.
- ✓ Take or teach a self-enrichment class.
- ✓ Join a book, tennis, quilt or knitting club.
- ✓ Travel.

EMOTIONAL NEEDS

Our emotional needs are met through understanding, empathy, and support.

- ✓ Surround yourself with others who speak your loss language.
- ✓ Develop friendships that are supportive.
- ✓ Talk to loved ones about your loss and how you are coping.
- ✓ Express your emotions in a journal.
- ✓ Engage in enjoyable outlets such as coloring, knitting, gardening, puzzles, etc.

SPIRITUAL NEEDS

Our spiritual needs are met through inner reflection.

- ✓ Each day write down one thing you're grateful for, or try spiritual journaling.
- ✓ Engage in reflective practices such as prayer or meditation.
- ✓ Try laughter yoga or forest therapy.
- ✓ Talk to clergy or a spiritual mentor.

MY CARING PLAN

Starting now, I will create a plan that tends to my emotional, physical, social and spiritual needs, and promise to do activities that activate my brain's happy hormones through the following:

Physical needs:

1. ______________________
2. ______________________
3. ______________________
4. ______________________

Emotional needs:

1. ______________________
2. ______________________
3. ______________________
4. ______________________

Social needs:

1. ______________________
2. ______________________
3. ______________________
4. ______________________

Spiritual needs:

1. ______________________
2. ______________________
3. ______________________
4. ______________________

WEEK 1 SPIRITUAL JOURNALING

What are you feeling this week? Pour your emotions onto this paper for nobody else to read.

SESSION 2

TOPIC: COMMUNICATING WITH FAMILY & FRIENDS

INTRO

This session focuses on hurtful things well-meaning people sometimes say, and how it's an opportunity to educate them so they don't hurt someone else.

SCRIPT

1. Last week's unfinished business.
2. Report on phone calls. How did they go?
3. Report on caring plan. How did they go?
4. NOTE: The next session is dedicated to sharing pictures and personal mementos with the group so we can all get to know your special person. Mementos of all sizes are welcome.

DISCUSSION

1. **Discuss how we are hurt by the ones we love**. What are some of the clichés and euphemisms we've heard?
    - You must get a hold of yourself.
    - Can't let yourself fall apart.
    - Be strong, or be strong for the children.
    - I know exactly how you feel.
    - Well, at least s/he didn't suffer.
    - It's over now. Let's talk about something pleasant.
    - The living must go on living.
    - S/he led a full life.
    - Time will take care of it.
    - God will never give you more than you can handle.

REMEMBER

- ✓ **Start and end on time.**
- ✓ **Keep conversation moving and productive.**
- ✓ **Ensure every participant has an opportunity to share or pass during the discussion.**
- ✓ **Protect the conversation from being monopolized.**
- ✓ **Stay supportive yet neutral.**

MATERIALS

- ❑ **Notebook & pen**
- ❑ **Index cards & pens**
- ❑ **Refreshments**
- ❑ **Nametags**
- ❑ **Tissue**

HOMEWORK

- ❑ **Please listen**
- ❑ **Empowerment**
- ❑ **Please see me through my tears**
- ❑ **Self-care assignment**

2. **What is happening when people use clichés and euphemisms?** Why do they do it?
    - How do you handle these statements and ones like them?
    - How do you feel about family or friends when they speak this way?
    - How do you begin to forgive them?
    - Do they really know what to say?
    - Did you know what to say before you had your direct experience confronting the feelings you're living with?
    - Are they afraid of our feelings? How do they feel about themselves?

3. Dr. Elisabeth Kübler-Ross called these statements phony baloney. Perhaps all we want is for someone to really listen to us. Perhaps just want a simple honest expression of feelings, like:
    - Could you tell me about it?
    - What happened?
    - I can't imagine how painful this must be.
    - What was your relationship like?
    - Simply saying "I'm so sorry," and then have them shut up and listen to us.

4. **Discuss Companions** (handout # 4). We really have a choice about how to deal with folks who seem unable to deal with us. We can get angry, write them off, and never speak to them again. We can tell everyone else how insensitive they are. Or, we can choose to recognize that they just never learned how to deal with pain, and we can try to preserve the relationship by educating them.

CONCLUSION

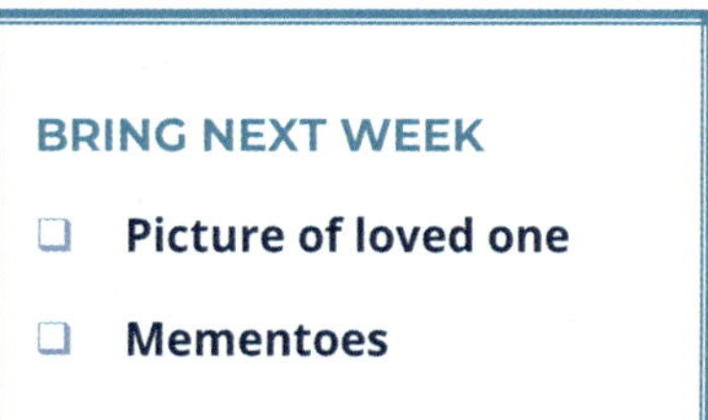

1. **Review this session**. Encourage participants to read handouts, journal their thoughts, and try this week's Resilience Rx self-care tip.
2. **Phone numbers for next week's calling**.
3. **Bring pictures or mementos to next week's session**.
   If you think you might have trouble with this, talk to your phone contact about those feelings, then come with a picture or memento and see if you really feel what you anticipated you would feel.
   It will be a good learning opportunity about yourself.

I02/SESSION 2 INSTRUCTIONS

SESSION 2 | HANDOUT 1

PLEASE LISTEN

When I ask you to **listen** to me
and you start giving advice
You really have not done what I asked.

When I ask you to listen to me
and you begin to tell me why I shouldn't feel that way,
my feelings feel trampled upon.

When I ask you to listen to me
and you seem intent on solving my problems,
you are failing me. Just listen.

All I ask is that you **listen**, please!
Don't **talk** or **do**,
just hear me.

Advice is cheap.
A quarter gets me both Dear Abbey and Billy Graham
in the same newspaper, and I can do that for myself.
I'm not helpless.
Maybe discouraged and faltering,
but not helpless.

Please try to understand.
When you do something for me that I can and need to do for myself,
rather than helping, you contribute to my fear and inadequacy.

When you accept as a simple fact that I really do feel the way I say I feel,
no matter how irrational, then I can conserve my precious energy.
I then have the energy to get about this business
of understanding what's behind my irrational feelings.

And when that's clear, the answers become obvious
and the advice becomes unnecessary.
I can make sense of my irrational feelings
when I begin to understand what's behind them.
So please listen and just hear me.

And if you want to or need to talk,
wait for your turn, and I'll **listen** to you.

H06/PLEASE LISTEN

DOODLES, THOUGHTS, NOTES & OTHER STUFF:

EMPOWERMENT

Some of us were brought up to merge our self with those around us: our family, our schools, churches and other social organizations.

Under the umbrella of family or group, we learned to subvert our interests and needs to others who were more powerful, such as a parent, older sibling, chronically ill family member, school system, government, etc.

In marriage, some of us continued subverting our needs to our spouse, children and aging parents. Our own self may never have had the opportunity to fully develop. We never learned to exchange information and emotions with others while maintaining individuality.

We never learned to connect without merging, without loss of our own self.

When we overly identify with others, we lose our boundaries. When we set boundaries, we are honoring that part of us which makes us a unique and important individual.

Much of our unhappiness and worry results from our inability to set boundaries. We have learned not to feel empowered to be our own self. We haven't learned how to be oneself as a separate entity from someone else.

As a result, inside ourselves, sometimes barely conscious, our body system continues to deny its unique existence.

In this session we will begin to acknowledge our unique personhood. We may need to learn how to undo years of practice where we gave priority to the needs of others rather than consciously acknowledging our own.

In this process, we will be careful of extremes. We are not trying to establish walls. We are not looking for boundaries so rigid that they are no longer permeable.

However, we're going to learn how to acknowledge, validate, and give importance to our needs as humans.

AFFIRMATIONS FOR EMPOWERMENT

- My emotions are allies
- I can heal
- I can trust
- I have resources
- I have boundaries
- I can experience intimacy
- My body belongs to me
- I have an unconscious
- I have a future
- I have inner guides
- My emotions are allies
- I can reject others
- I can release self-blame
- I can participate in a community
- I can enjoy my sexuality
- I can change my relationship to my memory
- I can support and respect myself

H07/EMPOWERMENT

DOODLES, THOUGHTS, NOTES & OTHER STUFF:

SESSION 2 | HANDOUT 3

PLEASE SEE ME THROUGH MY TEARS

You asked me how I was doing. When I replied, tears came to my eyes.

You immediately began to talk again. Your eyes looked away, your speech picked up, and all the attention you had given me went away. How am I doing?

I do better when you will listen to my response, even though I may shed a tear or two, for I so want your attention. But to be ignored because I am in indescribable pain, that hurts me and makes me feel angry.

So, when you look away, I feel alone.

Really, tears are not a bad sign you know.

They're nature's way of helping me to heal. They relieve some of the stress of sadness.

I know you fear that asking me how I'm doing brought this sadness to me.

No, it didn't. The memory of my loss will always be with me, only a thought away. It's just that my tears make my pain more visible to you, but you did not give me the pain, it's just there.

When I cry, could it be that you feel helpless?

You're not, you know.

When I feel your permission to allow my tears to flow, you've helped me more than you can know.

You need not verbalize your support of my tears. Your silence as I cry is my key. Do not fear my tears.

Your listening with your heart to, "How are you doing," helps relieve the pain, because once I allow the tears to come and go, I feel lighter.

Talking to you releases things I've been wanting to say aloud,

and then there's space for a touch of joy in my life.

When I tear up and cry, that doesn't mean I'll cry forever, maybe just a minute or two, and then I'll wipe the tears away. Sometimes you'll find I'm even laughing at something funny ten minutes later.

When I hold back tears, my throat grows tight, my chest aches and my stomach begins to knot up, because I'm trying to protect you from my tears.

But then we both hurt. Me, because I've kept the pain inside and it's become a shield against our closeness. You hurt because we're now distant.

Please take my hand. I promise not to cry forever; it's physically impossible, you know.

When you see me through my tears, then we can be close again.

DOODLES, THOUGHTS, NOTES & OTHER STUFF:

SESSION 2 | HANDOUT 4

COMPANIONS

ACTIVE LISTENING

One of the most important things someone can do for a person in grief is to listen, because we need to tell our story over and over again.

The head knows what's happened but it takes a long time for the heart to catch up, and telling the story is the way that is accomplished.

People are often worried about what to say, and not knowing what to say is what keeps them away from us. "I don't know what to say. I might say the wrong thing."

But really, you need to say very little. Active listening is what will help me heal most.

INTENSITY OF EMOTIONS

There are many emotions in grief, and the intensity of those emotions can be frightening. That's why people want to avoid grieving; it's hard work. Some of the hardest feelings are just plain sadness and feeling helpless.

We replay our loss again and again, trying to figure out whether we could have done something different. We always end up at the same point; there was nothing we could do.

Griefs that haven't been expressed never go away. They don't just disappear.

You have to grieve, you have to get it out. And if you don't, it's going to hurt you. It's going to hurt those around you, and it's going to affect you physically.

It's so important to get grief out. That's why we need people to listen to us.

IDENTIFY YOUR FEELINGS

You need to say what you're feeling—and keep talking about it. Listeners can help us by giving us a safe place to talk about our loss and all the feelings that are part of it.

The process is different for everyone, but the initial period of grief often includes shock, numbness, and even feeling disconnected from our body and can be frightening.

"I feel helpless."

"I feel sad."

"I feel angry."

Further along, you might obsess for your loved one, have dreams about him or her, think you saw or even heard them speak. These thoughts can make us feel crazy at times. It's frightening if you don't know that this is normal.

In another phase of the grief journey we often feel disorganized, physically depressed, and feel as though we're physically falling apart.

Eventually, things begin to normalize. We start to eat and sleep normally, and life starts to fit into a normal pattern that feels good enough to live with.

After the initial shock of grief wears off, you feel like other people don't want you around when you're feeling sad. Nobody likes to be sad, and nobody likes to be around sad people, so we hide.

It's hard going back to work, back to church, back to the office, back into a routine. If there's any one wonderful thing that a person can do to help a griever, it's to say "Come with me. I'll sit with you in church," or "Let's go together to the office today," or something like that.

You need someone to take your hand and help you back into your normal life—a companion along the way.

Adapted from an interview transcript with the Reverend Corrine Chilstrom, Associate Pastor at St. Luke's Lutheran Church in Park Ridge, IL., conducted by Richard A. Jensen, Director/Speaker of LUTHERAN VESPERS, a radio ministry of the Evangelical Lutheran Church in America, based upon Pastor Chilstrom's book: "Andrew, You Died Too Soon."

H09/COMPANIONS

SELF CARE TIP #2

Sensorial Therapy

Our five senses play a role in how we feel and can be influenced by what our senses take in.

Practice the Rule of 5s below to give yourself some form of sensory pleasure every day. With practice, the awareness and perception of delight eventually becomes effortless, and is an important step toward restoring balance after loss.

A treat is a small pleasure that we give to ourselves. GRETCHEN RUBIN

WHY IT MATTERS

When grief overwhelms you, treat your five senses to things that look, feel, smell, taste, or sound good. Treating yourself to something that evokes sensorial joy stimulates the feel-good hormones in your brain to help offset the stress of grief.

RULE OF 5s

Every day practice the Rules of 5 by enjoying the following:

- ✓ 5 things you can **see**
- ✓ 4 things you can **touch**
- ✓ 3 things you can **hear**
- ✓ 2 things you can **smell**
- ✓ 1 thing you can **taste**

Use the suggestions on the following page to stimulate your senses in pleasurable ways. In addition to stimulating your brain's feel-good hormones, research shows that certain actions such as coloring (sight) and foods (taste) also help reduce stress, including avocado, oatmeal, raspberries, blueberries, oranges, pistachios, walnuts, and chocolate.

VISUAL—SIGHT SUGGESTIONS:

- Watch a sunrise or sunset.
- Look at a cherished photo or a favorite memento.
- Use a plant or flowers to enliven your workspace.
- Enjoy the beauty of a garden, the beach, a park, or your own backyard.
- Surround yourself with colors that lift your spirits.

TACTILE—TOUCH SUGGESTIONS:

- Soak in a warm tub with Epsom salts or bath oil.
- Wear a pair of extra soft socks.
- Pet a dog or cat.
- Wrap yourself in a soft scarf or blanket.

HEARING—SOUND SUGGESTIONS:

- Listen to relaxing or upbeat music.
- Listen to laughter on YouTube or comedy sitcom.
- Listen to the sound of the ocean, waterfall, or fountain.
- Hang windchimes near a window.
- Seek silence.
- Listen to the birds or a soundtrack of nature.

OLFACTION—SMELL SUGGESTIONS:

- Shower or bathe with a lovely scented soap.
- Light a fragrant candle or burn incense.
- Apply a scented lotion to your skin before bed.
- Buy a fragrant floral bouquet for the kitchen or your office.
- Experiment with different essential oils in a diffuser.
- Enjoy clean, fresh air in the great outdoors.
- Spritz on your favorite perfume.

GUSTATION—TASTE SUGGESTIONS:

- Enjoy one of the foods listed on the prior page.
- Enjoy a mug of herbal tea, cocoa with whipped cream, or a cold drink.
- Chew flavored gum.
- Indulge in a piece of dark chocolate.
- Eat a ripe piece of fruit.

WEEK 2 SPIRITUAL JOURNALING

What are you feeling this week? Pour your emotions onto this paper for nobody else to read.

SESSION 3

TOPIC: CONFRONTING VS ESCAPING GRIEF

INTRO

This session focuses on how we sometimes want to escape the pain, and why it's important to confront and work though grief.

SCRIPT

1. Last week's unfinished business.
2. Report on phone calls. How did they go?
3. Report on caring plan. How did they go?
4. Review: How did it go with communicating with family and friends?
5. This session is dedicated to sharing pictures and personal mementos so we can all get to know your special person.

REMEMBER

- ✓ **Start and end on time.**
- ✓ **Keep conversation moving and productive.**
- ✓ **Ensure every participant has an opportunity to share or pass during the discussion.**
- ✓ **Protect the conversation from being monopolized.**
- ✓ **Stay supportive yet neutral.**

MATERIALS

- ❑ **Notebook & pen**
- ❑ **Index cards & pens**
- ❑ **Refreshments**
- ❑ **Nametags**
- ❑ **Tissue**

HOMEWORK

- ❑ **The Photo Album of my Mind**
- ❑ **Self-care assignment**

DISCUSSION

1. **Discuss escaping**. Our natural reaction as humans are to fight, flight or freeze—it's how our brain responds. While escape is sometimes appropriate, the only way to escape grief is to grieve. Therefore, the time comes when it is appropriate to confront our grief by outwardly mourning. We can easily put off facing the reality of our feelings maybe for days, weeks, months, years, or even a lifetime.
   - We aren't really escaping, there is no escape; but we give an appearance of escape.
   - By not confronting and working through the grief, the feelings may be ever present.
   - If not in consciousness, they will work on our physical or emotional system, leading to sickness and disease.

2. **How do some of us escape our feelings?** In what ways are you escaping? Examples include:
   - ✓ Addictions, work, prescription drugs, substance use, alcohol, inappropriate loving.
   - ✓ Overeating or undereating.
   - ✓ Activity frenzy through lots of travel and busyness.
   - ✓ Isolating and avoiding situations where we need to talk about our feelings.

3. **Discuss confronting our grief** and the need to deal with the reality of our feelings when we're ready to do so. This helps to relieve the physical and emotional self of the need to indefinitely carry the pain. How do we confront our feelings?
   - Do some writing about our loss.
   - Allow alone time to really **think** vs frantic busyness.
   - Talk about feelings and loss with others.
   - Consciously externalize (physically express) our feelings.
   - Dispose of clothing and personal effects, if desired.

ACTIVITY

In this safe environment, you will show your loved one's photo and/or mementoes, and also share your feelings about his or her death so you have an opportunity to confront and externalize some of those feelings. If this is not strange to you, it will reinforce what you're already skilled at. If it is, a beginning in this safe environment will help form a pattern for your future needs.

- Tell us what this picture means to you.
- What stories does it remind you of?
- What feelings does it bring to the surface for you?

CONCLUSION

- **Review this session**. Encourage participants to read handout, journal their thoughts, and try this week's Resilience Rx self-care tip.
- **Phone numbers** for next week's calling.

I03/SESSION 3 INSTRUCTIONS

THE PHOTO ALBUM OF MY MIND

BY JEANNE LOSEY

The photo album of my mind,
holds treasured thoughts of you.
And I can almost see again
the things we used to do.

I hear your voice, I see your smile,
I feel you close to me.
The photo album of my mind
shows how we used to be.

Time may have changed us through the years,
but I will always find,
you're just as I remember in
the album of my mind.

And, as I turn page after page,
such precious scenes I see,
the photo album of my mind
is very dear to me.

It holds the pictures of our past,
like reels of film unwind.
I cherish all those photos in
the album of my mind.

H10/PHOTOALBUM OF MY MIND

DOODLES, THOUGHTS, NOTES & OTHER STUFF:

SELF CARE TIP #3

Sleep well

Losing a loved one creates upheaval that can lead to many sleepless nights. Juggling such emotional strains often leads to serial tossing and turning, sleep disruption and insomnia. In turn, the ensuing sleep deprivation magnifies our emotions and reduces our ability to cope with the upheaval, creating what feels like an unending circle.

When you have laboriously accomplished your daily task, go to sleep in peace. VICTOR HUGO

WHY IT MATTERS

Studies show that receiving less than 7 hours of sleep at night may increase our risk of diabetes, heart conditions, obesity, or anxiety. Managing sleep disruption and insomnia by practicing good sleep hygiene, coupled with medical management when needed, can help restore a restful sleep pattern after loss, and lead to significant improvements in other distress symptoms (National Institutes of Health, 2008).

CREATE A RITUAL

Create a relaxing bedtime ritual gives your mind and body time to wind down. It sends a signal to your brain that bedtime is near, and trains it to go into quiet mode.

BENEFITS OF GOOD SLEEP HYGIENE

Healthy sleep habits are an essential part of caring for yourself, and can make a big difference in your quality of life. Studies show that good sleep helps you cope better in times of stress. It can also lower your blood pressure, improve your memory, help keep your immunity strong, and puts you in a better mood.

Known as good sleep hygiene, healthy bedtime habits can influence the body's circadian rhythms. Healthy daytime habits, including what you eat, drink, how much daylight and physical exercise you get, also play roles.

SLEEP HYGIENE TIPS:

Try the following suggestions from the National Sleep Foundation to help you reestablish a restorative sleep pattern after losing someone you love.

- To help regulate your body's clock, stick to a sleep schedule of the same bedtime and wake time, even on weekends.
- Exercise early in the day. Vigorous exercise is best, but even light exercise is better than no exercise.
- A sleep environment between 60 and 67 degrees is ideal.
- If your partner snores, consider using a fan, earplugs, or white noise.
- Use comfortable pillows and bed linen.
- Consider moving around the bedroom furniture, repainting the bedroom walls, and purchasing new bed linen.
- Avoid bright light in the evening to keep your circadian rhythm in check.
- Avoid alcohol, caffeine, cigarettes, and heavy meals later in the day.
- Try wearing a sleep mask or weighted blanket across your feet to help reduce stimuli and calm your mind.

If you continue to struggle with sleepless nights after trying the tips above, cognitive behavioral therapy is one of the top suggestions for treating long-term sleep disruption. Speak to your doctor to learn more about this process.

WEEK 3 SPIRITUAL JOURNALING

What are you feeling this week? Pour your emotions onto this paper for nobody else to read.

SESSION 4

TOPIC: CARING FOR YOURSELF

INTRO

This session focuses on the importance of self-care, and how we're doing with the caring plans we started in week 1.

SCRIPT

1. Last week's unfinished business.
2. Report on phone calls. How did they go?
3. Report on caring plan. How did they go?

DISCUSSION

Grief can make us feel out of control. Self-care helps to restore some of that control through managing our health and well-being. When we feel physically and spiritually stronger, our coping improves.

Take time to assess your physical, emotional, intellectual, and spiritual well-being. Be honest with yourself. Where can you improve? The healthier you feel, the better you cope.

REMEMBER

- ✓ **Start and end on time.**
- ✓ **Keep conversation moving and productive.**
- ✓ **Ensure every participant has an opportunity to share or pass during the discussion.**
- ✓ **Protect the conversation from being monopolized.**
- ✓ **Stay supportive yet neutral.**

MATERIALS

- ❑ **Notebook & pen**
- ❑ **Index cards & pens**
- ❑ **Refreshments**
- ❑ **Nametags**
- ❑ **Tissue**

HOMEWORK

- ❑ **Life quality inventory**
- ❑ **Controlling stress with your calm scene**
- ❑ **Self-care assignment**

Physical. How do you physically feel right now? Do you have any aches or pains? Do you feel physically strong or rundown? What measures do you take at home to ensure good health? Is there room for improvement?

Suggestions for tending to your physical self:

- ✓ Exercise: Walking, yoga, swimming, jogging, biking, chop wood. What else can you do?
- ✓ Rest and relaxation. Picking a time to rest and relax your physical self.
- ✓ Nutrition: Regular eating times, balanced meals.
- ✓ Massage, Reiki, acupuncture, etc. Try it; maybe you'll like it.

Emotional. How do you emotionally feel right now? Do you feel strong or fragile? Do you feel alert, engaged, and aware of the world outside your own? Suggestions for tending to your emotional self:

- ✓ Become aware of your emotional being. Keep a journal of your feelings.
- ✓ Give yourself permission to express emotions. Holler, scream, cry, laugh.
- ✓ Find a friend who you can share anything with.

Intellectual. How do you feel intellectually? How do you care for your intellectual self? Suggestions for tending to your intellectual needs:

- ✓ Take a personal enrichment course.
- ✓ Read a book every month, any book. Just read.
- ✓ Browse the community library.
- ✓ Play games.
- ✓ Do puzzles.

Spiritual. How are you feeling spiritually? Not necessarily religious, but spiritual? Suggestions for tending to your spiritual needs:

- ✓ Take a trip to the mountain or beach.
- ✓ Walk a trail.
- ✓ Book a retreat.
- ✓ Take a spiritual workshop.
- ✓ Revisit the religion of your childhood.

ACTIVITY

Split into groups of dyads or triads and share where you are with the caring plan you began in week one.

1. Share what activities you currently have on your caring plan, and why.
2. Talk about what part of your caring plan is hardest, and how you're managing those obstacles.
3. Write down one thing you are going to change or add to your caring plan during the next week.
4. List one area where you need help from someone else to make the changes you listed.

CONCLUSION

- **Review this session.** Encourage participants to read handouts, journal their thoughts, and try this week's Resilience Rx self-care tip.
- **Phone numbers** for next week's calling. Share your self-care progress with the person you're calling.

LIFE QUALITY INVENTORY CHECK

Grief can have a dramatic effect on our physical, emotional and spiritual systems. It can be difficult to bring these systems into balance, particularly so if we aren't fully clear about ourselves.

This inventory is worthless unless you are completely honest with yourself. You don't need to share your answers with anyone, so please be totally honest with yourself. This will help you clarify where you are and help you to establish goals for changes you may want to bring about. These questions also make excellent prompts for the confidential journal writing. Once you're clear on these topics, you may choose whether it will be helpful or appropriate for you to share portions with anyone else.

EATING PATTERNS:

- o Only eat when hungry
- o Eat to a schedule
- o Eat sit down meals
- o Eat on the fly
- o Balanced meals
- o Snack Food
- o Binge
- o Binge & purge
- o Eat for comfort whether or not hungry

WEIGHT:

_____ How much do I weigh?
_____ How much did I weigh a year ago?
_____ How much did I weigh 5 years ago?
_____ What is my ideal weight?
_____ Am I gaining or losing weight?
_____ Do I want that to happen?

SLEEP:

- o Am I able to go to sleep easily?
- o Do I wake up much at night?
- o I've had a change in sleeping patterns
- o It's hard to get out of bed

TEARS:

- o Is it easy or hard to cry?
- o When I start crying, I can't stop
- o Crying gives me relief
- o I can cry in front of others
- o I can't cry in front of others
- o I can cry only with someone I know well
- o I burst out crying sometimes
- o I'm embarrassed when I cry
- o I never know when I'll cry

ANGER:

- o I never show my anger
- o I can't contain my anger
- o My anger spills over to others
- o This bothers me or I'm okay with it
- o When I'm angry, I let it out
- o How do I let my anger out?
- o I bear grudges and it's hard to forgive

GUILT:

- o I feel guilty about_________________
- o I can talk freely about these feelings
- o I've never told anyone these feelings
- o I experience remorse at times
- o I find talking about my feelings helps

SEXUAL FEELINGS:

I have sexual feelings:

- Often
- Sometimes
- never have any sexual feelings

When I have such feelings

- I've gone with them
- repressed them
- I miss my former sexual activity to what degree___________________?

SPIRITUALLY:

I feel this way about my spiritual nature:

- Content
- Disturbed
- neutral

- My spirituality and my religion are merged
- My spirituality and religion are two separate dimensions for me
- I am at peace with myself
- I am in inner turmoil about my relationship with the universe

DREAMS:

I dream:

- frequently
- Occasionally
- Never

I remember my dreams :

- Always
- Sometimes
- Never

My dreams are mostly:

- pleasant
- unpleasant
- nightmares
- nightmares with physical effects
- I keep having the same dream

ANXIETY / PANIC:

I get panic attacks:

- Often
- Occasionally
- Never

They last for:

- Days
- Hours
- Just moments
- I can get them under control
- They are uncontrollable

FEARS:

My greatest fear right now is__________________

____

____

____

____

____.

CALM SCENE:

When I am calm, my visualization is ____________

____

____

____

____

____.

SHARING:

- I am aware of those parts of myself I am willing to share, and why
- I am aware of those parts of myself I am not willing to share, and why

H11/LIFE QUALITY INVENTORY

SESSION 4 | HANDOUT 2

CONTROLLING STRESS WITH YOUR CALM SCENE

The day-to-day difficulties of modern society is a cause of stress. You may not be able to avoid or get rid of it, but you can learn to control it.

TRY THIS APPROACH

In your mind, create and visualize a feeling where you can experience a unique sense of peace, a oneness with the world.

Some use a time when they recall being particularly connected with nature. Suggestions:

- On a mountaintop looking into the distant valley below, surrounded by silence
- At the seashore looking into the distant vastness of the ocean horizon

Some have associated **calm** with a single moment when, for an instant, they felt a certain peace or even absence of conflict, where there was a pause in the cares of the world and a sense of peace descended over them.

Whatever your unique visualization, there are certain guidelines to use in selecting a **calm scene** which will serve you as you continue on your journey.

SPECIFIC SCENE:

The scene should be a specific place, not a general or vague memory like "in the woods somewhere."

Use your senses:

To make your image clearer, use all your senses. What do you see? What do you hear? What do you smell? What do you feel?

No other people:

Select a scene where you are absolutely alone and safe.

Limited activity:

Your physical activity should be limited. Excessive activity tends to remove the aspect of calm you are looking for.

No substances:

Your remembrance of **calm**, in order to be useful in your journey, should not be influenced by drugs, alcohol or tobacco.

Write it down:

Now that you have selected your **calm scene**, write a short paragraph to describe it. Describe where you are, what you see, what you hear, what you smell or taste, how you feel, and where in your body you have this feeling.

MY CALM SCENE:

____

____

____

____

____

____

____

____

____

____

____

____

____

____

PUT IT TO USE:

Find a moment when you can relax and enter into your **calm scene**. Once you're there in that calm, serene space in your head, anchor it with a touch by clasping the fingers of one hand around the wrist of the other hand. Feel a gentle wave of calmness and peace surge through your mind and body.

Whenever you need to reduce stress, clasp your wrist in the same manner to trigger your calm scene.

SELF CARE TIP #4

Chromotherapy

Colors are all around us, and they aren't meaningless. They play a role in how we feel, and can influence our emotions and how we react.

Chromotherapy is an ancient practice, yet researchers are just beginning to understand how it works as a healing modality as they study how colors affect our brain and emotions.

There is not one blade of grass, there is no color in this world that is not intended to make us rejoice.
JOHN CALVIN

WHY IT MATTERS

What we know about chromotherapy is that it calms the amygdala, the fear center of the brain. It also takes you outside the thinking part of your brain. Certain colors can invigorate a depressed mood or soothe an agitated mind, lower blood pressure, and relax breathing.

SELF CARE

When you need to relax, grab a coloring book or color the following pages. Use crayons, colored pencils, gel pens or felt pens to color each picture using whatever colors match your emotions in that moment.

BENEFITS OF ADULT COLORING

Most of us loved coloring as a child. Its popularity as an activity for grownups has exploded, and for good reason. The repetitive hand motions used in coloring induces a meditative state. Focusing on the simple act of coloring gives our brain a respite from pain. It unplugs it from negativity and plugs it into positivity by focusing on the present rather than our worries. The beauty of coloring is that it can be done by anyone regardless of creative talent, and you can take it with you wherever you go. Pick colors that reflect your current mood to help safely externalize your feelings.

MORE WAYS TO USE COLOR TO TRIGGER POSITIVE HORMONES:

- Paint a color-by-number picture
- Color your bath water
- Plug in a colored nightlight
- Hang a colored glass prism
- Paint the walls of your bedroom or office
- Add colorful home décor
- Use colored bulbs in your lamps
- Enjoy a color wash YouTube video
- Download a color therapy app
- Enjoy a chromotherapy sauna

iCare

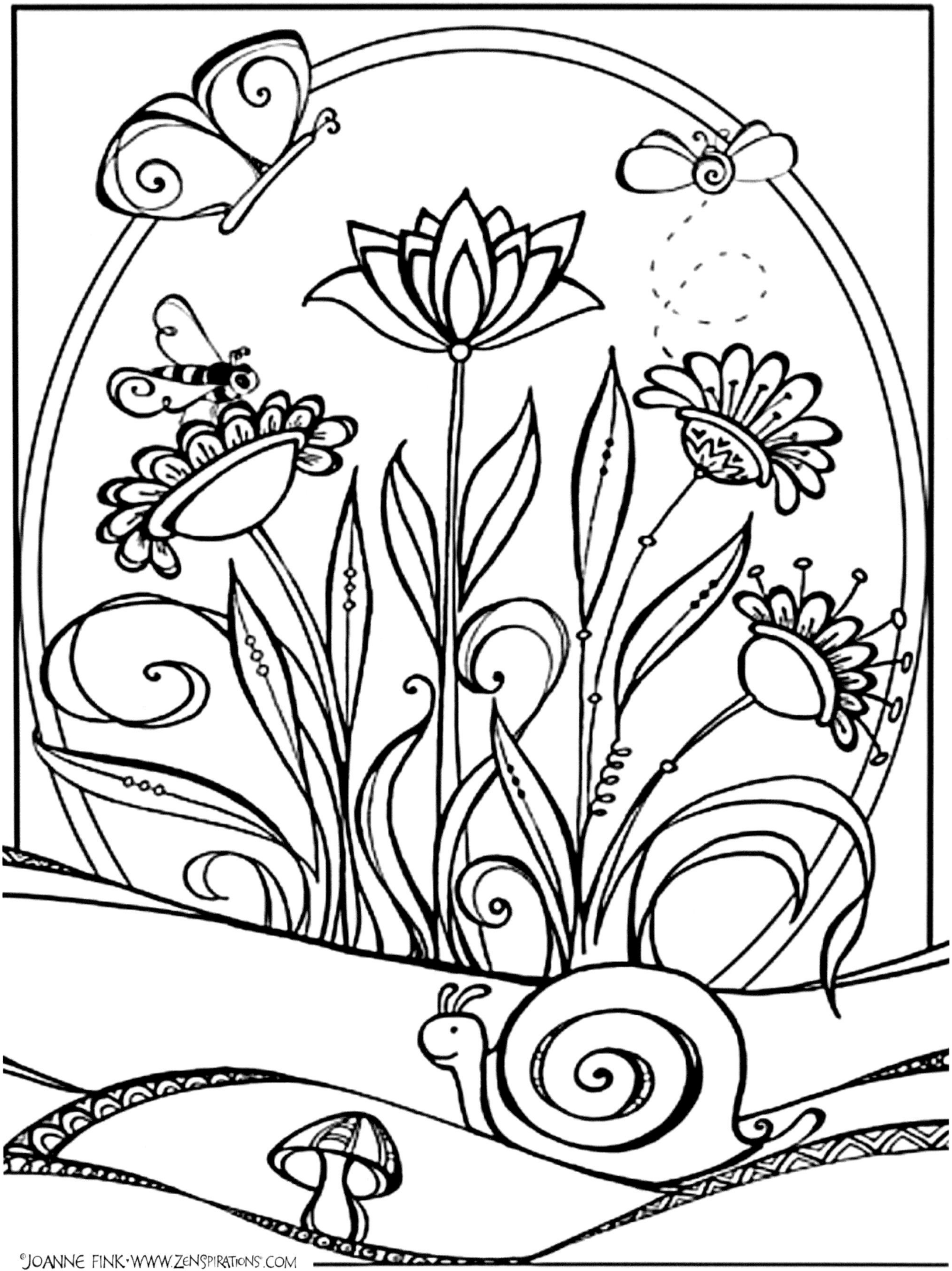

iCare

Love

MATTERS

WEEK 4 SPIRITUAL JOURNALING

What are you feeling this week? Pour your emotions onto this paper for nobody else to read.

iCare

SESSION 5

TOPIC: ANGER

INTRO

This session focuses on anger and how to release it.

SCRIPT

1. Last week's unfinished business.
2. Report on phone calls. How did they go?
3. Review: How did you do on your self-care commitment?
   - ✓ What did you do differently?
   - ✓ What changes are you making?

DISCUSSION

Anger is a natural emotion that needs to be expressed. When we get angry, a cortisol reaction occurs in the brain that causes an increase in our heart rate, blood pressure, respirations and core body temperature. Too much cortisol will decrease the brain's serotonin, a happy hormone. A decrease in serotonin can make you feel anger and pain more easily.

When we physically and emotionally restrain anger, it can be expressed or manifest in inappropriate ways. Sometimes it results in physical discharges into the body or is expressed through erratic behavior. Other times we suppress it until it becomes a lifetime of bitterness.

It is important to learn how to externalize anger so it can be released and resolved.

- It is not a sin to be angry; it is a sin against your being to hold repressed anger.
- Learn to release your anger safely and in a manner that is appropriate for you.

REMEMBER

- ✓ **Start and end on time.**
- ✓ **Keep conversation moving and productive.**
- ✓ **Ensure every participant has an opportunity to share or pass during the discussion.**
- ✓ **Protect the conversation from being monopolized.**
- ✓ **Stay supportive yet neutral.**

MATERIALS

- ❑ **Notebook & pen**
- ❑ **Index cards & pens**
- ❑ **Refreshments**
- ❑ **Nametags**
- ❑ **Tissue**

HOMEWORK

- ❑ **Hidden anger**
- ❑ **Anger quotes**
- ❑ **How to safely process anger**
- ❑ **Self-care assignment**

1. **Do you know when you're angry?** What happens to you physically?
   - ❑ Face turns red
   - ❑ Blood pressure goes up
   - ❑ Tight muscles
   - ❑ Clenched fists
   - ❑ Heart races

2. **What happens to you emotionally?**
   - ❑ Cry
   - ❑ Yell
   - ❑ Scream
   - ❑ Curse
   - ❑ Feel sad
   - ❑ Feel fear

3. **What happens to you spiritually?**
   - ❑ Feel guilt
   - ❑ Feel shame

4. **As a child, what happened when you displayed your natural anger?**

5. **Do you feel mad now?** If so, what are you mad at? Anger doesn't need to be reasonable or rational. You may be angry at:
   - ♦ Medical establishment, individuals or institutions, hospice, etc.
   - ♦ The person who died for leaving, not leaving soon enough, drain on finances, for beneficiaries in will, not listening to me about smoking, drinking, etc.
   - ♦ Relatives and friends for not visiting, insensitivity, not behaving to my expectations.
   - ♦ God for not minding the store, deserting me in hour of need, ignoring my prayers, letting my loved one suffer.
   - ♦ Others for murdering my loved one, or for letting him or her abuse oneself.
   - ♦ Myself. Anger directed inward is one form of guilt.

6. **Discuss how to form a plan to uncover and deal with your anger.**

CONCLUSION

- ♦ **Review this session.** Encourage participants to read handouts, journal their thoughts, and try this week's Resilience Rx self-care tip.
- ♦ **Phone numbers** for next week's calling. Share your plan to deal with anger with the person you're calling.

SESSION 5 | HANDOUT 1

HIDDEN ANGER

Anger is a natural human emotion. We are all born with the capability of letting others know we are distressed. As infants, we show natural anger by getting red in the face and crying at the top of our lungs. As toddlers, we threw ourselves down and screamed and kicked when we felt angry. Parents scolded or spanked us for doing this, and little by little we learned not to physically express our natural anger or act in a violent fashion.

Perhaps we learned to use words to express anger, such as profanity, sarcastic remarks and vindictive thoughts. Many of us were taught that, too, wasn't nice.

As we matured and grew into nice, polite, civil, socially responsible people, we became quite adept at hiding and repressing our natural anger, so much so that we often convince ourselves we aren't really angry, when deep down our insides might be raging.

Denial and self-deception are ways we learned to tell ourselves we're okay, even though the anger was still there, no matter how well we covered it up.

Would you call yourself an angry person? What do you do with your natural anger? Do you deny negative feelings or just don't get angry?

ACTIVITY

ANGER SIGNS

Mark the signs of hidden anger which apply to you. Be honest with yourself.

- ❑ Procrastination in the completion of imposed tasks.
- ❑ Perceptual or habitual lateness.
- ❑ A liking for sadistic or ironic humor.
- ❑ Sarcasm, cynicism or flippancy in conversation.
- ❑ Over-politeness, constant cheerfulness, attitude of grin and bear it.
- ❑ Frequent sighing.
- ❑ Smiling while hurting.
- ❑ Frequent disturbing or frightening dreams.

- ❑ Overcontrolled, monotone speaking voice.
- ❑ Difficulty in getting to sleep or sleeping through the night.
- ❑ Boredom, apathy, loss of interest and enthusiasm.
- ❑ Slowing down of movement.
- ❑ Getting tired more easily than usual.
- ❑ Excessive irritability over trifles.
- ❑ Getting drowsy at inappropriate times.
- ❑ Sleeping more than usual, maybe 12 to 14 hours a day.
- ❑ Waking up tired rather than rested and refreshed.
- ❑ Clenched jaws and/or grinding teeth, especially while sleeping.
- ❑ Facial tics, spasmodic foot movements, fist clenching and similar repeated physical acts done unintentionally or unawares.
- ❑ Chronic depression and/or extended periods of feeling down for no reason.
- ❑ Chronically stiff or sore neck.
- ❑ Stomach ulcers.

Don't be surprised if you marked more than a few. Majority of nice adults are going around with hidden anger. Some of us have learned how to discharge our anger in appropriate ways. Some of us have gotten—or will get—physically ill as our body tries to discharge the suppressed anger.

DISCUSSION:

Discuss anger, and safe and appropriate ways to deal with it.

H13/HIDDEN ANGER

ANGER QUOTES

Those tormented by the pain of anger,
will never know tranquility of mind,
strangers to every joy and pleasure;
sleep deserts them, they will never know rest.
~SHANTIDEVA -8TH CENTURY

The greatest remedy for anger is delay.
~SENECA

An angry man opens his mouth and shuts up his eyes.
~CATO

Anger begins with folly, and ends with repentance.
~H. G. BOHN

Anger blows out the lamp of the mind.
~ROBERT GREEN INGERSOLL

I was angry with my friend:
I told my wrath, my wrath did end.
I was angry with my foe:
I told it not, my wrath did grow.
~WILLIAM BLAKE

Keep cool; anger is not an argument.
~DANIEL WEBSTER

Men often make up in wrath what they want in reason.
~WILLIAM ROUNSEVILLE ALGER

Anger is a momentary madness, so control
your passion or it will control you.
~HORACE

When a man is wrong and won't admit it, he always gets angry.
~HALIBURTON

Anger is as a stone cast into a wasp's nest.
~MALABAR PROVERB

An angry man is again angry with himself when he returns to reason.
~PUBLILIUS SYRUS

Anger is seldom without argument, but seldom with a good one.
~LORD HALIFAX

When angry count four; when very angry, swear.
~MARK TWAIN

Anger and intolerance are the twin enemies of correct understanding.
~MAHATMA GANDHI

Anybody can become angry—that is easy; but to be angry with the right person, and to the right degree, and at the right time, and for the right purpose, and in the right way—that is not within everybody's power and is not easy.
~ARISTOTLE

Wise anger is like fire from a flint: there is great ado to get it out; and when it does come, it is out again immediately.
~MATTHEW HENRY

H14/ANGER QUOTES

HOW TO SAFELY PROCESS ANGER

The only way to escape from anger is by confronting it, listening to it, and working it through, just like grief. As a powerful emotion, some are frightened by it, or have been taught to avoid pain. Find ways that allow you to safely process and discharge the anger. Below are some examples to get you started.

PHYSICAL EXTERNALIZATION

Do something physical that doesn't make you more frustrated (don't continue hitting golf balls if you keep missing them).

- ✓ Hit the ground using a rubber hose.
- ✓ Beat on pillows.
- ✓ Throw a bowling ball.
- ✓ Hit golf balls at the driving range.
- ✓ Run.
- ✓ Chop wood.
- ✓ Pound nails.
- ✓ Stomp on bubble wrap.

INTELLECTUAL EXTERNALIZATION

- ✓ Keep a journal and write down how your anger started and how you feel about it. Does it scare you? What do you do about it? Where does it cause you to choke up?
- ✓ If you're angry at an individual, write a letter and let it all hang out, and then burn it. If your writing skills need development, take a writing workshop.
- ✓ Give yourself permission to talk about your anger in your support group.

EMOTIONAL EXTERNALIZATION

Do something that allows you to express your frustration and anger.

- ✓ Cry, yell and scream.
- ✓ Throw a tantrum in your bedroom (this combines physical and emotional release).
- ✓ Allow yourself to gut cry.

SPIRITUAL EXTERNALIZATION

- ✓ Give it to God. Talk to him.
- ✓ Spend time in still meditation or listen to spiritually soothing music.
- ✓ If your spirituality is closely aligned to your faith or religion, revisit your association with the faith of your youth or the faith of your rebirth.

ACTIVE FORGIVENESS

It is difficult to get on with your own life without forgiving those who anger you. This is why externalizing anger is very important, otherwise it's just words without action.

Active forgiving involves letting issues pass through, noticing them, and letting them go. The confessional works for some, personal confession and prayer works for others.

H30/HOW TO SAFELY PROCESS ANGER

DOODLES, THOUGHTS, NOTES & OTHER STUFF:

SELF CARE TIP #5

Forest Therapy

Forest therapy is rooted in the Japanese practice of Shinrin-yoku, which is often translated as "forest bathing." A stroll of any length through the forest offers one of the most reliable boosts to your mental and physical well-being.

There are moments when all anxiety and stated toil are becalmed in the infinite leisure and repose of nature.
HENRY DAVID THOREAU

WHY IT MATTERS

Exposing your brain to restorative environments by immersing yourself in the atmosphere of the forest helps with mental fatigue by eliciting feelings of awe. This triggers the brain to release feel-good hormones that counteract the stress hormones of grief.

NATURAL THERAPY

Stress, anxiety, and depression may all be eased by some time in the great outdoors, especially when combined with exercise. The natural environment is restorative, and one thing that a walk outside can restore is your waning attention.

Doses of nature have found to improve concentration after just 20 minutes in a park. Studies show that walks in the forest were specifically associated with decreased levels of anxiety and bad moods. The effects of nearby water such as a stream, waterfall or fountain improves it even more.

SELF CARE

Try to spend at least twenty minutes outside every day. Even a walk around the block can help. During inclement weather, eat your breakfast or lunch near a window, look at forest images, or watch forest videos on YouTube.

WHAT RESEARCH SAYS

One study found that people's mental energy bounced back even when they just looked at pictures of nature (Psychological Science, 2012). Another study showed decreased stress hormones in those who spent time in the forest. Even the view of nature out a door or window is associated with lower stress and higher job satisfaction (Scandinavian Journal of Forest Research, 2007; Environmental Health and Preventative Medicine, 2010; Japanese Journal of Hygiene, 2011; Biomedical and Environmental Sciences, 2012).

WAYS TO ENJOY OUTSIDE

- ❑ Walk or run
- ❑ Garden
- ❑ Bike ride
- ❑ Hike
- ❑ Kayak
- ❑ Sail or go fishing
- ❑ Golf, play tennis, or swim
- ❑ Team sports such as soccer
- ❑ Kite flying
- ❑ Geo-caching
- ❑ Pokemoning
- ❑ Metal detecting
- ❑ Mining for gems
- ❑ Outdoor photography

WEEK 5 SPIRITUAL JOURNALING

What are you feeling this week? Pour your emotions onto this paper for nobody else to read.

SESSION 6

TOPIC: GUILT

INTRO

This session focuses on how to release guilt and resentment.

SCRIPT

1. Last week's unfinished business.
2. Report on phone calls. How did they go?
3. Report on caring plan. How did they go?
4. Review: How did you do on anger and/or resentment?

DISCUSSION

Last week we mentioned that guilt is often a result of being angry with ourselves. However, that's only part of it.

1. What is guilt?
   - If you had to put guilt in your body, where would it be?
   - If you gave guilt a color, what color would it be?
   - If guilt had a sound, how would it sound?
2. What is your first remembrance of feeling guilty?
   - What were the circumstances surrounding it?
   - Who labeled it for you and told you it was guilt?
3. What productive thing does guilt do for you? Is this thing really productive?
4. Does knowing you are not alone in your guilt help in any way?
5. Who do we need forgiveness from in order to get over the intensity of our feeling? How do we sand down the rough edges?
6. If we need forgiveness from our dead loved one, how are we going to go about getting it?
7. What has to happen to be free from our feelings of guilt?

REMEMBER

- ✓ **Start and end on time.**
- ✓ **Keep conversation moving and productive.**
- ✓ **Ensure every participant has an opportunity to share or pass during the discussion.**
- ✓ **Protect the conversation from being monopolized.**
- ✓ **Stay supportive yet neutral.**

MATERIALS

- ❑ **Notebook & pen**
- ❑ **Index cards & pens**
- ❑ **Refreshments**
- ❑ **Nametags**
- ❑ **Tissue**

HOMEWORK

- ❑ **Guilt**
- ❑ **Regret & guilt**
- ❑ **Self-care assignment**

ACTIVITY

Substitute the word guilt for resentment and see what happens.

I feel **guilty** about not taking good enough care of ______________________________.

I **resent** the demands placed upon me when I was taking care of ____________________.

ACTIVITY

Do an intensification meditation.

- ❑ Select a positive incident.
- ❑ Describe the good feeling associated with it.
- ❑ Now intensify that feeling by stepping into that memory—feel just the way you felt when the incident occurred. See the things you saw, hear the things you heard, smell the smells and feel the feelings.
- ❑ Intensify those sights, sounds, and feelings. Make them bigger, brighter, stronger, nearer.
- ❑ Where in your body do you feel this good sensation? Trace this good sensation as it moves through you.
- ❑ Amplify good feelings by making the movement bigger, stronger, and faster until you are bathed all over in this good feeling.
- ❑ Find something to anchor this feeling to, such as wrapping the right index finger and thumb around your left wrist. With practice, you'll soon be able to trigger the good feeling simply by wrapping your right finger and thumb around the left wrist.

CONCLUSION

- **Review this session.** What happened for you tonight? Encourage participants to read handouts, journal their thoughts, and try this week's Resilience Rx selfcare tip.
- **Phone numbers** for next week's calling. Share your progress with the person you're calling.

GUILT

Even though we intellectually know we can't undo the past, our inner self will sometimes not let us off the hook. For many of us, the perceived deeds or omissions of the past keep coming back, again and again and again, as if a needle were stuck in an old record. Over and over it keeps whispering . . .

- **you should have . . .**
- **you shouldn't have . . .**
- **If only you had . . .**

Sometimes it is an incessant inside voice which will just not stop, even at 3 in the morning. Sometimes we know our fault is imagined. Though it is not visible to the rest of the world, we still cannot seem to let go.

Sometimes our fault is real—we really were clearly wrong. If we only had a chance to do it over, we would now want to do something quite different.

The uncomfortable feelings we have are known as **guilt**.

- Does it help us to know that guilt is common?
- Does it help to know that in most cases, we couldn't or wouldn't really do anything different if we had another chance, particularly if we were operating with the same information we had at the time?
- Does it help to know we are already forgiven by God?
- Our problem may be that we never really learned how to forgive ourselves.

HOW THEN, DO WE DEAL WITH GUILT?

Acknowledge its presence by verbalizing it first to ourselves, and then to another person. Make it a clear statement:

- "When Fred was dying, I was cranky and irritable and never really told him I loved him."
- "Would Joan have died by suicide if she hadn't discovered me having an affair?"
- "I knew Joseph's smoking was killing him, and I never successfully got him to stop."
- "I should have stayed at the hospital the night Harvey died. I was tired, and didn't listen to myself. He died alone and I'm so unhappy that we never got to say goodbye."

We may need to express it in many ways, perhaps in writing or in conversation. We may need to act it out. We may need to identify a color, sound or picture to it. A hidden guilt seems to stay with us forever. A guilt that's brought out into the open loses its power to haunt us.

HOW DO WE DEAL WITH OTHERS?

Some people want to tell us that our guilt is groundless, that we couldn't have acted any other way and shouldn't feel the way we do. While most of these comments are gratuitous, at some level it may be helpful to hear that the rest of the world doesn't appear to judge us as harshly as we are judging ourselves. We sometimes have a difficult time listening to these well-meaning people because we know they are incapable of really knowing what we are feeling.

CLARITY

Our feelings are justified in our eyes at the moment we are feeling the way we do. What we often don't recognize is that our perspective is frequently obscured by the traumatic events which have taken place. As we gain clarity, our perspective changes. Our feelings of guilt also have the ability to change.

How do we go about gaining clarity?

Once acknowledging our guilty feelings and listening to others tell us why we should or shouldn't feel this way, it is helpful to clearly review the circumstances which led to our feelings. These should be written down to ensure we haven't missed anything. The next step is to list all the reasons we might be feeling and reacting the way we are. Also list the mitigating circumstances which help to explain why we acted that way.

RESENTMENT

Many psychologists have found a link between resentment and guilt. Since guilt is often a reaction to things resented, it is sometimes useful for us to list all the people, circumstances or things we resented which feeds our guilt.

Examples:

- I resent having had the responsibility to decide whether Henry remained on life support.
- I resent that I was put in the position of needing to be Harry's nurse for the last 3 years. I never asked for that role nor was I particularly qualified for it.
- I resent that Joan treated me so poorly that I felt I needed other personal companionship.
- I resent that I wasn't able to say goodbye.

EXERCISE

For each guilt, put the words **I resent** before the situation. Does it talk to you? Can you associate with the resentment within the situation which you are now using to abuse yourself?

H15/GUILT

REGRET & GUILT

You might feel that you could have had more patience, spent more time, given more care, had more concern, done things differently, or made different decisions or different choices.

Whatever your thoughts of regret or guilt may be, know that these responses are a common part of the grief experience and, for some, are even necessary. This isn't a bad thing.

Some people will tell you not to think like that, and not to put yourself through that. Yet we need to define all the ways that we feel **guilty**.

It is healthy to define our regrets.

The process of doing this is painful. It's hard for others to witness. Some might feel you're overreacting.

When you're grieving, there is no such thing as overreacting.

Your feelings are very powerful. You need to express them. Doing so will help you examine your circumstances and come to a resolution in your own time.

One widow said, "At one point, I was so angry that I gathered an old set of dishes my mother-in-law had given me many years earlier. I went out to my firepit in the yard and broke every single dish into the pit that night." She went on to say she hadn't had a very healthy relationship with her mother-in-law, for she had caused great stress in the widow's marriage. "Breaking those dishes brought me such relief and satisfaction."

A bereaved husband said, "I wish I had taken my wife on that trip she had always talked about. I just never wanted to spend the money. I feel so awful, maybe I would feel better if I had."

A grieving son said, "After I married and moved to a nearby town, I did not spend too much time with my parents. I was so busy with my own life. When Dad died, I held up okay, staying strong for my mom. Three weeks later, Mom died suddenly. I wish I had made a better effort to spend time with both of them." He further said, "Having to take care of their final affairs and settling their estate, I have spent more time in their home since their death than I had in the previous four years."

A bereaved parent said, "My daughter had been treated for what we thought was an occasional dizzy spell. She died three months later following brain surgery to remove a cancerous tumor. I can't help but think that the doctors missed something. I constantly think about obtaining all her medical records in hopes of finding something that would justify pursuing legal action."

This parent was hurting so badly, she needed a better reason for her daughter's death. She believed there must be something more that caused her daughter to die.

Although typically not the fault of anyone or anything, her concerns about her daughter's death were perfectly legitimate. Often times there are no answers to be found, but being allowed to explore the possibility of finding one is a part of the grief journey for some.

Sometimes people feel as though their loved one had not received proper medical care. You might have questions surrounding your loved one's death that you feel may not have been addressed sufficiently or with the right person.

Communicate your concerns and share your questions with those who had been involved with your loved one's care. Even if you already asked the question, it is okay to ask it again.

Communicating with your loved one's caregiver(s) is vital in order to obtain whatever information will help you resolve lingering concerns.

SELF CARE TIP #6

Dance/Movement Therapy

Feelings can influence your movement, and movement can impact your feelings. When we feel tired and sad, we tend to move slower. Moving your body improves your mood, helps combat anxiety and depression, and promotes a safe space for the expression of feeling.

When you dance, your purpose is not to get to a certain place on the floor. It's to enjoy each step along the way.

DR. WAYNE DYER

WHY IT WORKS

Any form of exercise is great for relieving stress in the mind and body. Dancing is also emotionally therapeutic, especially when paired with music we love. Since movement can be related to thoughts and feelings, dance/movement therapy (DMT) benefits us both physically and mentally through stress reduction, mood management, decreased muscle tension, increased mobility and more. Further, it oxygenates the brain, which helps clear the mind and allows you more clarity and focus.

SELF CARE

Put on music you love, and dance for ten minutes every day like nobody's watching. If you feel inhibited, dance in the shower, your bedroom, or a corner of your garden.

PHYSICAL BENEFITS

Dancing helps to oxygenate the brain and fight illness. Unlike the circulatory or respiratory systems, the lymphatic system— the body's defense mechanism against illness—does not have a pump. It relies on your motion to circulate the fluid that contains infection-fighting white blood cells around the body. Each time you move large muscles of the body, you help pump lymphatic fluid through your body, keeping your systems circulating.

TAKE A MENTAL RECESS

School recess was invented for a reason. Movement improves cognitive performance for people of all ages. In one study, children who participated in physical activity demonstrated increased electrical activity in the brain, as well as improved mental accuracy and reaction times during learning. Dancing and moving offer a mental recess through physical release.

Movement is one of the most basic functions of the human body, making it easy to incorporate motion into daily life in a way that feels good. If dancing isn't your thing, try one of the alternatives below.

ALTERNATIVE OPTIONS TO DANCING:

- ✓ Shake a bed sheet.
- ✓ Run in place or jump up and down.
- ✓ Stretch or roll your head in circles.
- ✓ Go for a short walk.
- ✓ Squeeze a rubbery stress ball.
- ✓ Window shop.
- ✓ Garden.
- ✓ Stretch.
- ✓ Clean a closet.
- ✓ Grocery shop with a basket instead of a cart.
- ✓ Romp around with the kids or grandkids
- ✓ Walk, bike, or hike.

WEEK 6 SPIRITUAL JOURNALING

What are you feeling this week? Pour your emotions onto this paper for nobody else to read.

SESSION 7

TOPIC: SPIRITUAL LESSONS & RECONCILIATION

INTRO

This session focuses on the grief reconciliation process, how proactive we are in our own healing, and spiritual lessons.

SCRIPT

1. Last week's unfinished business.
2. Report on phone calls. How did they go?
3. Report on caring plan. How did they go?
4. Review: How did you do on last week's topic of guilt?

REMEMBER

- ✓ **Start and end on time.**
- ✓ **Keep conversation moving and productive.**
- ✓ **Ensure every participant has an opportunity to share or pass during the discussion.**
- ✓ **Protect the conversation from being monopolized.**
- ✓ **Stay supportive yet neutral.**

MATERIALS

- ❑ **Notebook & pen**
- ❑ **Index cards & pens**
- ❑ **Refreshments**
- ❑ **Nametags**
- ❑ **Tissue**

HOMEWORK

- ❑ **What I need**
- ❑ **Griefwork & boundaries**
- ❑ **Reconciliation**
- ❑ **Grief & drugs**
- ❑ **Self-care assignment**

DISCUSSION

Spiritual Lessons. In the early days of loss, the thought that anything good can come from our experience is beyond comprehension. Yet spiritual lessons are God's nuggets of wisdom—collateral blessings—we learn from hardship. Have you discovered a lesson learned or collateral blessing from your loss?

Reconciliation. We've all heard the cliché "time heals," yet we know that time itself just doesn't make it suddenly all right. We know that from moment to moment we are never quite the same.

The experience of each moment changes our outlook on the next moment. The changing of perspective can work for you, once you realize and accept that the world is never static.

1. What are your feelings?
2. What have you been experiencing?
3. What are you looking forward to experiencing?

ACTIVITY

Review the steps of reconciliation. Where are you with these?

- ☐ Learn to effectively experience and express the reality of the death of your loved one.
- ☐ Learn to lean into the pain of the loss, while learning how to nurture yourself physically, emotionally and spiritually.
- ☐ Learn to convert your relationship with the person who died from one of interactive presence to one of appropriate memory.
- ☐ Learn to develop a new self-identity based on a life without the person who died.
- ☐ Learn to relate the experience of the death to a context of new meaning in your life.
- ☐ Learn to develop a lasting network of support to help you through the process.

NEEDS WE HAVE BEEN DISCUSSING & WORKING ON

- ☑ Learning to express your grief.
- ☑ Learning to take care of ourselves physically, emotionally, intellectually, and spiritually.
- ☑ Learning how to develop new relationships. While honoring the memory of your loved one, learning to replace the day-to-day relationship with other types of experiences.

WHERE ARE WE NOW? WHERE DO WE GO FROM HERE?

- Some need alone time for reflection and integration.
- Some need to continue some sort of group contact.
- Some may need professional social or psychological support.
- Some may need additional individual intensive work in expressing grief.
- Each person needs to work out a plan for his/herself.

CONCLUSION

- **Review this session**. Encourage participants to read handouts, journal their thoughts, and try this week's Resilience Rx self-care tip.
- **Phone numbers** for next week's calling. Share your progress with the person you're calling.

WHAT I NEED

TIME

I need time alone, and time with others whom I can trust and will listen when I need to talk. I need time to feel and understand the feelings which go along with loss.

REST

I may need extra amounts of things I needed before. Relaxation, exercise, diversion, nourishment, hot baths, afternoon naps, a trip, a cause to work for to help others, any of these may give me a lift. Grief is an emotionally exhausting process. I need to replenish myself, to follow what feels healing, and connects me to the people and things I love.

SECURITY

I need to reduce or find help for financial or other stresses in my life. I need to allow myself to be close to ones I can trust. It helps when I allow myself to get back into a routine, and to do things at my own pace.

HOPE

I find hope and comfort from those who have experienced a similar loss. Knowing some things that helped them, and realizing that they have recovered and that time does help, gives me hope that sometime in the future my grief will be less raw and less painful.

CARING

I try to allow myself to accept the expressions of caring from others, even though they may be uneasy and awkward. Helping a friend or relative also suffering from the same loss often brings me a feeling of closeness with that person.

BACKSLIDING

Sometimes after a period of feeling good, I find myself back in old feelings of extreme sadness, despair or anger. Intellectually, I know the nature of grief is up and down, and it may happen over and over for a time. Humans cannot take in the pain and the meaning of death all at once. So, I give myself permission to let it in a little at a time.

SMALL PLEASURE

I no longer underestimate the healing effects of small pleasures. Sunsets, a walk in the woods, a favorite food all are small steps toward regaining pleasure in life itself.

GOALS

It can sometimes feel that much of life is without meaning. At times like these, small goals are helpful. Giving myself something to look forward to, like playing tennis with a friend next week, a movie tomorrow night, a trip next month, helps me get through the moment. Living one day at a time is a good rule of thumb. At first, my enjoyment of these things just isn't the same. I know this is normal. As time passes, I will work on longer range goals to give some structure and direction to my life. It is okay to get some guidance or counseling to help with this.

MEDICATION

Unless carefully managed under professional supervision, medication is not always the answer. Drugs intended to help me get through periods of shock may sometimes prolong and delay the necessary process of grieving. I cannot prevent or cure grief. The only way **out** is **through**.

GRIEFWORK & BOUNDARIES

A boundary is a limit or edge that defines you as separate from others. When that boundary is indistinguishable from the boundary of others, the relationship is called **enmeshed**. When someone crosses your boundary without your full consent, your boundary has been **violated**.

An understanding of boundaries, those which have been appropriately healthy for you and your past, current and future relationships, is particularly useful when dealing with the changes brought by the death of someone who has been a significant part of your life.

You might discover that your boundaries were inappropriately enmeshed with a deceased partner, or even violated by that partner. In order to constructively deal with your loss, you may need to better understand that relationship and learn whether or not there is a danger of having it adversely affect your future well-being.

Many changes will be brought about by your loss, and a better understanding of your rightful boundaries is an important part of shaping that change in a healthy manner.

While problems in life are inevitable, suffering is not. You are allowed to make appropriate changes in your image, outlook and behavior.

BOUNDARY TYPES

- **Physical.** A boundary may be physical, like where and when you are comfortable being touched by others, how close you want to be to others, how physically involved you are comfortable being with others. It is in respect for the accidental violation of another's physical boundary that in our first session we asked you not to hug or physically comfort another without first getting that person's consent. We cannot assume that someone else's boundary is the same as our own.
- **Emotional.** A boundary may also be emotional, a result of how you act with others or will permit others to act with you, communicate with you, be with you, and how you permit yourself to feel in a variety of life situations.
- **Visible.** A boundary may be visible, obvious or apparent to you and to others, or invisible, where you or others are not aware that it exists or even that it has been violated.

Given a particular relationship or situation, your boundary may be different than usual. There are appropriate boundaries and inappropriate boundaries for you in varying situations and relationships. Your boundaries were learned as a result of your experiences as children and in the process of growing up. Because you may have learned a set of inappropriate boundaries, this doesn't mean that you can't change your life and learn to practice more appropriate boundaries.

PHYSICAL BOUNDARIES

You have a right to have control of your body. You need not let anyone get closer to you than what is comfortable for you. Sometimes we're conditioned to accept something as outwardly comfortable which, had we been in good communication with our inside feelings, would have realized was making us uncomfortable. Incidentally, this is true for emotional as well as physical boundaries. Insist that your boundary of physical closeness, sexual contact, and degree of touch are honored and not **violated**.

EMOTIONAL BOUNDARIES

Emotional boundaries are more varied, more invisible, more deeply ingrained in your upbringing, and sometimes more difficult to change.

ACTIVITY

Do you:

- Pretend to agree when you really disagree? "I love that color" when you really don't?
- Conceal your true feelings? "That's okay, I'm not hurt," when you were terribly hurt?
- Go along with an activity you really don't want to do, never stating your preference? "That movie is fine with me," when you would rather have taken a walk.
- Declining to join an activity you really want to do? "No thanks, you guys go ahead."
- Work too hard or work too long?
- Do too much for others?
- Not rest when tired?
- Ignore your needs; not eat regularly, not get sufficient sleep?
- Get too little or too much alone time?
- Get too little of too much exercise?
- Have too little or too much leisure activity?
- Have insufficient contact with persons who really care about you?
- Use chemicals to avoid yourself: alcohol, drugs, tranquilizers, caffeine sugar, etc.?
- Use compulsions to avoid yourself: eating, starving, exercise, work, shopping, spending, TV, sex, games, sports? All can be done appropriately or can be done compulsively.

To the degree that you are comfortable, let's discuss some of the boundary issues you have had in previous relationships as well as desirable future changes.

Should you realize you've had a problem with boundaries in the past and wish to prevent similar problems in the future, a more intensive work on your personal boundaries may greatly benefit from the professional direction of a therapist or trained counselor

H19/GRIEF WORK

SESSION 7 | HANDOUT 3

RECONCILIATION

Dr. Alan Wolfelt's six reconciliation needs of the mourner emphasizes the following activities.

I will learn to effectively express the reality of the death.

Choosing to attend a support group is a positive initial step. I tell my story and express my feelings over and over again to whomever will listen without wanting to offer inane advice. I need compassionate listeners now, not advice that will cause me to shut off my feelings.

I will learn to embrace pain while nurturing myself.

This means I don't shut off my feelings, and will permit myself to cry in appropriate places and in appropriate times. I permit myself to feel depressed and scared, and to share this with others. I also commit to establishing a routine which provides exercise, nutritious meals, a time to memorialize, a time for friends, and journal keeping with particular regard to my feelings and speculation on meaning in my life.

I will learn to convert my relationship with my loved one from an interactive presence to one of appropriate memory.

This is a process which cannot be deliberately willed. I won't even try. I just make a mental note of it as something that's in the process of happening, and allow my subconscious to do its work without interference.

I will learn to develop a new self-identity.

Over time, I will learn that I am an important person in my own right. I inventory my needs and create a plan to fill in areas where needed. This may involve establishing new friendships and relationships which I will do without guilt. I am a worthy human being who deserves the company of others and has value to offer. My new relationships will be just that—new, not a replacement of my old relationships.

I will learn to relate the experience of the death to a context of new meaning in life.

In this process of reconciliation, I have learned much about myself and my life. I have slowly developed a new perspective on living which honors each relationship as a unique gift from my higher power—most particularly my new relationship with myself. I find that I have much to offer others who are traveling my road.

I will learn to develop a lasting network of support to help me get through the process.

I realize there are others who can help me. Perhaps I've reconnected or strengthened the bond with my immediate or extended family. Perhaps I've discovered the nature of true friendships and am more discriminating in whom I place my confidence. It is so difficult to do it all alone, and I've learned I can count on the love and help of others who have had similar experiences.

H27/RECONCILIATION

DOODLES, THOUGHTS, NOTES & OTHER STUFF:

GRIEF & MEDICATION

Perhaps you've heard the expression, "The only way out is through." The only way out of grief is to go through the pain and let the natural process work. Only then will you find the light at the other end of the dark tunnel.

Our natural body requires externalization of emotional pain before we can heal.

In a day of pharmacology, people are denied the opportunity to work through their pain by externalizing their feelings. Medication offers only temporary cessation of the pain, and robs those around the mourner the experience of witnessing someone grieving. The mourner is able to mask his or her feelings and look okay to the outside world.

But where do the emotions and feelings go?

They remain unprocessed in the mind, body, and soul.

When the medication stops, grief emotions will again surface in their natural effort to be expressed.

Many will again attempt to shut off the pain with drugs instead of naturally externalizing it, and thus become addicted in a similar manner to those addicted to alcohol, tobacco, cocaine and other chemical substances.

So, what's wrong with taking away the pain?

There is nothing wrong with removing pain as long as it doesn't set you up for more pain and trauma in the future.

H29/GRIEF AND MEDICATION

Unless the natural feelings and emotions of grief are somehow expressed—gotten out of the system—they remain inside, perhaps masked or disguised by the drug.

Is it ever appropriate to take drugs?

Yes, when prescribed by a competent clinician who has training and experience with the grieving process, and will continue to follow the patient during the grieving process.

It is not appropriate when prescribed by a well-meaning professional who is only concerned with the cessation of immediate symptoms and will have no responsibility for continually working with the patient during the grieving process.

It is never appropriate for medication or drugs to be administered by family or friends.

Even when their motivation is the griever's emotional stability, all too often they have a hidden motivation to make that person more comfortable to be around.

The only way out of the pain is to go through it, to fully experience it.

Only then can we reconcile it within our heart and learn to move forward.

This will require lots of support to guide us through the rough spots, but the end result will be reconciliation—a working through of the grief—instead of a lifetime of drug-assisted avoidance.

DOODLES, THOUGHTS, NOTES & OTHER STUFF:

SELF CARE TIP #7

Laugh Therapy

Those who need a good laugh are usually the ones who feel least like laughing, yet the heart can hold joy the same time as sorrow, so go ahead and laugh. One laugh can scatter a hundred griefs, and help lift your spirits. Even in difficult times, a laugh—or even simply a smile—can go a long way.

Laughter is an instant vacation.
MILTON BERLE

WHY IT MATTERS

Laughter creates the perfect diaphragmatic breath that oxygenates the brain. It also stimulates the brain into a positive state, which helps clear the mind and allows you more clarity and focus. When you're having a tough time, laughing creates psychological distance and can slow the momentum of overwhelm, frustration or disappointment.

A powerful healing modality, studies show that laughter offers many physical, psychological, and emotional benefits. Smiling and laughter stimulate the facial muscles that trigger the brain to release happy hormones called endorphins, the body's natural feel-good chemicals that promote an overall sense of well-being, temporarily relieves pain, decreases stress, and increases immune and infection-fighting antibodies.

SELF CARE

Enjoy a good belly laugh at least once every day to oxygenate the brain and trigger feel-good hormones. Ten minutes of laughter is equivalent to thirty minutes on a cardio machine.

BENEFITS OF LAUGH THERAPY

Because the body can't tell the difference between a real or fake smile, hold a pencil between your teeth to "fake it until you make it." When you smile, the stimulation of the involved facial muscles trigger the brain to release the chemicals that cause the feeling of happiness. A phenomenon called facial feedback, this works even if you weren't feeling happy in the first place. The brain can't tell the difference and will be tricked into releasing those feel-good chemicals anyway. No matter how you choose to induce a good belly laugh, the bottom line is that whatever makes you laugh is truly good medicine.

WHY IT WORKS:

- Laughter and crying are like yin and yang, they both release energy.
- Laughing bypasses the mind and helps us keep a positive attitude.
- Laughter engages in perfect diaphragmatic breath. When we laugh, we exhale completely and then inhale completely, which oxygenates the brain and body. When our brains are fully oxygenated, our minds become calm and clear.
- Laughter releases endorphins which help us feel good. The brain oxygenation and endorphins combination are like a Joyful cocktail.
- When we feel good and the mind is clear, we feel grounded and peaceful, less stress and less reactive.
- Laughter doesn't change reality but does help us to cultivate a positive mental attitude.
- Be silly, be playful. Laughter is contagious and allows our inner child to come out.
- Fake laughter often turns into authentic laughter. The body can't tell the difference, and the health benefits are the same.

HOW TO LAUGH WHEN YOU DON'T FEEL LIKE IT:

- Watch a comedy movie or TV show
- Watch funny YouTube videos
- Listen to children laughing
- Watch blooper reels on TV
- Read a funny book
- Try laugh yoga
- Look at funny pictures
- Read funny social media memes
- Listen to funny jokes

WEEK 7 SPIRITUAL JOURNALING

What are you feeling this week? Pour your emotions onto this paper for nobody else to read.

SESSION 8

TOPIC: TURNING PAIN INTO PURPOSE

INTRO

This session focuses on how helping others helps our own heart to heal. It concludes with a memorable **closing candlelight ceremony** (instructions in next chapter).

SCRIPT

1. Last week's unfinished business.
2. Report on phone calls. How did they go?
3. Report on caring plan. How did they go?
4. Review: Have you discovered a spiritual lesson in your loss?

DISCUSSION

In session 7, we talked about what spiritual lessons can be gained through the pain of loss. In this final session, we encourage you to explore how you can turn pain into purpose either by helping others who are grieving, too,
or finding a new purpose in life. Use **Give Joy** (handout 1) for discussion.

- ❑ How do you view your life now?
- ❑ What meaning have you found, and how can you use that new meaning to create joy?

REMEMBER

- ✓ Start and end on time.
- ✓ Keep conversation moving and productive.
- ✓ Ensure every participant has an opportunity to share or pass during the discussion.
- ✓ Protect the conversation from being monopolized.
- ✓ Stay supportive yet neutral.

MATERIALS

- ❑ Candlelight supplies
- ❑ Notebook & pen
- ❑ Index cards & pens
- ❑ Refreshments
- ❑ Nametags
- ❑ Tissue

HOMEWORK

- ❑ Turning pain into purpose
- ❑ From despair to hope
- ❑ As we close
- ❑ What now?
- ❑ The holidays
- ❑ God's script
- ❑ Self-care assignment

CONCLUSION

- **Review this session.** Encourage participants to read handouts, journal their thoughts, and try this week's Resilience Rx self-care tip.
- **Continue phone calls**, a valuable asset. Call those not here tonight.
- **Closing candlelight ceremony**

DOODLES, THOUGHTS, NOTES & OTHER STUFF:

GIVE JOY

Winston Churchill once said, "We make a living by what we get. We make a life by what we give." In other words, helping others helps our own heart to heal.

Giving is good for the giver in that it induces a natural high. It generates positive emotions that trigger a release of dopamine which regulates pleasure in the brain. It also evokes internal gratitude which helps to heal our heart.

Additional bonuses are the multiple—and proven—health benefits of giving: less stress, lower blood pressure, improved sleep, increased self-esteem, and greater happiness.

WAYS TO GIVE:

- Distribute blessing bags to the homeless.
- Volunteer in the community.
- Donate to a charity.
- Smile at a stranger.
- Give a compliment.
- Leave a nice note for someone at work or school.
- Let a driver merge in front of you during rush hour traffic.
- Do random acts of kindness.
- Leave a bouquet of balloons in a park for children to find.
- Feed the homeless in a soup kitchen.
- Hold the door open for someone behind you.
- Send an anonymous care package to someone who is struggling.

She who heals others heals herself.

LYNDA CHELDELIN FELL

H39/GIVE JOY

DOODLES, THOUGHTS, NOTES & OTHER STUFF:

SESSION 8 | HANDOUT 2

TURNING PAIN INTO PURPOSE

When I was a kid, I wanted to be a doctor. A brain surgeon. But God has a way of throwing us curve balls that force us down a different path.

Sometimes those paths are most welcome, like mothering four wonderful children. My least favorite? Losing a child. That path is long and torturous, and took me straight through the belly of hell.

My story began one night in 2007, when I had a vivid dream. I was the front passenger in a car and my daughter Aly was sitting behind the driver. Suddenly the car missed a curve and sailed into a lake. The driver and I escaped the sinking car, but Aly did not.

My beloved daughter was gone. The only thing she left behind was a book floating in the water where she disappeared.

Two years later, in August 2009, that horrible nightmare came true when Aly died as a back seat passenger in a car accident.

Returning home from a swim meet, the car carrying Aly was T-boned by a father coming home from work. My beautiful fifteen-year-old daughter took the brunt of the impact and died instantly. She was the only fatality.

Life couldn't get any worse, right? Wrong. Hell wasn't done with me yet.

My dear hubby buried his grief in the sand. He escaped into 80-hour work weeks, more wine, more food, and less talking. His blood pressure shot up, his cholesterol went off the chart, and the perfect storm arrived on June 4, 2012.

My husband suddenly began drooling and couldn't speak. At age 46, my soulmate was having a major stroke.

My dear hubby lived, but he couldn't talk, read, or write, and his right side was paralyzed. He needed help just to sit up in bed. He needed full-time care.

Still reeling from the loss of our daughter, I found myself again thrust into a fog of grief so thick, I couldn't see through the storm. Autopilot resumed its familiar place at the helm.

I needed God's reassurance that the sun was on the other side of hell. As I fought my way through the storm, He showed me that helping others was a powerful way to heal my own heart. I began reaching out to individuals who were adrift and in need of a warm hug.

In 2013, I formed AlyBlue Media to house my mission. Comforting people who spoke my language and listening to their stories, my mission took on a life of its own and came in many forms: a radio show, film, webinars, and writing. I also hosted a national convention. I wanted to bring the brokenhearted together.

I had many wonderful speakers, but the one who excited me most was a woman who had faced seven losses in a few short years—Martin Luther King's youngest daughter.

I didn't bring Dr. Bernice King to the convention to tell us about her famous father—we already knew that story. I wanted to know how she survived.

Over the course of that weekend, I was deeply moved by watching strangers swap stories and become newfound friends. These were stories born from hardship and yet remarkable on many levels.

Touched to the core, I set out to capture them into a book series aptly named Grief Diaries.

Now home to 5 literary awards and more than 700 writers spanning the globe, Grief Diaries has over 35 titles in print. Two years later I founded the International Grief Institute to help others invest in community resilience and strengthen the pipeline of hope.

I wanted to be a brain surgeon, but God had other plans. Being thrown into the forge so He could mold my soul was necessary for Him to accomplish those plans.

Life's lessons aren't easy because as humans, we don't learn from the easy stuff. It's sometimes necessary to reduce us like molten metal before we can be forged into a pillar of hope, courage, strength—or whatever God wants us to be—so we can serve others.

Once the forging was done, He filled my life—and heart—with blessings for which I am truly grateful, blessings that wouldn't have come about any other way. He'll do the same for you.

Where am I today?

Once a bereaved mother, always a bereaved mother. My heart is a bit like a broken teacup that's been glued back together. All the pieces are there, but they might not fit as seamlessly as they once did.

Some days the glue is strong and unyielding. Other days that glue is soft and threatens to spring a leak. Nonetheless, that teacup still holds water and serves God's purpose.

It's important to hold out hope that the sun can be found at the end of the path. But until you find it, it's comforting to know you aren't alone. God is there, even when you don't think He is.

For the record, I've found the sun. Some days I marvel at its beauty. Other days it hides behind clouds. But I now know those days don't last forever. And thanks to the lessons I've learned from my loss and trusting God along the way, my umbrella is stronger than ever.

Long story short, if I can turn pain into purpose, you can, too. Maybe not right this minute, but when God feels you're ready, he'll point you in the right direction.

Just trust that there is a bigger picture at play, and remember that He's not asking you to save the world, just help one person at a time.

In doing so, you'll help your own heart to heal.

LYNDA CHELDELIN FELL

H32/TURNING PAIN INTO PURPOSE

SESSION 8 | HANDOUT 3

FROM DESPAIR TO HOPE

On September 1, 1989, I lost my baby. She died two hours and nine minutes after birth. We named her Aubrie Marie.

During my pregnancy we'd been told that there might be a problem, but everything could be fixed. Although we anticipated a crisis, never did we expect our baby to die.

The year prior, in December 1988, my mother died from a sudden heart attack. She was just fifty-three years old. Six months later I lost a dear friend who had been a mother figure to me. I was no stranger to loss, even then.

My grandmother, who raised me, died when I was fifteen following complications of surgery for brain cancer.

When my baby died, I had no idea where I was to go from there.

After five long days in the hospital, I remember waiting in the doorway for my husband to pull the car around. I wondered, how do I step foot outside without my baby in my arms?

The pain and sorrow were excruciating.

I spent five days physically recuperating after the birth of my first baby following a cesarean section. It happened to be Labor Day weekend that year. The hospital staff was scarce. We were left pretty much alone to deal with our loss.

We weren't told much. As a matter of fact, we weren't even told what the sex of our baby was. We didn't find out that she was a girl until my discharge, when a vital statistics lady came to my room to ask why we hadn't checked the box indicating the sex of the baby on the birth certificate form.

She couldn't believe nobody had told us whether our baby was a boy or girl.

She left our room, went down to the morgue to speak with the pathologist who performed the autopsy, and returned twenty minutes later to tell us that we had had a baby girl.

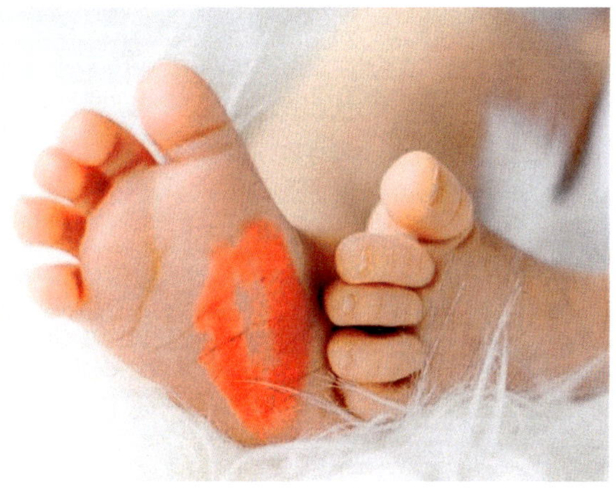

During the five days that followed the birth and death of our baby, we were told the following:

- You are young, you can have another baby.
- God must have wanted an angel in heaven.
- God wanted a grandchild to give to your mother in heaven.
- These things are meant to be.
- Why do you have to name it?
- It's suggested you get pregnant right away.
- This usually happens to boy babies.
- You have to call a funeral home.

Overcome with shock, I couldn't imagine why we had to call a funeral home. Some of these things were told to us by well-meaning friends and family. We were devastated, in shock.

There were no answers, only lots of painful questions coupled with confusion and great sorrow.

The following months were terrible. I didn't have the support I needed. But not because nobody cared—it was because nobody understood.

Because of my loss and the short life of my first baby, Aubrie Marie, it has become my life mission to provide that understanding and support to other people who are grieving. As a result, I founded Mourning Discoveries Grief Support Services.

I wanted to provide a place where people can receive the support and understanding they need following death of a loved one.

I've since partnered with over three hundred funeral firms in twenty-five states and Canada, and have mailed thousands of publications to grieving families. I have talked to thousands of grieving individuals, and spent countless hours listening to their stories of loss.

Mourning Discoveries is now part of the International Grief Institute.

We continue to have the honor of providing bereavement support services, facilitate grief support groups, and make a difference in the lives of those who walk the road of grief.

Because of my own loss, I've helped many navigate through grief towards healing.

Most importantly, I have been a witness to the power of God's love and the miracle of healing and human resilience.

If it hadn't been for the loss of my precious baby, Aubrie Marie, none of this would've been possible. I am grateful.

LINDA FINDLAY

H33/FROM DESPAIR TO HOPE

AS WE CLOSE

I do not know if you feel it as I feel it.

Perhaps so . . . maybe not . . .

For me, I sense here a dimension of love for each other

that is absolutely unique.

I know for sure that with each passing week

we have become more precious to each other.

And one of the reasons this is so,

is that here we didn't need to hide behind a mask.

That this corner of our world was safe for us to share a bit of our

hurts and sorrows, worries and dreams,

fantasies and pleasures, anger and insights.

Each struggle shared brought a new dimension to my being.

And to those who witnessed and shared with you,

thank you for sharing with me.

I hurt with you.

Though capable of just a tiny bit of your hurt, that tiny bit was often hard for me to bear.

There is no doubt that I feel weak yet thankful for the ability to so feel.

For somehow or other, In the sharing of our vulnerability,

there has emerged a meaning and strength.

Never experienced when we were strong,

with our weakness unable to emerge.

Namaste . . .

An ancient Sanskrit salutation:

"I honor that place deep within, where you . . . and I . . . are one."

H17/AS WE CLOSE

DOODLES, THOUGHTS, NOTES & OTHER STUFF:

WHAT NOW?

So, you've been attending a support group for two months. What were your expectations?

Some entered this experience with hopes that something would happen which would make the pain go all away. Others suspected that the support group would not be a magic pill, yet it might help. Some had no defined expectations, just knew inside that they needed to do something, and this was here to do.

Early on, we learned that this is griefwork, with an emphasis on **work**. Take a measurement of where you are in the reconciliation process. This may help to focus your energies as you continue your work outside the support group.

- We learned to effectively experience and express outside ourselves the reality of the death. For many, this group was the first opportunity to do this. For others, it was a continuation and reinforcement of what was started elsewhere. It is necessary to continue the process of outside expression of our feelings, whether that be talking regularly to others, writing in our journals, or any other form of outside expression.
- We have learned to allow ourselves to embrace the pain of the loss while learning how to nurture ourselves physically, emotionally and spiritually. Over and over we heard that the only way **out** is **through**. When I am in a safe place, I will permit my feelings to surface and be experienced. Stifling the pain prolongs the agony. This is also a time for learning or relearning how to care for our physical, emotional, and spiritual selves.
- We are learning how to convert our relationship with the person who died from an interactive presence to one of appropriate memory. This is a process which can't be deliberately willed. We have learned to just make a mental note of it as something which is in the process of happening at a subconscious level, and to allow our subconscious to do its work without interference.
- We are learning how to develop a new self-identity based on a life without the person who died. Each person's journey is different, and our individual timing is unique. Each day, some experience takes place which continues to build our new self-identity. For some who had a deeply enmeshed relationship, this may be a difficult task. It isn't a sign of weakness to seek professional help.

- We've begun to relate the experience of the death to a context of new meaning in our lives. For many, death provokes questions regarding the meaning of life and its transitory nature. There are no universal answers to many of these questions, however the process of seeking them often brings a meaningful answer to each of us. I will allow myself time for my own discovery of meaning. I won't permit others to rush me with their pat conclusions.
- I am developing a lasting network of support to help me through the process. This group was a useful step toward learning to establish lasting support. Through our emphasis on phone calls and networking, it reinforced my ability to reach out. Sometimes this was easy, other times it wasn't. I will keep trying because I know that continuing to reach out will help my reconciliation timetable. I will find it also causes other miracles in the world. I will try to notice them when they occur.

H18/WHAT NOW

SESSION 8 | HANDOUT 6

THE HOLIDAYS

The holidays are a time of remembrance of past celebrations, of present get-togethers, and of future opportunities to break away from everyday stress. But for people who are grieving, the holidays may be a time of mixed emotions, feelings of being overwhelmed with multiple demands, and the pain of loves lost. As the holidays approach, think about how you take care of yourself during this vulnerable time.

HELPFUL HINTS

- Acknowledge griefwork as real work. Adjustment to the death or dying of someone close to you does not simply come with time. The work of grief demands that you deal with all the feelings that loss engenders. This work takes emotional and physical energy that can leave you unable to deal with the extra demands of the holiday season.

- Allow yourself to be merely human. Avoid perfectionistic expectations during the holidays. Let some things slide. If you really want to do all the cooking and baking, let the dusting go. Enlist the aid of others in the spirit of holiday sharing. You do not have to do it all yourself this year.

- Plan ahead. Sit down with your family and friends ahead of time to discuss and decide those activities, experiences, and people that make the holidays special. Decide to do a few special things with a few special people, not everything with everybody.

- Set limits. Tell your family, friends, and yourself now—and continue to remind them— that you are on a stress-reduction diet this holiday season. You will not be overdoing, over-cooking, over-shopping, over-complying or over-worrying this year. Put a sign on your bathroom mirror or refrigerator to remind yourself (or others).

- Change **shoulds** to **wants**. Be aware of your own statements to yourself. Are you saying "I should do this or that?" Decide which of your shoulds you really want to do, and make those your priorities. Remember: You should not should yourself; there are enough other people doing that already.

- Strive for a balanced lifestyle. With all the parties and demands of the holidays, it is difficult for anyone to get enough rest and exercise. It is easy to overindulge.
    - Set exercise as a priority. It is an antidote to depression.
    - Learn relaxation techniques. They are an antidote to stress.
    - Don't overdo the eggnog. Alcohol is an antidote for nothing.

- Tell others clearly what you want and need for the holidays. Do not be embarrassed or shy to let others know what you want from them in terms of emotional support, help, or sharing. Mindreading is best left to fortunetellers. Unknown expectations generally go unfulfilled and lead to disappointment and bad feelings.

- Honor the old, create the new. If this is the first holiday without your family member, include your deceased loved one to the extent that you can. The memory of him or her will be with you this holiday season no matter what you do. Consider giving gifts in acknowledgment of your dying family member or in memory of the deceased; consider giving love to others in honor of the love you have received. Only you can put the joy into the holidays.

- Be generous to yourself. The holidays are a time of real and symbolic gift-giving. What are you giving yourself this season? When the new year rolls in, what will be your answer to the question, "What supportive and caring thing did I do for myself this holiday season?"

- Celebrate life. It seems like an impossibility for someone in grief to find joy and peace at any time, but especially during the season for joy and peace. This is your challenge. Life is worth living only to the extent that we make it so. Survivorship means more than merely surviving; it means fully living. Search for the living path for you and start now!

This material was prepared by Ellen S. Zinner, Psy.D., and based on materials developed in part by Sally Featherstone, RN.

H21/HOLIDAY COPING SKILLS

GOD'S SCRIPT

On the night of the accident, I sat next to my daughter's body at the scene of the two-car collision. As I sought to find her hand under the white sheet, God handed me a new script. I handed it back.

I wanted my old life, not a new one.

I wanted my daughter to open her eyes, to say "Hi, Mom."

Surveying the car's damage, instinctively I knew that wasn't going to happen. Yet shock, and the horror of seeing my daughter's bare toes peeking out from under the white sheet protected my mind from reality.

God again handed me the new script. I tore it up and handed it back.

"I don't want your new script!" I yelled.

I had a wonderful life as a mother of one college graduate, one college student, and two teenagers. My husband and I were even blessed with our first grandchild. Life was wonderful! There was no need for God to go changing it.

But I didn't win. God did. I had no choice but to take the new script.

I ignored it for three years. And then tragedy struck again.

My dear hubby's grief consumed him, and he suffered a life-threatening stroke that left him disabled. He was just 46 years old.

I gave in and waved the white flag. There was nothing left of me. I was done. Exhausted. Here I was facing a new kind of grief, and I had hardly begun to process the first.

God's script laid there for months and months. My heart broken in so many places, I had no energy to read it. The lines blurred together, the words indistinguishable.

And then one day out of anger, I picked it up.

The first line said, "When you help others, you help your own heart to heal."

Seriously, God? I felt like a regressed teenager challenging a parent. I could hardly put one foot in front of the other, how was I supposed to help someone else?

But God didn't include instructions. I wasn't amused.

Yet I needed God. Desperately.

I gave in and waved the white flag. I was standing squarely in the belly of hell; I had nothing more to lose.

I wasn't entirely sure how to go about this new script, but herein lies the answer: I didn't have to figure it out all on my own.

One door opened, then two doors, then four. And so on and so forth.

It's now been seven years since the loss of our daughter and four years since my husband's life-changing stroke. I haven't figured it all out yet, but God's script gave me a life purpose far better than I could ever have imagined.

Where am I now? Today, I help others. Because this helps my own heart to heal.

There. I said it. Script accepted. God was right.

Helping others has come in many forms. One of my most joyous endeavors was creating the book series, Grief Diaries, an anthology of stories about surviving loss.

When I set out to compile these stories, some questioned whether I had lost my final marble. Who would want to read tales of life's most challenging moments? Yet, God had laid this on my heart. And I trusted him.

I knew, without a shadow of a doubt, that the collection was going to change lives around the world.

I trusted God's script, and strangers I've never met handed me the most precious of gift of all: their own loss experiences.

They entrusted me to handle each with kid gloves, package them oh-so-carefully, and present them to the world for the sole purpose of helping others not feel so alone. Each stranger became my friend who enriched my world beyond measure.

So, I no longer questioned the script. I just followed it, never once forgetting that every story I now held in the palm of my hand is sacred. Not just to the writer, but to the world.

And to God.

Suddenly, this crazy book series about sharing true stories about loss has given a platform to more than 700 writers. It feels good to share our experiences with others. Why? Because it helps both readers and writers feel less alone.

So, it's true. When we help others, we help our own heart to heal.

Baring and sharing to comfort others like ourselves. Healing hearts by sharing journeys.

Script accepted.

Thank you, God.

LYNDA CHELDELIN FELL (2016)

H34/GOD SCRIPT

SELF CARE TIP #8

Hug Therapy

Giving is good for the giver in that a hug benefits ourselves and others. Connections are fostered when people acknowledge and appreciate one another. Hugging is also known to boost self-esteem in people of all ages.

A hug is a free, easy, and—at 20 seconds—a quick way to show love and appreciation.

We need 4 hugs a day for survival, 8 hugs a day for maintenance, 12 hugs a day for growth. VIRGINIA SATIR

WHY IT MATTERS

From the time we're born, our family's touch shows us that we're loved and special. The associations of self-worth and tactile sensations from our early years become imbedded in our nervous system as we grow into adults.

A sincere embrace triggers the brain to release the love hormone oxytocin. This substance has many benefits in our physical and mental health. A natural tranquilizer, it helps us to relax, to feel safe and calm our fears and anxiety. And it's free every time we hug, cradle a child, cherish a dog or cat, slow dance, or simply hold the shoulders of a friend.

SELF CARE

The average length of a hug between two people is 3 seconds. Research shows that a hug lasting at least 20 seconds has a therapeutic effect on the body and mind. Hug something or something for at least 20 seconds every day.

BENEFITS OF HUG THERAPY:

Almost 70 percent of communication is nonverbal. Hugging is an excellent method of expressing yourself nonverbally to another human being or animal. Not only can they feel the love and care in your embrace, but they can actually be receptive enough to pay it back.

Hugs stimulate oxytocin, a neurotransmitter that acts on the limbic system, the brain's emotional center. Oxytocin is known to:

- promote contentment
- reduce anxiety and stress
- lower our heart rate
- lower our cortisol level, the hormone responsible for stress
- Released during childbirth, helping mothers forget about the labor they endured and fall immediately in love with their newborn

HUGS ALSO . . .

Affection also has a direct response on the reduction of stress which prevents many diseases. Touch Research Institute at the University of Miami School of Medicine has carried out more than 100 studies on the power of touch, and discovered evidence of improved immune system, reduced pain, lower glucose levels, and faster growth in premature babies.

- ✓ Hugs apply gentle pressure on the sternum which stimulates the thymus gland, which regulates and balances the production of white blood cells, which keep you healthy and disease free.
- ✓ Hugs stimulate brains to release dopamine, the pleasure hormone, which helps to negate sadness.
- ✓ Hugging also releases serotonin levels, elevating mood and creating happiness.
- ✓ Hugs balance out the nervous system. Skin contains a network of tiny pressure centers that can sense touch and notify the brain through the vagus nerve. The galvanic skin response of someone receiving and giving a hug shows a change in skin conductance which suggests a more balanced state in the parasympathetic nervous system.

WEEK 8 SPIRITUAL JOURNALING

What are you feeling this week? Pour your emotions onto this paper for nobody else to read.

CLOSING CEREMONY

CANDLELIGHT PROGRAM

MATERIALS

- ❑ **Refreshments**
- ❑ **Candles**
- ❑ **Wax catchers**
- ❑ **Music**
- ❑ **Poems**
- ❑ **Tissue**

A closing candlelight ceremony is a powerful remembrance ritual that gives participants a memory they'll treasure. In general, it includes music, poems, and candles as a symbolic release of their sadness. The following instructions use two facilitators to coordinate and lead a candlelight ceremony. Modify as needed.

PLAN

1. Allow 30 minutes at the end of your final group session for the closing candlelight ceremony.
2. Confirm whether use of lit candles are allowed within the facility. If not, consider LED candles or glowsticks.
3. If desired, invite one or two church leaders to attend and give opening prayer and/or read poems.
4. Secure music. Invite an a cappella singer or use CD or digital music. Song suggestions:
   - ❑ Somewhere Over the Rainbow
   - ❑ I Will Always Love You, by Whitney Houston
   - ❑ Amazing Grace
   - ❑ To Where You Are, by Josh Groban
   - ❑ Wind Beneath my Wings, by Bette Midler
   - ❑ Go Light Your World, by C. Rice

PREPARE

5. Purchase candles with wax catchers online, from religious store, or arts & crafts store. Assemble candles inside wax catchers prior to ceremony. Don't forget matches or lighter.
6. Secure use of mic and speakers for the music, if needed.
7. Purchase or find donated cookies and bottled water to serve.
8. Secure bucket of water for participants to drop candles in when finished.

SUGGESTED SCHEDULE

1. Opening prayer.
2. Comments about past 8 sessions, importance of continued use of self care tips, continued support of one another, and local grief resources.

3. Start music. While music is playing, facilitators light each other's candle. Participants should be close enough together so they can safely dip their candlewick into the flame of the closest facilitator.
4. After all candles are lit, facilitators may each recite one poem.
5. Allow music to finish, and then ask for a moment of silence. Play second song if desired.
6. End with closing prayer.
7. Distinguish candles and dispose of in bucket of water.

SUGGESTED POEMS

FIVE CANDLES

UNKNOWN AUTHOR

The first candle represents our grief.
The pain of losing you is intense.
It reminds us of the depth of our love for you.

This second candle represents our courage.
To confront our sorrow,
To comfort each other,
To change our lives.

This third candle we light in your memory.
For the times we laughed,
The times we cried,
The times we were angry with each other,
The silly things you did,
The caring and joy you gave us.

This fourth candle we light for our love.
We light this candle that your light will always shine.
As we enter this season and share this night of remembrance with our family and friends.
We cherish the special place in our hearts
that will always be reserved for you.

This fifth candle we light to thank you for the gift your living brought to each of us.

We love you.

We remember you.

TIME WILL EASE THE HURT

BY BRUCE B. WILMER

The sadness of the present days
is locked and set in time.
And moving to the future
is a slow and painful climb.

But all the feelings that
are now so vivid and real
can't hold their fresh intensity
as time begins to heal.

No wound so deep will
ever go entirely away,
yet every hurt becomes
a little less each day.

Nothing can erase the painful
imprints on your mind.
But there are softer memories
that time will let you find.

Though your heart won't let
the sadness simply slide away,
the echoes will diminish
even though the memories stay.

H35/CLOSING CEREMONY

ADDITIONAL HANDOUTS

RESILIENCE RX™

10 tips to surviving the holidays

After losing someone you love, the holidays can feel anything but joyful, especially when faced with what to do with our loved one's empty place at the table and Christmas stocking. Allow yourself to try a handful of the suggestions below to guide you through the hustle and bustle, and gift yourself with plenty of compassion, kindness, and grace by doing whatever feels best to your heart.

TIP #1: MAINTAIN YOUR ROUTINE

A familiar routine offers a sense of reassurance that at least one thing in life hasn't changed, and the familiarity can help ground us through the holiday hustle. But if the idea of sticking to routine is more than you can bear, then honor your need to break tradition. In short, do what feels most soothing to your heart and apologize to no one.

TIP #2: PROTECT YOUR TIME

Give yourself lots of breathing room and avoid packing the schedule too full. Grieving is emotionally exhausting; plenty of rest will help minimize raw nerves through the flurry of shopping, school performances, and parties.

TIP #3: CUT YOURSELF SOME SLACK, NOT YOUR FINGER

Cut some slack and buy store-bought. Grieving is naturally distracting, and the ER isn't a great place to dine. Even the smallest kitchen disaster can quickly deplete coping skills. If the family expects your legendary dinner rolls, then cheat with gourmet mashed potatoes and gravy from the deli.

TRIP #4: SKIP THE CHAOS

Turn off the computer, light a fragrant candle, grab a soft blanket, and binge-watch a good comedy. Take time to create peaceful surroundings to soothe your nerves.

TIP #5: CRY

Give in to the tears. There is no shortage of raw emotions over the holidays, and crying is not a sign of weakness. It's how we release intense feelings. A good cry can be very healing and serves as an important part of our journey.

During the holidays, self gift with compassion, kindness, and grace.

TIP #6: THE RULES OF 5

Treat your senses to the Rule of 5. Your emotions are raw, but your body could use some TLC. Each day acknowledge 5 things you can see, 4 things you can feel, 3 things you can hear, 2 things you can smell, and 1 thing you can taste. Wear a soft scarf (feel). Enjoy an eggnog latte (taste). Use aromatherapy soap in the shower (smell). You get the idea. Small gestures like these offer your physical body a reminder that not all pleasure is lost and allow us to deposit small moments of joy in our hearts to help balance the sadness.

TIP #7: WHEN THE MOOD STRIKES . . .

Feel joy without guilt. Give yourself permission, because it releases positive hormones that are good for your brain. If you find yourself humming to holiday music, don't stop. The heart can feel joy the same time as sorrow, and it helps to balance the sadness. Allow yourself to experience moments of joy without guilt. Your spirit needs it.

TIP #8: HONOR THE PAST

Find a way to include your loved one's memory in the festivities. Hang their stocking and fill it with cat toys or dog treats to share with the family pet on Christmas morning. Visit your loved one's favorite coffee stand and pay it forward. Buy a small bouquet of balloons in your loved one's favorite color and leave it in a public spot for a stranger to find.

TIP #9: HEAL OTHERS

Do something in the community that lifts your spirits. It induces a helper's high that's good for the brain, it's gratifying to the heart, and is a good reminder that we aren't alone in our struggles. It helps us keep perspective that the holidays can be hard for a variety of reasons, and helping others helps our own heart to heal.

TIP #10: SEEK OUT SUPPORT.

Surround yourself with others who speak your loss language. A quick internet search will likely reveal a number of local groups led by seasoned grievers trained to hold a sacred space for your sorrow. If that isn't your style, grab one of the books in the Grief Diaries series, take a self enrichment class, or join the growing number of live Facebook events without leaving your living room. No matter how you seek support, surrounding yourself with others who speak the language of sorrow is an important part of healing.

RESILIENCE RX™

Coping with grief at work

The wealth of a company is built on the health of its employees. When grief impacts our life, the emotional stress and mental exhaustion make us less organized, less productive, and less efficient. Emotional depletion can lead to other health problems such as insomnia, hypertension, and more. Use the tips below manage grief when you return to work. Stay in contact with your boss or human resources to make sure they are supporting you in your time of need.

Self-compassion involves a consistent attitude of kindness and acceptance toward ourselves as a whole.

LISA FIRESTONE, Ph.D.

SELF CARE TIPS FOR WORK:

- Work with your employer to identify a safe room you can use for 10 to 15 minutes when emotions bubble to the surface. This gives you the space to collect yourself in a private setting away from clients and colleagues.
- Compartmentalize if needed at work but give yourself time to grieve, too.
- If possible, request short-term light cognitive duty to minimize mistakes and injuries.
- Avoid operating dangerous equipment until the fog lifts. This will maximize safety and minimize risk management issues.
- Learn to let go, say no, and ask for help from others. Honor your own limits.

SELF CARE TIPS FOR HOME:

- Talk about your loss for at least 15 minutes every day. It's okay to ramble, rant, and repeat yourself. Talking is how we process. Processing is how we heal.
- Carve time in your schedule to do things you love. This will help recharge your battery.
- Eat healthy and stay hydrated to boost immunity and physical well-being.
- Engage in light exercise and practice good sleep hygiene.
- Sing. In the shower, in the car, in your bed. It releases muscle tension and stress.
- Enjoy a good belly laugh every day. Laughter releases tension, boosts your mood, and lightens a heavy heart. Watch a comedy or funny videos.
- Engage in activities involving repetitive hand motions such as beading, painting, pottery, knitting, gardening, woodworking or coloring. Repetitive hand motions calms the mind.
- Use journaling to release inner thoughts and feelings.
- Recognize that you can't fix grief. It's a rite of passage for everyone.

DOODLES, THOUGHTS, NOTES & OTHER STUFF:

THE WAILING TENT

Dear grieving mother,

Welcome to the sisterhood of the wailing tent. With profound condolences, I know you'll soon forget my greeting, for your heart and soul have sustained a terrible blow.

The shock known as "the fog" will accompany you for some time, greatly impacting your memory. So I offer you this written welcome to refer to when your recollection falters.

The wailing tent is an honored place where only mothers with a broken spirit can enter. Admittance is gained not with an ID card bearing your name, but with the fresh sorrow etched on your heart.

Membership is free, for you have already paid the unfathomable price.

Directions to the wailing tent are secret, available only to mothers who speak our language of everlasting grief.

No rules are posted, no hours are noted. There is no hierarchy, no governing body.

Your membership has no expiration date, it is lifelong.

The refuge offered within its walls does not judge members based on age, religious belief, or social status. Hang your mask outside, and if you can't make it past the door, we will surround you with love right where you lay.

The wailing tent is a shelter where mothers shed anguished tears among her newfound sisters. A haven where all forms of wailing are honored, understood, and accepted.

In the beginning, you will be very afraid, and will hate the wailing tent and everything it stands for. You will flail, thrash about, and spew vile words in protest. You will fight to be free of the walls, wishing desperately to offer a plea bargain for a different tent, learn a different language. Those emotions will last for some time.

Your family and friends cannot accompany you here. The needs of the wailing tent are invisible to them. Though they'll try, they simply cannot comprehend the disembodied, guttural howls heard within.

In the beginning, your stays here will seem endless. Over time, the need for your visits will change and eventually you will observe some mothers talking, even smiling, rather than wailing. Those mothers have learned to balance profound anguish with moments of peace, though they still need to seek refuge among us from time to time.

Do not judge those mothers as callused or strong, for they have endured profound heartache to attain the peace they have found. Their visits here are greatly valued, for their hard-earned wisdom offers hope that we, too, will learn to balance the sadness in our hearts.

Lastly, you need not flash your ID card or introduce yourself each time you visit, for we know who you are. You are one of us, an honorary lifelong sister of the wailing tent.

Welcome, my wailing sister.

LYNDA CHELDELIN FELL (2014)

DOODLES, THOUGHTS, NOTES & OTHER STUFF:

THE YOUNG WIDOW

While the grieving process is similar to those experiencing any loss, the content and prescription for reconciliation of young widows requires an emphasis on a number of special activities.

For many young widows, this is the first time there has been a major loss—of any kind. Until now, life was normal and predictable, filled with school, perhaps college, idyllic romance, a home, children, developing careers, and more. They had everything according to the American dream and expectation—ever onward and upward, each year better than the last.

Of course, there was nothing to prepare them to deal with major and often sudden reversal.

The statements below represent many of the feelings and concerns of women who are widowed early in their married life.

- In one moment, my life, my hopes, my dreams turned upside-down so completely.
- After years of preparation for life together with a man I admire, respect and love, I find myself overwhelmed with responsibilities and aloneness.
- I find myself with so many unsatisfied needs—physical needs, emotional needs, intellectual needs, and spiritual needs.
- I really don't know how to be a single parent. I'm scared.

ALONENESS

There've always been people around. Father, mother, sisters and brothers, college roommates, the old high school gang, hanging out with friends, my special boyfriend, fiancée, lover, husband, and perhaps children. Now it is me alone or me and my kid(s).

No adult to talk to, to listen to me, to touch me, to take care of me, to sleep with me, for me to listen to, care about and take care of.

The world is organized for couples and I'm not part of that anymore. It is all gone, and I am alone with myself or kid(s) who are demanding of my nonexistent energy.

PARTNER DEPENDENCY

Can I be a fulfilled woman without intimacy in my life? My social modeling has always been centered around being with a partner.

All my physical, emotional and social needs require the close presence of a partner in my life. Am I capable of attracting someone else now that I'm older and perhaps have kids?

Am I going to change my attitudes about the need for companionship?

How am I going to find someone else, anyone else?

LONELINESS

This is separate from aloneness. Aloneness is being alone and perhaps missing the adult activity I once enjoyed. But this overwhelming feeling of loneliness is separate and apart from being alone.

It is my wave of depression which may be present even when I'm at work or around others. I can feel lonely even when I'm not alone. It's just different and I'm not certain I want to go on living this way.

My loneliness really stems from my feelings of worthlessness. I've needed the company and admiration of others to feel valuable. I have lost what I had, and I am lonely.

RESPONSIBILITY

I am a responsible person, but I never had this degree of responsibility thrust upon me before and don't know how to handle it. I'm really scared.

There is the financial concern of how I'm going to support myself and perhaps my kid(s). Just being alone and raising the children alone in this day and age is frightening.

How am I going to provide? How am I going to take care of all these possessions? How am I going to ensure proper childcare when I go back to work?

THE UNKNOWN

What will become of me?

Will I ever love again?

Will I live the rest of my life feeling the way I do right now? If so, is it all worth it?

This decision, that decision, am I doing it correctly?

What would my partner have done?

FOR MY COMPASSIONATE FRIENDS

BY MARILYN ROLLINS
The Compassionate Friends
Lake-Porter County, Indiana

How is it that I know you?
How'd you get into my life?
Sometimes when I look at you,
It cuts me like a knife.

I do not want to know you,
I don't want to cross that line.
Let's both go back into the past,
When everything was fine.

You've held me and you've hugged me,
And dried a tear or two,
Yet, you're practically a stranger,
Why do you do the things you do?

Of course, I know the reason,
We are in this club we're in,
And why we hold on to each other
Like we are long lost kin.

For us to know each other,
We had to lose a kid,
I wish I'd never met you,
But, I'm so thankful that I did.

DOODLES, THOUGHTS, NOTES & OTHER STUFF:

THE FAMILY MEETING

The family meeting process has been used successfully by family units to establish and maintain an elevated level of communication based upon honesty and openness in the disclosure of feelings. This process will work with any family unit of two or more people living together. To be effective, all persons living together under the same roof must participate; it just doesn't work if any member is excluded.

THE FAMILY MEETING PROCESS

1. Select a sacred time that's agreeable to all family members. It is **essential** the sacred time be honored; all other family and individual activities must be planned around this time. Keeping this sacred time is a covenant by each individual which gives honor to the importance of the family unit.
2. The family meeting is held once a week at the agreed upon sacred time.
3. Family members will take turns convening the meeting. The convener will begin the meeting by sharing his/her own reality with other family members. This self-disclosure is designed to include all positive and negative feelings. For example:
    - **"This is my hurt, my pain . . . "**
    - **"I am feeling guilty for having done . . . "**
    - **"I feel angry when . . . "**
    - **"I feel proud of myself for . . . "**
    - **"This is the space I am in right now . . . "**

    It is extremely important that the person sharing only talk of his or her own feelings. This is not the time to talk about others, nor is this the time to lecture, preach or gripe.
4. No one is allowed to interrupt the one who is disclosing him or herself. Other family members must listen until it is their turn to share.
5. When the first person is finished sharing, the next person is not to answer or defend against feelings previously shared by another, but begins to share his or her direct feelings.
6. This process continues uninterrupted until all have shared.

7. When all family members have finished sharing, a discussion period is held only for the purpose of clarification. It is important to keep this time free from advice, argument and problem solving. Stick only to clarifying what was heard to be certain it was what the other person really meant to convey.
    - **"I heard you say . . . , does that mean you were . . . ?"**
    - **"I didn't understand what you meant when you said . . . "**
    - **"Please repeat . . . I'm not sure I really understood you."**

8. In the event of a disagreement or fight, no one is allowed to leave the room until an agreement has been reached which is satisfactory to all family members. Difficulties can be solved by honest conversation which honors each person's individual feelings. Fighting is not necessarily bad. If the fighting is fair, communication continues. The real enemy of communication and relating is silence.

REMEMBER:

- ☑ Never attack. Keep the focus on self, using **I** statements. I feel, I sense, I think, I will...
- ☑ Repeat everything you think you hear to the person who said it. "I heard you say...." Then listen for the confirmation.
- ☑ Regardless of how foreign to your own ideas and values, take everything that is said seriously. Making light of another's honest feelings is a devastating putdown.

This process is not intended to solve individual problems which are best served by qualified therapists. It is an excellent means of how to use openness and honesty to help nurture the family unit by promoting self-disclosure and the art of listening.

MARRIAGE AFTER DEATH OF A CHILD

Don't expect your spouse to be a tower of strength when he or she is also experiencing grief. Be sensitive to your spouse's personality style. In general, he or she will approach grief with the same personality habits used in approaching life. It may be very private, very open and sharing, or somewhere in between.

- ✓ Find a sympathetic friend, someone who cares and will listen without judgment or interruption.
- ✓ Do talk about your child with your spouse. If necessary, set a daily or weekly time for this.
- ✓ Seek the help of a counselor if grief or problems in your marriage are getting out of hand.
- ✓ Do not overlook or ignore anger-causing situations. It's like adding fuel to a fire—eventually there will be an explosion. Deal with things as they occur.
- ✓ Remember, you loved your spouse enough to marry. Try to keep your marriage alive by having dates or time alone together to create new memories.
- ✓ Join a support group for bereaved parents. If you are unable to attend as a couple, come by yourself or with a friend. It is a good place to learn about grief and to feel understood. Do not pressure your spouse to attend with you if it is not to his or her preference.
- ✓ Join a mutually agreeable community-betterment project as common ground between you.
- ✓

REMEMBER

Men and women are wired differently. You won't react to the loss the same way. Don't try to understand one another's way of coping, just honor it.

- ✓ Be gentle with yourself and your mate. Have grace.
- ✓ Do not blame yourself or your mate for what you were powerless to prevent. If you blame your spouse or personally feel responsible for your child's death, seek counseling for yourself and your marriage.
- ✓ Realize that you are not alone. There are many bereaved parents who survived loss of a child.
- ✓ Choose to believe that one day your heart will again know the joys of life.
- ✓ Recognize your extreme sensitivity and vulnerability, and be alert to the tendency to take things personally.
- ✓ Read about grief, especially the books written for bereaved parents.

- ✓ Take your time with decisions about your child's things, change of residence, etc.
- ✓ Be aware of unrealistic expectations for yourself or your mate.
- ✓ Remember, there is no timetable. Everyone goes through grief differently, even parents of the same child.
- ✓ Try to remember that your spouse is doing the best he or she can.
- ✓ Marital friction is normal in any marriage. Don't blow it out of proportion.
- ✓ Try not to let little everyday irritants become major issues. Talk about them and try to be patient.
- ✓ Be sensitive to the needs and wishes of your spouse as well as yourself. Sometimes it is important to compromise.
- ✓ It is very important to keep the lines of communication open.
- ✓ Work on your grief instead of wishing that your spouse would handle his or her grief differently. You will find that you will have enough just handling your own grief. Remember, when you help yourself cope with grief, it indirectly helps your spouse.

Value your marriage—you have lost enough.

PANIC ATTACKS

Panic attacks are episodes of acute fear that can appear suddenly and incapacitate without apparent cause or rational explanation. For many, it is so irrational that they are afraid to tell anyone about their incident for fear they will be judged mad, crazy, or insane. Some have described their attacks as feeling like they will faint or even die on the spot. They can't breathe, their hyperventilating, their heart is pounding like a drum, their hands are trembling, and their legs feel like jello.

Typically, a panic attack is preceded by a period of stress overload. The person experiencing it may feel generally rundown, poorly nourished for the amount of stress being carried. Frequently he or she is exercising a great deal of introspection and worry about stress-related symptoms.

Before proceeding with the strategies outlined below, it is necessary for a medical doctor, one with a good understanding of nutrition and the effect of body chemistry on the autonomic nervous system, to eliminate certain conditions which could be organic causes for episodes of panic. Let your doctor know you wish to eliminate potential causes. Take control of your body and mind. Don't permit anyone to get you into a chemical drug/medication trap without a second opinion and clear evidence of an organic problem.

RECOVERY

This is an outline of a 7-step program utilized by the Panic Attack Sufferers Support Group (PASS). It is basic and easy to understand. It is easy to accomplish but requires a major willingness to make changes. If we continue to do the same things, we continue to get the same results. A willingness to do something different from what we currently do is necessary for this program to minimize your attacks of panic, fear and terror.

STEP 1: DIET

- As panic attacks are often related to the body's blood sugar, eat balanced meals based on the basic four food groups. Eliminate simple sugars such as corn syrup.
- Avoid alcohol.
- Spread out your meals, eat 5 or 6 small meals each day.
- Have small amounts of protein with each meal.
- Avoid caffeine.
- Take a daily multivitamin.
- Go easy on fats and salt.

STEP 2: RELAXATION

Relaxation is a learned skill that needs daily practice. Body chemistry changes with relaxation. Endorphins which promote good, calm feelings are produced under circumstances of relaxation, and adrenalin—which is often associated with panic and fear—is lessened. Practice diaphragmatic breathing (laughing creates the perfect diaphragmatic breath). Learn to stretch your body with slow soft stretches through tai chi or dancing. Learn progressive relaxation from audio or videos.

Learn this quieting reflex which you can do unobtrusively anywhere, anytime. Practice this until you can perform it instantly at times of panic onset. It really help.

- Smile inwardly. Unclench your teeth and jaw.
- Tell yourself, "My eyes are twinkling and sparkling."
- Imagine inhaling through the soles of your feet, up through your legs and into your stomach. Feel the upward flow of warmth and heaviness.
- Imagine the air flowing back down through your feet and out the soles, taking all the tension along with it. Let your jaw, tongue and shoulders go limp.

STEP 3: EXERCISE

A regular exercise routine provides effective oxygenation of your body. It need not be overly strenuous, just regular. Try swimming, brisk walking, running in place, bike riding, rowing, dancing, jogging, rope jumping, calisthenics. Among all its other benefits, exercise also helps dissipate anger. Common sense precautions:

- Check with your doctor before beginning an exercise program.
- Don't begin if you are just recovering from a cold, flu or other illness.
- Start gradually and don't overdo it. Pace yourself. Work at a comfortable speed.
- Always begin by warming up with stretches to wake up the body and prevent injury.

STEP 4: ATTITUDE

Letting go to be in control. Paradoxical? Yes. But it works. Learning to honor and develop your courageous self. Using positive imagery and affirmations.

STEP 5: IMAGINATION

Be open to new situations, be open to learning. Use visualization and positive affirmations.

STEP 6: SOCIAL SUPPORT

Network and spend time with others who speak your loss language.

STEP 7: YOUR SPIRITUAL SIDE

Tap into your spiritual side.

H23/PANIC ATTACKS

SHOULDS OR SHOULD NOTS

Following are common questions about what people should or should not do, and in what timeframe. There are no **should** or **should not** standards. Your journey through grief and the reconciliation process is unique to you. Do whatever feels right to your heart.

If the question concerns the space you personally live in, the decision is yours alone. If other family members share that space, then it is important to communicate with one another about what your needs and expectations are.

Following are common questions and suggestions.

Should I clear out my loved one's personal belongings? How soon should I be doing this?

Some people find it cathartic to handle their loved one's belongings. Others find it painful. Still others find comfort by leaving their clothes, personal items, tools, and other such stuff in place. There is no inappropriate window. As long as keeping your loved one's belongings does not involve any bizarre behavior or cause ongoing stress, there is no time limit. If these things are perceived by others as taking up space, it is your decision how you fill your space. This may upset family members who believe that they know what is best for you. Gently remind them that this is something you need to do in your own time, and you'll know when the time is right.

Should I sell my home or move to a different location?

If possible, wait to make this decision as long as it is financially reasonable to do so. The process of packing and moving adds extra stress to your life, and can distract you from your griefwork. Additionally, moving to new, unfamiliar surroundings can be very stressful for some. Changing your surroundings will not take your grief away. Your grief will move with you wherever you go. If you need to move, know that you will need additional support, emotionally and otherwise.

How regularly should I visit the cemetery?

How often you visit your loved one's final resting place is a very personal choice. Some people find comfort by doing so, and report feeling closer to their loved one. Others cannot bring themselves to go to the cemetery. Some people visit every day, even several times a day. Others feel guilty for not visiting enough, or not at all. Go if it brings you comfort. If you would like to visit and cannot do this alone, bring along a trusted friend or family member for emotional support.

Should I celebrate the upcoming holiday or my loved one's birthday?

The first birthday and holidays following a loss can be very difficult. Many people feel anything but festive, and just want the holidays to go away.

Anticipating an upcoming holiday, birthday or anniversary creates a great deal of stress for people who are grieving. Oftentimes, the anticipation of the day can be worse than the day itself. Do only what you can in the days prior.

It may be helpful to ask a friend to take care of the things that are making you feel anxious. Try not to worry about expectations of others. You do not have to take care of anyone or anything, unless you choose to do so.

If you have family traditions in which you feel you cannot host or participate, communicate your feelings to those who are involved in the festivity. If at first you feel you can participate, know that it is okay to change your mind. On the other hand, you may not accept an invitation, and when the day arrives, you feel you could go. Do what feels right to you **in the moment**. Most people will understand, and you do not have to explain yourself either way.

I'm mad at God but afraid to admit that. Should I tell someone?

Many mourners find themselves mad at God or their church. Sometimes they even question their faith. This is more common than not. Find a spiritual mentor whom you can talk to freely, and be honest about your feelings. Chances are that you aren't the first person who has come to them with such feelings, and he or she might have sage advice that will help you process the strong emotions.

If you aren't comfortable talking to someone in your church, give it to God. He hears you, loves you, and won't strike you down for mourning so deeply. He created you as a human, with human emotions. Remember that your grief is a testament to the love you have for one of His children. He gets it. He really does.

THE POWER OF PRAYER

Stacy Roorda, a busy 37-year-old mother of two young girls, had noticed a lump in her left armpit for some months. Having moved into a larger home the previous winter, she had long attributed the pestering symptom to the strain of moving.

Nine months later, in November 2006, Stacy finally went to see her naturopath. Suspicious of something sinister, the doctor immediately sent Stacy for a battery of tests. The results rocked her world.

She had stage 4 breast cancer with metastases to the bone.

With two little girls at home, surgery was immediately scheduled to remove the primary mass in Stacy's left breast.

Then the other shoe dropped.

Pre-op labs revealed Stacy was unexpectedly expecting—and the cancer was feeding on the very hormones her unborn baby needed to survive.

It was gloom and doom. Tears were shed, prayers were said, and she handed it over to God.

"I immediately got an image of a harness that racecar drivers wear. The feeling was instant. 'Sit down and buckle up. It's going to be a rough road, but you'll be fine.' I grabbed onto that thought and never let go," shares Stacy.

Finding her case beyond his scope, the local oncologist sent Stacy and her husband south to Seattle.

Because the pregnancy hormone was the cancer's food source, the team of specialists offered few options. Stacy's best chance for survival depended on immediate termination of the pregnancy followed by aggressive treatment. They had no time to waste. The doctors told her it was her only hope. The cancer was too advanced.

It was either Stacy's life, or the baby. They couldn't save both.

Against medical advice, she refused to abort the baby. The doctors gave her three years to live at best.

News of Stacy's plight spread rapidly in her small hometown of Lynden, Washington. With a 2-year-old and 4-year-old at home, and the very lives of Stacy and her unborn child at stake, family and friends sprang into action.

Meals were brought, childcare was juggled, and a church prayer chain was started.

Stacy was known for her devout faith. And her stubbornness. Despite pressure from the best oncologists in the state, she refused to terminate the unexpected pregnancy.

An older, less effective chemotherapy deemed safer for the developing baby was planned. Nicknamed Red Death, the goal was to slow down the cancer and buy Stacy some time until the baby could be born. Treatment began immediately.

Back home, news of the family's troubles spread. So did the prayer chain.

While bolstered by the many petitions, Stacy wasn't about to be left out of the prayer party held on her behalf.

"Before every round of chemo, I would go into the bathroom by myself. I would take a few moments to look directly at Jesus. You can always look around in the world and listen to the negative stuff, but if you look up to Jesus, that is where you find peace that surpasses all understanding. And I prayed that Jesus would fill the room with angels. I felt that as long as Jesus was there with me, I could do it," she said.

But after five rounds of Red Death, the unborn baby started showing signs of distress. They had to stop.

Things went from bad to worse.

An MRI showed the cancer had advanced to Stacy's spine, and was marching downward. At 32 weeks gestation, they needed to deliver the baby before the cancer reached the womb.

"Once again I was totally shocked. I thought back to the image of the seat belt. I had a very serious conversation with God.

"I don't remember signing up for this part. I've done everything you asked, and I've trusted you. You brought us through and we've been lifted up in prayer by loved ones and complete strangers around the world. How could this be?"

"Once again, I got the feeling God was indeed there and would bring me through it. He gave me a peace that surpassed all understanding, all I had to do was keep praying," she said.

By this time, reports of Stacy's dire situation had spread far and wide.

"I heard that my story reached missionaries, and that people all around the world were praying. That was the most humbling part, is that people were praying for me who had never met me. That is what carried Matt and I through the whole thing," she said.

With news that such a premature delivery was imminent, the prayers that surrounded Stacy and her family took on a new urgency.

Less than 48 hours later, Jazmine Stacy Roorda was born.

Weighing just 3.5 pounds and lacking the sucking reflex that hadn't yet developed, their new daughter was otherwise perfect.

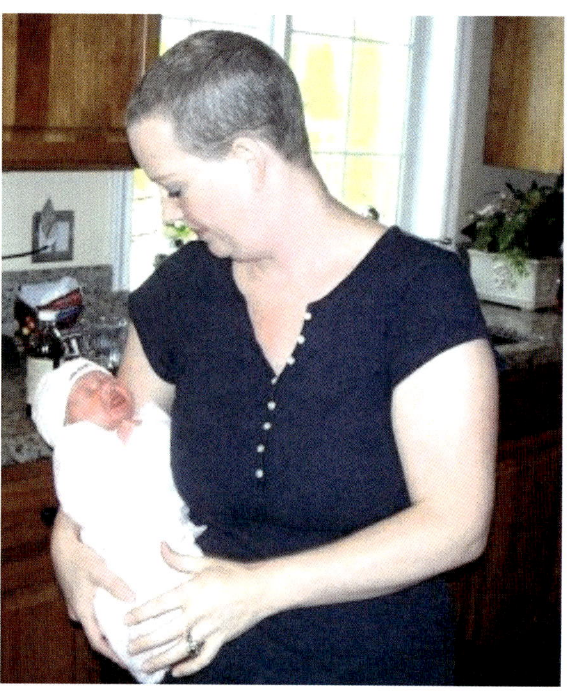

The announcement of the baby's birth spread along the prayer chain, but the petitions on their behalf didn't stop.

With the pregnancy behind her, two young daughters at home, a preemie in the NICU, Stacy now faced the cancer treatment head on.

The intensity of the prayer chain now stretched around the world fortified Stacy's determination. She believed without a doubt that the positive, loving energy contained in a prayer chain is a force that cannot be denied.

What happened next is what some might call a miracle: the treatment designed to buy Stacy a bit more time with her family instead, and inexplicably, brought the cancer to a standstill. It hasn't budged since.

Fast forward thirteen years. Against the odds, Stacy not only survived the doctors' prognosis, so did her baby.

With bone mets, Stacy will never be free from cancer. But for reasons doctors can't explain, it inexplicably fossilized in the various parts of her body.

Stacy gives much of the credit to the prayers that came from strangers across the globe.

What is prayer? It's love in an energetic form. Many use it to talk to God. Others use it to spread light in the world.

No matter how you use or label it, it's a powerful energy, love in its purest form.

"The power of prayer is how God works in this world, through people and their petition. Their desire to pray for a complete stranger is out of their love for Jesus. Love trumps everything," Stacy says.

Stacy Roorda is aware that skeptics are still waiting for proof in the power of prayer. But it doesn't faze her.

The prayer party that spanned the world on her behalf is all the proof she needs.

STACY ROORDA WITH DAUGHTERS HANNAH, ZOE AND JAZMINE (2019)

NOTES:

CHAPTER 7

NONTRADITIONAL SUPPORT PROGRAMS

IN THIS CHAPTER

✓ Nontraditional support groups

Grief is unique as a fingerprint.

LYNDA CHELDELIN FELL

Nontraditional support programs serve those who are resistant to traditional support yet open to other options. Because nontraditional methods engage different regions of the brain, it shifts mourners from the pain into learning mode while helping them battle the sense of isolation that often accompanies grief. From an emotional standpoint, the learning brain is calm, peaceful, open to new information, excited about what they're learning, and curious. They're not thinking of only themselves, and have a bit of confidence that they can apply what they learn.

Each group provides value to those who wouldn't otherwise have support. The bonus to you and your organization for hosting such a group is a stronger community connection with those who lead and/or attend nontraditional groups.

Make a list of nontraditional grief support groups you can host, and brainstorm with community leaders and teachers on how you can make them come to fruition.

SUGGESTIONS

- iCare Café™
- Family Days
- Drum circles
- Walking clubs
- The Dinner Party
- Knitting groups
- Book clubs
- Quilting, sewing, or knitting group
- Gardening club (ecotherapy)
- Laughter yoga
- Music therapy
- Adventure therapy

NOTES:

CHAPTER 8

RESILIENCE TOOLS

Life doesn't get any easier or more forgiving. We get stronger and more resilient.

JAMAIS CASCIO

IN THIS CHAPTER

- ✓ About resilience
- ✓ Resilience Rx™
- ✓ More tools

Resilience is the ability to recover from, or adapt to, difficulties—an individual's ability to take something positive from adversity. Supporting resilience means building resilience through strategies that support the brain, body and emotions during a critical time. When faced with death of a loved one, there are three possible outcomes:

1. Full emotional adaptation and ability to function in a meaningful way
2. Partial emotional adaptation and stunted ability to function
3. No emotional recovery nor adaptation, and halted function.

Because of the stress hormones that flood the brain during grief, the goal of peer support is to offer not just comfort and understanding. Our role is to also provide self-care tips and self-help techniques and modalities that support the mourner as they move forward.

Because grief isn't one size fits all, neither are support tools. What works for one mourner may be ineffective for another. Having a robust toolbox of modalities and techniques will ensure that you have plenty to draw from. Print the handouts from **www.icarelibrary.com/specialists** to keep on hand, or refer to this manual as needed when working with your families.

KEYNOTE

While resilience tools don't erase the grief, they empower the mourner to take care of themselves when they need it most.

GOAL

To foster emotional recovery, restore hope and a return to full function and a meaningful life.

IMPORTANCE OF RESILIENCE TOOLS

Trauma creates fear and grief creates sadness, both of which trigger the brain to release stress hormones (cortisol, adrenaline, norepinephrine). While it's normal to feel anxious during stressful times, the uncertainty brought about by death of a loved one can suck mourners into a constant state of worry and anxiety, thereby compounding their sadness. This is where resilience tools come in.

Neuropsychological research shows that the brain's prefrontal cortex, the area responsible for rational thinking and decision-making, is inhibited when the amygdala is activated by the stress hormones. This means that when we feel anxious or angry, we can't think clearly. Focusing attention on self-care tips and self-help techniques will focus the mourner's attention on something positive and help them feel calm and more in control.

WAYS TO STRENGTHEN INNER RESILIENCE:

The first step is to understand stress and how it affects us (see chapter 4). The second is to encourage mourners to minister to their own needs. We can't always predict stress and the outcome, yet we are in control of how we care for ourselves physically, mentally, emotionally, and spiritually. Providing resilience-building tools and techniques that trigger the brain's positive hormones will help offset the stress hormones, and encourage the mourner to engage in further modalities.

Most people know how to take care of themselves under ordinary circumstances. When facing death of a loved one, the shadow of grief can eclipse common sense. While we can't stop the grief journey from happening, we can empower mourners to help themselves along the way.

Resilience Rx™

Resilience Rx™ promotes nurturing self-help techniques and positive coping strategies that support mourners through loss. They also help to mitigate compassion fatigue.

Resilience Rx™ handouts are available for you to print for your families at www.icarelibrary.com/specialists. Use these to help your families develop a self-care plan they can stick with along with the following self-help techniques.

Following is a comprehensive list of self-care tips and self-help techniques and modalities to share with your families, along with a link to print any associated handouts to pass along.

KEYNOTE

Resilience tools help empower mourners to care for them-selves, offer activities to focus on, and give their brain a respite from the grief pain.

MODALITY 1: SELF-CARE PLAN

Losing someone we love changes how we live and who we are. According to the American Psychological Association, a good self-care routine can help manage grief stress, prevent illness, protect inner resilience from eroding, and maintain equilibrium. It is also an important way to help anchor emotions and honor one's own needs when grieving the death of a loved one.

Help your families create a self-care plan and encourage them to fill it with things they enjoy so they can design a unique and helpful plan they'll stick with. Use the template here to get started, and modify as needed.

PRINT:
https://www.internationalgriefinstitute.com/wp-content/uploads/2020/06/Self-Care-Plan.pdf

RESILIENCE RX™ INTERNATIONAL GRIEF INSTITUTE

SELF CARE PLAN

Losing someone we love changes how we live and who we are. The first step is to take good care of yourself.

Creating a self care plan and practicing those techniques that tend to our physical, emotional, social, and spiritual needs can help anchor you in times of stress and upheaval.

The love in the world begins with the love within ourselves. DEEPAK CHOPRA

WHY IT MATTERS

Self care can improve our well being, minimize stress, reduce the damaging effects of grief, and help us adjust as we learn to live with our loved one in our heart instead of our arms. By identify things you enjoy, you'll be able to create a unique and helpful self-care plan you'll stick with.

CREATE YOUR PLAN

STEP 1: Identify your emotional, physical, social and spiritual needs.

STEP 2: Create your self care plan and fill it with activities you enjoy.

STEP 3: Put it into action and stick to it.

STEP 4: Reassess it every 3 months and adjust as needed.

EMOTIONAL NEEDS

Our emotional needs after loss are met through understanding, empathy, and support from others.

- Surround yourself with others who speak your loss language.
- Develop friendships that are supportive.
- Talk to loved ones about your loss and how you are coping.
- Express your emotions in a journal.
- Engage in enjoyable outlets such as coloring, knitting, gardening, puzzles, etc.

PHYSICAL NEEDS

Nourishing your body with oxygen, hydration, and healthful food will help you physically feel better. When you feel better, you cope better.

- Practice good sleep hygiene. Use a body pillow to help the marital bed feel less empty.
- Engage in light exercise, housekeeping or dancing to keep the body moving.
- Stay hydrated and eat for health.
- Make time for restorative relaxation.
- Enjoy a good belly laugh at least once daily.
- Join a walking or hiking club.

SPIRITUAL NEEDS

Our spiritual needs are met through inner reflection.

- Each day write down one thing you're grateful for, or try spiritual journaling.
- Engage in reflective practices such as prayer or meditation.
- Attend church, mosque, temple or a spiritual center.
- Try laughter yoga or forest therapy.
- Talk to clergy or a spiritual mentor.

SOCIAL NEEDS

Fulfilling engagements and interactions help guard against depression, anxiety and isolation after loss.

- Volunteer in the community.
- Take or teach a self enrichment class.
- Join a book, tennis, quilt or knitting club.
- Travel

MORE TIPS

- Paint a color-by-number picture.
- Join a monthly potluck club.
- Stomp on bubble sheets.
- Listen to music you love.
- Start a garden.
- Pull weeds.
- Get a pet.

iCare ICARE AFTERCARE™ Resilience Rx™ promotes nurturing self-help techniques and positive coping strategies that support you through loss.

ACTIVITY

CREATE CARE PLAN

Help the mourner create a self-care plan and encourage them to fill it with things they enjoy so they can design a unique and helpful plan they'll stick with.

Step 1: Identify emotional, physical, social and spiritual needs.

Step 2: Create a self-care plan and fill it with activities they enjoy.

Step 3: Put it into action and stick with it.

Step 4: Reassess every 3 months and adjust as needed.

MODALITY 2: LISTENING CALENDAR

The first step toward helping a mourner reconcile their head with their heart is to validate the grief they're feeling and associated emotions. When you hold the space for the mourner to talk about his or her heartbreak, we aren't encouraging them to ruminate in their sorrow or feel sorry for themselves. By allowing them to discuss it, we give them the space to process it. If they aren't allowed to process it, it becomes silent grief. Silent grief can be deadly grief.

When sitting with a mourner, invite them to talk about their loss for fifteen minutes. Set the timer, and avoid interrupting the mourner during those fifteen minutes. Explain that it is important for him or her to just ramble without interruption, guidance, or judgment.

ACTIVITY

DEVELOP LISTENING CALENDAR

Help the mourner develop a calendar that assigns individual family and friends to a 15-minute slot of listening once weekly. For example, Neighbor Betty might serve as Monday's listener while coworker Alice might serve as Thursday's listener. The time of day isn't important, but having the daily opportunity to talk about their loss uninterrupted is the goal.

EXAMPLE:

SUNDAY	MONDAY	TUESDAY	WEDNESDAY	THURSDAY	FRIDAY	SATURDAY
Betty (neighbor)	Fran (oldest sister)	Marcie (friend)	Scott (brother)	Stacy (book club)	Evelyn (coworker)	Bill (peer support)

MODALITY 3: NURTURE SUPPORTIVE RELATIONSHIPS

Nourishment is life sustaining. We eat nutritious foods to fuel our bodies. We engage in activities to nourish the soul. We volunteer time and resources to nourish those around us. Yet we often neglect to develop nourishing relationships—an essential element of happy lives.

It's important to find friends with whom we can share stories and express ourselves freely without judgment. Seek out those who settle for less than perfection and make allowance for human weaknesses. Those types of friendships are fulfilling and rewarding for everyone, and can last for life. Because loving bonds come in a variety of flavors, look for healthy friendships in a variety of places.

TIPS TO GOOD RELATIONSHIPS:

- Be authentic. Honesty is a cornerstone.
- Be one another's cheerleader. Inspire.
- Listen. Avoid starting any sentence with "You should . . . "
- Cultivate joyful memories together.
- Give without expectations.
- Protect confidentiality.
- Love yourself first.

DIFFICULT RELATIONSHIPS

Although most people naturally stay away from whiners, sometimes we are forced to interact with others who are less than nurturing, and suck what little energy a mourner has left. Equally important to nourishing good relationships is the need to set down boundaries with challenging relationships. The activity below empowers mourners to set down boundaries when needed.

ACTIVITY

SET BOUNDARIES

- Close your eyes. Envision yourself on a stage. Notice where you are on that stage.
- Envision the person who sucks the energy from you plopping from thin air onto the stage. Where do they land in relation to you? How does your body react?
- Notice what s/he is doing. Laughing? Talking? Criticizing?
- Envision a glass dome going down around yourself, keeping you safe from energy vampires.

MODALITY 4: SENSORIAL THERAPY

Our five senses play a role in how we feel, and can be influenced by what our senses take in. Sometimes when life feels stressful or hopeless, treating our five senses to something that looks, feels, smells, tastes, or sounds good serves as an important reminder that not all pleasure is lost. Further, treating ourselves to something that evokes sensorial joy also stimulates our brain to trigger positive hormones (oxytocin, dopamine, serotonin).

Include the activity below in self-care plans. With practice, the awareness of delight eventually becomes effortless, and is an important step toward restoring balance in times of stress.

ACTIVITY

RULE OF 5

Every day, practice the following:

- ✓ 5 things you can **SEE**
- ✓ 4 things you can **TOUCH**
- ✓ 3 things you can **HEAR**
- ✓ 2 things you can **SMELL**
- ✓ 1 thing you can **TASTE**

SIGHT—Visual suggestions:

- Watch a sunrise or sunset.
- Look at a cherished photo or a favorite memento.
- Use a plant or flowers to enliven your work space.
- Enjoy the beauty of a garden, the beach, a park, or your own backyard.
- Surround yourself with colors that lift your spirits.

TACTILE—Touch suggestions:

- Soak in a warm tub with Epsom salts or bath oil.
- Wear a pair of extra soft socks.
- Pet a dog or cat.
- Wrap yourself in a soft scarf or blanket.

HEARING—Sound suggestions:

- Listen to relaxing or upbeat music.
- Listen to laughter on YouTube or comedy .
- Listen to the sound of the ocean, waterfall, or fountain.
- Hang windchimes near a window.
- Seek silence.
- Listen to the birds or a soundtrack of nature.

OLFACTION—Smell suggestions:

- Shower or bathe with a lovely scented soap.
- Light a fragrant candle or burn incense.
- Apply a scented lotion to your skin before bed.
- Buy a fragrant flower bouquet for the kitchen or your office.
- Experiment with different essential oils in a diffuser.
- Enjoy clean, fresh air in the great outdoors.
- Spritz on your favorite perfume .

GUSTATION—Taste suggestions:

- Enjoy a favorite food.
- Enjoy a mug of herbal tea, cocoa with whipped cream, or a cold drink.
- Chew flavored gum.
- Indulge in a piece of dark chocolate.
- Eat a ripe piece of fruit.

MODALITY 5: CHROMOTHERAPY

Colors are all around us, and they aren't meaningless. They can change the way we feel and react. Although chromotherapy has been around since the time of Ancient Egypt, Western researchers are now adapting to the idea of chromotherapy as a healing modality, and studying the scientific properties of how colored lights affect our brain and emotions. Although the science behind how chromotherapy works isn't yet clear, several ancient cultures including the Egyptians and Chinese practiced the use of colors to heal.

Chromotherapy is sometimes referred to as light therapy or colorology, and is widely used today as a holistic or alternative treatment.

WHAT WE KNOW ABOUT CHROMOTHERAPY:

- Calms the amygdala
- Takes you outside the thinking part of your brain
- Certain colors can invigorate a depressed mind or soothe an agitated mind
- Lowers blood pressure
- Relaxes breathing
- The repetitive hand motions used in coloring induces a meditative state

DIFFERENT METHODS OF USING COLOR:

For those who are resistant to coloring, encourage an alternative such as a colored light bulb, color-wash video, or chromotherapy sauna.

- Paint a color-by-number picture
- Color your bath water
- Plug in a colored nightlight
- Hang a colored glass prism
- Paint the walls of your bedroom or office
- Add colorful home décor
- Use colored bulbs in your lamps
- Enjoy a color wash YouTube video
- Download a color therapy app
- Enjoy a chromotherapy sauna

ACTIVITY

COLORING

- Grab a fresh box of crayons or colored markers and use the pages in this manual or a coloring book to get started.
- Let your emotions guide the colors you choose. The repetitive movements of your hand induces a calm meditative-type state.

MODALITY 6: LAUGH THERAPY

Those who need a good laugh are usually the ones who feel least like laughing, yet the heart can hold joy the same time as sorrow, so go ahead and laugh. It's actually good for us.

A powerful healing modality, studies show that laughter offers many physical, psychological, emotional, and social benefits. It decreases stress and increases immune and infection-fighting antibodies. Smiling and laughter stimulate the facial muscles that trigger the brain to release happy hormones called endorphins, the body's natural feel-good chemicals that promote an overall sense of well-being and can even temporarily relieve pain.

KEYNOTE

No matter how you induce a good belly laugh, the bottom line is that whatever makes you laugh is truly good medicine.

HOW IT WORKS:

- Smiling and laughter stimulate the facial muscles that trigger the brain to release endorphins, the body's natural feed-good hormones.
- Like crying, laughter releases emotional energy. And studies show that 10 minutes of laughter is equivalent to 30 minutes of cardio.
- Laughter engages in perfect diaphragmatic breath. When we laugh, we exhale completely and then inhale completely, which oxygenates the brain. When our brains are fully oxygenated, our minds become calm and clear. The brain oxygenation and endorphin combination is like a joyful cocktail.
- When we feel good and the mind is clear, we feel grounded, less stress and less reactive.
- Laughter doesn't change reality but does help us to cultivate a positive mental attitude.
- Be silly, be playful. Laughter is contagious and allows our inner child to come out.
- Fake laughter often turns into authentic laughter. The body can't tell the difference, and the health benefits are the same.

ACTIVITY

DAILY BELLY LAUGH

- Watch funny YouTube videos, a comedy TV show or movie, or listen to baby giggles.
- Try laughter yoga.
- Because the body can't tell the difference between a real or fake smile, hold a pencil between your teeth to "fake it until you make it." The brain can't tell the difference and will be tricked into releasing those feel-good chemicals anyway.

MODALITY 7: HUG THERAPY

Connections are fostered when people take the time to appreciate and acknowledge one another, and a hug is a free, easy, and—at 20 seconds—is a quick way to show love and appreciation. Research shows that a hug lasting at least 20 seconds has a therapeutic effect on the body and mind. A sincere embrace produces the love hormone oxytocin which helps us feel relaxed, feel safe, and calms fears and anxiety. This substance has many benefits in our physical and mental health. A natural tranquilizer, it helps us to relax, to feel safe and calm our fears and anxiety. And it's free every time we hug, cradle a child, cherish a dog or cat, slow dance, or simply hold the shoulders of a friend.

HOW IT WORKS

- Affection has a direct response on the reduction of stress which prevents many diseases. Touch Research Institute at the University of Miami School of Medicine has carried out more than 100 studies on the power of touch, and discovered evidence of improved immune system, reduced pain, lower glucose levels, and faster growth in premature babies.
- Hugs stimulate brains to release dopamine, the pleasure hormone. Low dopamine levels play a role in neurodegenerative diseases and mood disorders such as depression. Dopamine is responsible for giving us that feel-good feeling, and it's also responsible for motivation.
- Hugging releases serotonin into the blood vessels which cause pleasure and negate pain and sadness. It also reduces the risk of heart problems, helps fight excess weight, and prolongs life. Hugging raises our serotonin levels, elevating mood and creating happiness.
- Hugs apply gentle pressure on the sternum which stimulates the thymus gland, which regulates and balances the production of white blood cells, which keep you healthy and disease free.
- Hugging boosts self-esteem, especially in children. From the time we're born our family's touch shows us that we're loved and special.
  The associations of self-worth and tactile sensations from our early years become imbedded in our nervous system as we grow into adults. They become imprinted at a cellular level, and therefore connect us to our ability to self love.

ACTIVITY

DAILY HUG

- Embrace someone you love for 20 seconds
- Cradle a child
- Snuggle with a pet
- Hug a stuffed animal or doll
- Self hug
- Try a weighted blanket

MODALITY 8: FOREST THERAPY

Forest therapy is rooted in the Japanese practice of Shinrin-yoku, which is often translated as "forest bathing." Exposing your brain to restorative environments by immersing yourself in the atmosphere of the forest helps with mental fatigue by eliciting feelings of awe. One study found that people's mental energy bounced back even when they just looked at pictures of nature (Psychological Science, 2012).

Another study found that students sent into the forest for two nights had lower levels of cortisol, the stress hormone, than those who spent that time in the city. In another study, researchers found a decrease in both heart rate and levels of cortisol in subjects in the forest when compared to those in the city.

HOW IT WORKS

The natural environment is restorative, and time outdoors offers many benefits. Even viewing a natural scene on the computer or through a window can help. Doses of nature have found to improve concentration after just 20 minutes in a park (Environment & Behavior, 1991; Journal of Environmental Psychology, 1995 (2); Journal of Attention Disorders, 2008).

- Stress, anxiety, and depression may all be eased by time outdoors, especially when combined with exercise.
- One study found that walks in the forest were specifically associated with decreased levels of anxiety and bad moods. The effect of nearby water improves it even more.

- Restores waning attention
- Improves focus
- Rejuvenates mental fatigue
- Improves concentration
- Decreases anxiety
- Improves bad mood

ACTIVITY

DAILY DOSE OF NATURE

Engage in one or more of the following nature activities each day:

- Stroll through a park or forest for 20 minutes
- Try gardening, fishing, kayaking, golfing, or other outdoor activities
- Hike, bike, jog, walk, swim or fly a kite
- Take nature photos with your phone
- Try geo-caching or Pokemoning, mine for gems or metal detecting

MODALITY 9: DANCE/MOVEMENT THERAPY

Feelings can influence your movement, and movement can impact your feelings. When we feel tired and sad, we tend to move more slowly. Dance/Movement Therapy gets us moving and yields many positive benefits along the way.

HOW IT WORKS

Movement is one of the most basic functions of the human body. Dance/movement therapy (DMT) uses movement to help achieve emotional, cognitive, physical and social integration. Dancing benefits us both physically and mentally through stress reduction, mood management, increased mobility, decreased muscle tension, and more. DMT promotes self-awareness, self-esteem, and offers a safe space for the expression of feelings.

Further, the lymphatic system—an important part of your body's immune system—is a series of channels and nodes dispersed throughout the body that move lymph fluid containing infection-fighting white blood cells. Unlike the circulatory or respiratory systems, the lymphatic system does not have a pump. It relies on our motion to circulate lymph fluid around the body. Each time we move large muscles of the body, we help pump lymphatic fluid through your body, keeping your systems circulating.

The creative expression of dancing is commonly used to treat issues such as:

- Chronic pain
- Obesity
- Depression, anxiety, trauma
- Poor self esteem
- Hypertension
- Cardiovascular disease

SONG SUGGESTIONS:

- "Uptown funk," by Bruno Mars
- "Walking on sunshine," by Katrina and the Waves
- "Can't stop the feeling," by Justin Timberlake
- "Better when I'm dancing," by Meghan Trainor
- "Dancing Queen," by ABBA
- "Shut up and dance," by Walk the Moon
- "I want to dance with somebody," by Whitney Houston

ACTIVITY

JUST DANCE

Each day, pick a 3-minute song to dance to.

- Pick something upbeat.
- Select a private room where you can dance uninhibited. Consider playing the song from YouTube (watching others dance helps us feel less awkward, even in private).
- Turn the music up or wear headphones.
- Allow yourself to sing while dancing, if inspired to do so (it's good for the lungs).

MODALITY 10: COMPASSIONATE THOUGHTS

Self-kindness is about gifting ourselves with the same kindness and understanding we give others. Rather than being critical or judging ourselves harshly when we already feel pain, we can learn to treat ourselves with compassion and patience instead.

HOW IT WORKS

According to Dr. Kristin Neff, self-compassion is a practice of goodwill, not good feelings. With self-compassion we mindfully accept that the moment is painful, and embrace ourselves with kindness and care in response, remembering that imperfection is part of the shared human experience.

The following activity can be done any time of day or night, and is a wonderful way to gift ourselves with compassion when we need it most.

ACTIVITY

SELF COMPASSION EXERCISE

Find yourself a quiet spot. It can be your favorite chair, in your car, in your office, or even in your garden. Then clear your head and for five minutes think nothing but compassionate thoughts about yourself. Not your spouse, not your children, not your coworkers, but yourself. Having trouble? Fill in the blanks below, and then give yourself permission to really validate those positive qualities. Do this every day.

I have a ____

Example: good heart, gentle soul, witty personality

I make a ____

Example: good lasagna, potato salad, scrapbook, quilt

I'm a good____

Example: friend, gardener, knitter, painter, poem writer

People would say I'm ____

Example: funny, kind, smart, gentle, generous, humble, creative

MODALITY 11: HOBBY THERAPY

For a long time in the grief journey, everything is painful. In the early days, just getting out of bed and taking a shower can be exhausting. Housecleaning, grocery shopping, and routine errands often take a back seat or disappear altogether. As painful as it is, it's very important to find an outlet that gets you out of bed each day. Beginning a new outlet may feel exhausting at first, but remember that the first step is always the hardest. And you don't have to do it forever, just focus on it for the time being.

HOW IT WORKS

Doing something productive occupies your mind and provides a respite for your brain pain, both which help to relax raw nerves. Embarking on a new hobby will help your brain focus on something besides the pain, and can help to channel emotions. As a bonus, any hobby that requires repetitive action of the hands, such as knitting or clay work, induces a meditative state that calms your mood, and can even result in gifts to give, inducing a "helpers high."

SUGGESTIONS:

- Learn to mold chocolate or clay
- Learn to make soap
- Learn how to bead, knit, crochet, or quilt
- Volunteer at a local shelter
- Learn a new sport such as golf or kayaking
- Create a memorial garden in a forgotten part of the yard
- Join Pinterest
- Doodle or draw
- Paint-by-number
- Join a book club
- Create a scrapbook
- Write poetry and start a poem collection
- Learn to play an instrument

ACTIVITY

PICK AN OUTLET

1. Create a list of hobbies or activities you might enjoy. Pick something that doesn't require a lot of setup; if it's less complicated, you're more likely to stick with it.
   - ______________________________
   - ______________________________
   - ______________________________
   - ______________________________
   - ______________________________
   - ______________________________
2. Engage in one activity for at least 15 minutes each day. Play around with different hobbies until you find one you enjoy enough to stick with for the time being.

MODALITY 12: GIVING THERAPY

Winston Churchill once said, "We make a living by what we get. We make a life by what we give." In other words, helping others helps our own heart to heal.

Using something that comes naturally to help others is a win-win. Gallup conducted a study that showed people who use their gifts to help others experience the same benefits of giving. You get to exercise your talent and receive all the benefits of giving while others benefit from the giving of your talent. Can you crochet? Create a prayer shawl so the newly bereaved can wrap themselves in a warm hug. Are you a good hugger? Volunteer as a baby cuddler at your local hospital. Don't be afraid to think outside the box.

HOW IT WORKS

Giving is good for the giver in that it induces a natural high. Biologically, the act of giving activates regions in the brain associated with pleasure, and raises serotonin, dopamine, and oxytocin, generating positive emotions. Proven health benefits of giving include less stress, less depression, lower blood pressure, improved sleep, increased self esteem, and greater happiness.

WAYS TO GIVE:

- Distribute blessing bags to the homeless
- Volunteer in the community
- Smile at a stranger
- Give a compliment
- Leave a nice note for someone at work or school
- Let a driver merge in front of you during rush hour traffic
- Do random acts of kindness
- Leave balloons in a park for children
- Hold the door for someone
- Send an anonymous care package to someone who is struggling
- Knit a prayer shawl or warm socks
- Sew a memorial quilt
- Join a community choir
- Lead a painting class
- Read to children at the library
- Teach theater production
- Translate for a community organization

ACTIVITY

ACTS OF KINDNESS

Create a list of things you can do for others. Do one thing every day.

- ____________________
- ____________________
- ____________________
- ____________________
- ____________________
- ____________________
- ____________________
- ____________________
- ____________________
- ____________________

MODALITY 13: GRATITUDE JAR

A grateful heart is a happy heart. Gratitude is an intentional mindset and powerful healing modality because it involves recognition of the positive things in life and how they affect us, and allows us to acknowledge appreciation for it.

HOW IT WORKS

Studies show that people who consciously count their blessings tend to be happier because it fosters positive feelings and optimism. It encourages us to check in with ourselves and provides a respite for the brain pain. Practicing gratitude fosters positive feelings and can contribute to a sense of well-being when done regularly.

ACTIVITY

CREATE A GRATITUDE JAR

Decorate a can or jar, or buy one from a craft store. Using a prompt below, write down one thing you're grateful for each day. Once you're done, fold the statement and add it to the jar as a reminder of that gratitude.

- I'm grateful for my faith because ______________________________
- I'm grateful when someone smiles at me because ______________________________
- I'm grateful for the sound of laugher because ______________________________
- I'm grateful for hugs because ______________________________
- I'm grateful for the sunset because ______________________________
- I'm grateful for my dinner tonight because ______________________________
- I'm thankful for my pet because ______________________________
- I'm grateful for my friend because ______________________________
- I appreciate my loved one because ______________________________
- I'm grateful for ______________________________
- I'm grateful for ______________________________
- I'm grateful for ______________________________
- I'm grateful for ______________________________
- I'm grateful for ______________________________
- I felt happy today when ______________________________

MODALITY 14: VISUALIZATION

Elite athletes use it. The super rich use it. And peak performers in all fields use it. It works because your mind can't tell the difference between reality and imagination. Successful people use this to their advantage, and we can, too.

When thinking of transformation, it's natural to notice the challenges in our way instead of focusing on the outcome. Visualizing things we want to attract into our lives help keep life's speedbumps from becoming obstacles that prevent us from moving forward d. It also reminds us that our own negative experiences aren't destiny—we can still lead and deserve a good life in spite of our loss.

HOW IT WORKS

Creative visualization is a mental technique that uses the imagination to make dreams and goals come true by harnessing the power of the mind to attract events, situations, or an object into your life. One study found that imagining to move certain parts of your bodies almost trains the muscles as much as the actual movement (Neuropsychologia, Volume 42, Issue 7, 2004).

ACTIVITY

5-MINUTE EXERCISE:

- Visualize yourself feeling joy and enjoying life.
- Get as detailed as possible because the little details increase the likelihood of the big picture coming to fruition.
- Do this for 5 minutes every day.

MODALITY 15: JOURNALING

Journaling is a simple yet powerful form of self-expression that can help us externalize complex emotions and process difficult experiences. It can help us shift from a negative mindset to a more positive one, can be done anytime, and requires nothing more than a pen/pencil and paper.

HOW IT WORKS

Journaling occupies the analytical, rational left side of the brain, which leaves the right hemisphere (the creative side) the freedom to wander and play (Grothaus, 2015). Studies show that journaling can lead to "extinction" of negative emotions, reduce depression, intrusion and post traumatic avoidance, enhance a sense of well-being and even improve our memory (Baikie & Wilhelm, 2005).

TIPS

- ✓ Buy an inexpensive wide-lined spiral notebook or one of those expensive designer journals.
- ✓ Give yourself permission to write without perfection.
- ✓ Keep it private so you feel free to write what you feel without fear.
- ✓ Forget erasers. It is easier, quicker and more spontaneous to cross out words. Give yourself permission to be as sloppy or as neat as you wish.
- ✓ There are no errors when writing for yourself, so allow yourself to write spontaneously and forget about erasers. Rather than erasing or tearing out pages, cross out words or try putting a big X through a page.
- ✓ When staring at a blank page and unable to think of anything to say, write from your stream of consciousness or try the 5-minute exercise below.

ACTIVITY

10-MINUTE WRITE EXERCISE:

- **I**dentify a private, personalized space free from distraction. Make this your writing space.
- **W**rite down 2 emotions you are currently feeling. Write down why you think you're feeling each emotion. Are you angry at someone? Are you pleased with someone? What are you feeling sad about? What are you thinking about? Be specific and don't criticize.
- **R**eview or reflect on what you wrote.
- **I**nvestigate your feelings through your writing. If you run out of things to write about, allow yourself to "brain dump."
- **T**ime yourself to ensure you allow at least 10 minutes.
- **E**xit with introspection. "I now feel . . . ."

MODALITY 16: TOUCH THERAPY

Touch is naturally nurturing, especially when it's intentional. Two common touch therapies are reflexology and acupressure. Touch therapy is instinctive, like rubbing our temple for a headache, and is thought to signal the body to turn on its own self healing.

Acupressure deals with thin energy lines called meridians that run most of the length of the body. There are more than 800 pressure points along these lines. In contrast, reflexology has an entire reflex map of the body on the feet, a second complete reflex map of the body on the hands, and a third complete reflex map of the body on the outer ear.

HOW IT WORKS

Using touch to apply self massage helps relax the muscles, and it's thought that pressure applied to specific points triggers the brain to release endorphins, our body's own natural pain-relieving hormones.

ACTIVITY

5-MINUTE EXERCISE:

- Find a relaxed, comfortable position, close your eyes, and breathe deeply.
- Using your fingertips, find your own acupoints that elicit "Ahhh" by applying firm pressure to massage the area. Don't get hung up on exact point locations. If you can't find that sensation above, then simply massage around the point.
- Focus on the angle. Try pivoting your finger a little to the right, left, up or down to achieve your optimal sensation. You'll need very little pressure when you find your optimal angle.
- Avoid pressing on wounds, rashes, and varicose veins.
- Repeat the massage as often as you like.
- Tai Chong is located on your foot about two finger widths above the place where the skin of your big toe and the next toe join. Locate the point then use deep, firm pressure to massage and stimulate the area for 4-5 seconds.

- Zhong Zhu is located in the groove formed by the tendons of the 4th and 5th fingers behind the knuckles. Locate the point in the groove then apply deep, firm pressure to massage and stimulate the area for 4-5 seconds.

MODALITY 17: HYDROTHERAPY

Known as water therapy, cultures around the world have used water for centuries to treat mental stress, muscle pain, arthritis, promote relaxation, and more. From bathing in hot mineral springs to ice baths, the history of hydrotherapy dates back to ancient times. Today's applications encompass a broad range of methods that harness the physical properties of water, such as temperature, pressure, and sound, and use it to relax muscles, stimulate circulation, reduce stress, and more.

HOW IT WORKS

In hydrotherapy, water plays a dual role of providing support and warmth, while simultaneously promoting muscle relaxation, reduction in gravitational forces, and increased circulation. Further, when a person's body is submerged in water, we experience a weightless feeling that offers a respite from pain. Hydrotherapy has also been shown to have immune stimulating effects (Brenner et al., 1999).

APPLICATIONS:

- Saunas
- Steam baths
- Foot baths
- Sitz baths
- Cold/warm compresses
- Cold/warm showers
- Lap swimming
- Immersion tanks
- Hot tubs
- Whirlpools

ACTIVITY

WARM COMPRESS

A warm compress is a home hydrotherapy remedy that triggers our brain to relax, and is very soothing.

- Soak a small towel in water that feels hot to touch, not scalding.
- Remove from water, wring out excess.
- Roll towel and apply around your neck for 20 minutes.

MODALITY 18: MEDITATION

Meditation is the process of training your mind to focus and redirect your thoughts. By tuning into our body, meditation can increase awareness of how we're feeling, and allows us to focus on reducing stress through mindful breathing which, in turn, oxygenates the brain, which helps us feel calmer and more relaxed.

In fact, meditation can reverse our body's stress response pretty quickly, which is what makes it so helpful.

HOW IT WORKS

Mental and emotional stress triggers the brain to release stress hormones, which produce inflammatory chemicals called cytokines which affect sleep, depression, anxiety, blood pressure, fatigue, and more. Studies show that among the many benefits, mindfulness meditation reduces the inflammatory response, and promotes a positive mood, healthy sleep patterns, and increased pain tolerance (Brain, Behavior, and Immunity, January 2013).

ACTIVITY

5-MINUTE MEDITATION

Set a timer for 5 minutes.

- Find a comfortable position.
- Close your eyes and consciously relax your body.
- Slowly inhale from the belly, then into the ribs, then into the chest, and up into the crown of your head.
- Reverse the process for the exhale. Visualize the tension leaving your body from your head to your feet. Imagine the stress literally draining out from your toes, away from your body.
- Concentrating on your breath while imagining the stress draining away gives your mind something to focus on while reaping the benefits of deep breathing.

MODALITY 19: PET THERAPY

Interacting with pets stems from a human-animal bond that's embedded in our genes. Falling under the realm of Animal Assisted Intervention, the American Veterinary Medical Association has deduced that animal-assisted therapy creates an ideal environment for individuals suffering from stress.

In addition, pets can also provide recreational exercise and motivational opportunities, as well as an ongoing opportunity to nurture something we love.

HOW IT WORKS

Dr. Boris Levinson was a pioneering psychologist who theorized that pets had therapeutic benefits. In the 1960s, he reported that having his dog present at talk therapy sessions led to increased communication, increased self-esteem, and increased willingness to disclose difficult experiences.

Studies show that interaction with pets triggers our brain's endorphins, and the natural ease of a relationship void of expectations naturally reduces our stress and lowers feelings of loneliness. The innocent nature of animals plays a critical role in reducing stress through the rewards of unconditional love. One study concluded that people feel more energized with a pet around, even when we're doing critical tasks.

The physical act of cuddling our pet provides both hug therapy and sensorial therapy.

SUGGESTIONS

HOW TO ENGAGE IN PET THERAPY WITHOUT A PET

Individuals who aren't equipped to own or care for a pet still have opportunities to indulge in pet therapy. Encourage him or her to consider the following:

- Volunteer at an animal shelter
- Borrow a neighbor's dog for a daily walk
- Cat sit for a friend
- Watch pet videos on YouTube
- Watch a pet-centered movie
  - ✓ Disney's Zootopia
  - ✓ March of the Penguins
  - ✓ The Lion King
  - ✓ Homeward Bound
  - ✓ Babe

MODALITY 20: HYPNOTHERAPY

Hypnosis can be a valuable tool in managing and even reducing stress. Whether you engage in professional hypnotherapy at the hands of a skilled clinician, or practice self-hypnosis, it promotes stress management by inducing a deeply relaxing state.

Hypnosis can be used for stress management in two ways.

- First, you can use hypnosis to get into a deeply relaxed state, which will help prevent health problems due to chronic stress.
- Hypnosis can also be used to achieve lifestyle changes, if desired, such as weight loss.

HOW IT WORKS

Hypnosis involves entering a deeply relaxed but focused state. It's so effective, mothers have been known to use it to help manage pain during childbirth. Like meditation, hypnosis requires focus and practice but offers a good alternative for those with physical limitations that make exercise like yoga more difficult.

RESOURCES

WHERE TO FIND INFORMATION:

- Medical clinics
- Libraries
- Naturopaths
- Hypnotherapy organizations and associations
- Local community colleges
- Local technical colleges
- Universities

CHAPTER 9

ALTERNATIVE TECHNIQUES

Love knows no difference between life and death.

KHAN GHALIB

IN THIS CHAPTER

- ✓ **EMDR**
- ✓ **Flotation therapy**
- ✓ **EFT tapping**
- ✓ **Binaural beat meditation**

Nontraditional modalities are non-mainstream techniques performed by a licensed and skilled professional. According to one 2012 survey, more than 30 percent of adults use complementary healthcare approaches that originated outside traditional Western medicine. Because grief tools are not one-size-fits-all, empowering your clients to explore some of these modalities may be beneficial.

When a nontraditional modality is used alongside traditional Western medicine, it's considered complementary. When it is used in place of conventional medicine, it's considered alternative. Because the amount of available research varies depending upon the practice, it is important to encourage your clients to explore each modality with due diligence beforehand and find a highly skilled clinician who is familiar with grief's influence on the mind and body.

Many of these modalities include breathing exercises, guided imagery, progressive muscle relaxation, and more. Rolfing, hypnotherapy, Feldenkrais method, Trager psychophysical integration, and more. In this chapter, we'll explore a few to get you started.

TYPES

- EMDR
- Flotation therapy
- EFT tapping
- Binaural beat meditation
- REST
- Acupuncture
- Rolfing
- Feldenkrais method
- Trager psychophysical integration
- Aromatherapy
- Feng shui
- Herbal therapy
- Bio feedback therapy
- Transcranial magnetic stimulation
- Garden therapy
- ____________________

EMDR

Eye Movement Desensitization and Reprocessing, EMDR, is a psychotherapy modality originally designed to alleviate distress associated with traumatic memories.

EMDR therapy works on the premise that the mind can heal from psychological trauma much like the body recovers from physical trauma. When you cut your hand, your body works to close the wound. If a foreign object or repeated injury irritates the wound, it festers and causes pain. Once the block is removed, healing resumes.

EMDR therapy demonstrates that a similar sequence of events occurs with mental processes. The brain's information processing system naturally moves toward mental health. If the system is blocked by the impact of a disturbing event, the emotional wound festers. Once the block is removed, healing resumes.

EMDR therapy is an eight-phase treatment. Eye movements are used during one part of the session. After the clinician has determined which memory to target first, he asks the client to briefly hold different aspects of that event in the mind while watching the therapist's hand as it moves back and forth across the client's field of vision. The lateral eye movements are the most commonly used external stimulus but a variety of other stimuli including hand-tapping and audio stimulation are often used (Shapiro, 1991).

In successful EMDR therapy, the meaning of painful events is transformed on an emotional level. For instance, a rape victim shifts from feeling horror and self-disgust to holding the affirmation that, "I survived it and I am strong." Unlike talk therapy, clients gain insight from their own emotional processes that now empowers them.

HOW IT WORKS

It is hypothesized that EMDR facilitates the accessing of the traumatic memory network so that information processing is enhanced, with new associations forged between the traumatic memory and more adaptive memories or information. It is believed that through EMDR, affective distress is relieved, negative beliefs are formulated, and physiological arousal is reduced.

More than 30 positive controlled outcome studies have been done on EMDR therapy. Some of the studies show that 84%-90% of single-trauma victims no longer have post-traumatic stress disorder after only three 90-minute sessions. Another study, funded by the HMO Kaiser Permanente, found that 100% of the single-trauma victims and 77% of multiple trauma victims no longer were diagnosed with PTSD after only six 50-minute sessions. In another study, 77% of combat veterans were free of PTSD in 12 sessions.

EMDR therapy is now recognized as an effective form of treatment for trauma and other disturbing experiences by organizations such as the American Psychiatric Association, the World Health Organization and the Department of Defense.

FLOTATION THERAPY

Floatation therapy centers on reducing the body's internal stress response by eliminating the forces of gravity while simultaneously removing external sources of distraction. The use of water removes any pressure points on the body, as though it is floating on a cloud or in space, and encourages the mind to relax and reset. The addition of salt aids in buoyancy, allowing us to float effortlessly atop the water.

HOW IT WORKS

Floating appears to take us out of "flight or fight" stress response by decreasing the production of cortisol, leaving us feeling serene. The brain enters the theta brainwave state, and provides an environment that is the exact opposite of stress. The spine naturally elongates and straightens, and the body undergoes the same regeneration process that transpires during sleep. There's also a growing body of research that demonstrates the potential for floatation therapy to significantly improve physical pain with promising results. Studies also show that it offers a cumulative benefit, meaning that the more you float, the more your mind learns to relax.

ACTIVITY

ALTERNATIVES

Flotation therapy involves Epsom salt for buoyancy. Most people don't have access to the amount of Epsom salt needed to float at home, but a handful of salt can still be useful to aid in relaxation.

- Add Epsom salts to warm bath water before bathing.
- Add Epsom salt to a child-size pool. Jump in and relax.
- Add Epsom salt to a foot bath.

EFT TAPPING

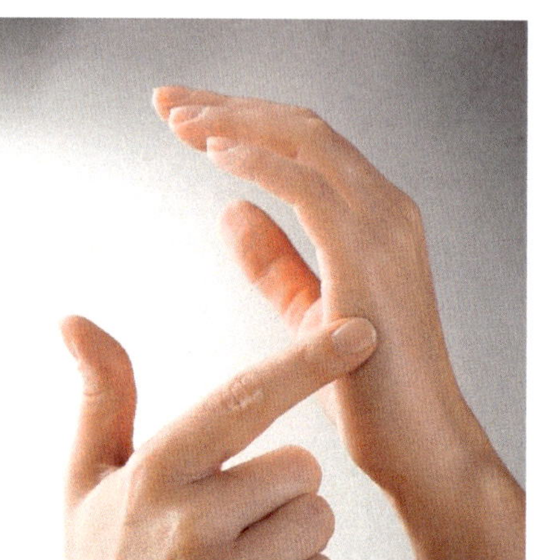

Also referred to as simply tapping or psychological acupressure, emotional freedom technique (EFT) is an alternative modality for anxiety and posttraumatic stress.

Chinese medicine teaches that energy flows through the body by way of channels, known as meridians, and any imbalance in this energy can result in disease and sickness. While acupuncture uses needles to apply pressure to these energy points, EFT uses fingertip tapping in place of needles. It is believed that stimulating the meridian points through tapping sends a signal to the part of your brain that controls stress, and can therefore help restore balance to the body's energy system.

Although further research is needed, recent studies have concluded that EFT tapping appears to show a significant decrease in stress and anxiety in subjects compared to other cognitive therapy techniques.

BINAURAL BEAT MEDITATION

Dating back to ancient times, binaural beat meditation is a type of sound therapy that is used to entrain the brain through sound repetition. Known as Frequency Following Response, it naturally occurs in the human brain when a different sound (tone) frequency is sent to the left and right ears through headphones.

Upon hearing different frequencies sent simultaneously to the left and right ears, the brain perceives a new tone, or third tone, based on the mathematical difference between the two frequencies. The brain then follows along with this auditory illusion at the new frequency, and produces brainwaves at the same rate of Hertz (Hz), thus becoming "entrained" to that frequency.

Understanding this information, we can listen to binaural beats to encourage the brain to produce brainwaves of a specific type, such as delta, theta, alpha, beta, and gamma, to help us relax and even fall asleep.

MORE WAYS TO RELEASE STRESS

- Chew gum
- Stomp on bubble sheets
- Meditate
- Pray
- Change the channel
- Yoga
- Deep breathing
- Kiss
- Acupressure
- Listen to music
- Watch a viral video
- Paint the walls
- Plant flowers
- Weed
- Deadhead the roses
- Dry skin brushing
- Buy a plant
- Get a pet

CHAPTER 10

COMMUNITY CONNECTIONS & EVENTS

The greatness of a community is most accurately measured by the compassionate actions of its members.

CORETTA SCOTT KING

IN THIS CHAPTER

- ✓ Speaking
- ✓ Workshops
- ✓ Holiday HUGS
- ✓ iCare Café
- ✓ Reunion Service
- ✓ Crisis gatherings
- ✓ Candlelight vigils

Connecting and aligning with similar organizations inside your community can be of mutual benefit. It can help you become visible, expand your own knowledge, stay current on the changing climate of the funeral and after-care industry, and even problem solve. Consider creating a local coalition of grief professionals. This is an excellent place to learn what others are doing, they'll learn what you're doing (market, market, market), and you can discuss resources that might be lacking in your community and how to fulfill them.

PLAN

1. Identify your goals for connecting with other organizations. What do you want to accomplish?
2. List the organizations that make up your care community.
   a. Hospice
   b. Religious organizations
   c. Therapists and counselors
   d. Chapter leaders of national bereavement groups
   e. Bereavement organizations
   f. Funeral service organizations
3. Decide who to approach that will benefit you both.
4. Develop an outreach plan for each of the groups listed above.

COLLABORATE & LEAD

5. Invite organizations to cohost or cosponsor community workshops for widows, widowers, bereaved families, and other mourners. Ideas include:

   a. How to organize your loved one's belongings (cohost with a professional home organizer).

   b. How to cook for one for widows or widowers (cohost with a personal chef or other organization).

   c. Banking needs (cohost with a banker).

   d. Managing household maintenance issues, cleaning, etc. (cohost with a home maintenance and/or cleaning business).

   e. Landscaping issues (invite local Boy Scouts group or professional business).

   f. Sponsor a movie night.

Speaking engagements

Speaking engagements are a tool to grow your business and draw in customers. The purpose of speaking is to get you and your name in front of clients. It gives you an opportunity to engage with your community and establish your credibility as an expert. When people are in the market for your services, they're more likely to remember you and have a higher level of confidence in your ability to serve them.

Learning how to create and use speaking engagements and presentations to engage with community members is an excellent marketing opportunity and a cost-effective way to subliminally market your products. It's important to recognize different presentation types, reasons for hosting a community presentation, understanding your audience, and learning how to create compelling and memorable content.

In general, a speaking engagement is a one-way presentation that allows you to educate your audience about a specific topic. Think of it as a college classroom—you're the instructor and the audience are your students.

TYPES OF EVENT

Speaking engagements can be informative, instructional, persuasive, and more. Decide on the purpose of your engagement. What would you like to accomplish? Consider the following possibilities.

- Provide educational information
- Provide instructional step-by-step information
- Connect and network
- Promote your organization

VENUES

Speaking opportunities and workshops are best held in a neutral environment. Consider using one of the library's conference rooms, or check with your local Chamber of Commerce to find what's available in your community. Some venues are free or low cost. Do not expect the venue to do any advertising on your behalf. If you want people to show up, you need to market the event.

ENTRY FEE

Decide whether you're going to charge an admission fee. If you do, consider online registration vs. paying at the door. If you opt for guests to pay at the door, consider a price that doesn't involve handling lots of change or one dollar bills.

SPEAKING TOPICS

Consider the needs of the community and your families. What information do you want them to know? What are you passionate about sharing? Also consider the audience. Don't be afraid to host a workshop that's never been taught before.

TIPS

- Use lots of powerful language
- Be enthusiastic and enjoyable to watch
- Incorporate stories or real life examples
- Offer supporting facts to reinforce credibility
- Engage the audience. "Raise your hand if you . . . "
- Problem solve
- If using a PowerPoint, purchase a quality template that pairs fonts, colors, and design elements for a polished look that's esthetically pleasing to the audience

PLAN

1. Determine your subject matter.
2. Create a catchy marketing title.
3. Select date and time.

4. Secure a venue of appropriate size.
5. Determine whether to charge an entry or registration fee.
6. Advertise the event:
    - press release
    - social media
    - newsletters
    - email blasts
    - website
7. Find volunteers to help manage the event.
8. Determine a refreshments budget and what refreshments you're going to provide.
9. Determine whether you wish to invite other professionals to co-host or join you.
10. Secure a display screen, projector, mic, sound system, etc
11. Choose a color theme to set the intended mood. Use these colors in your tablecloths, informational material and marketing, refreshment cups, display elements, etc.
12. Determine the delivery method of your information. Consider using a PowerPoint.
13. Determine visual displays and informational material you want to provide. What are the takeaways for your audience?

PREPARE

1. Set up an entry/registration table. Cover it with a tablecloth in one of your theme colors. Solid colored tablecloths work best (patterns compete for visual attention, drawing the eye away from more important tabletop items).
2. Display informational and marketing material (use separate table if needed).
3. Make it warm and welcoming. Consider adding a seasonal floral or holiday display.
4. Pens, dish of hard candies or chocolate kisses, free marketing gadgets
5. Set up refreshments table using matching tablecloth.
6. Set up A/V equipment.

LEAD

- Begin on time. Introduce yourself (5 minutes).
- Share your story (10 minutes).
- Discuss your topic and intended key points (30 minutes). Use PowerPoint if desired.
- Promote your organization (5 minutes).
- Invite audience to ask questions (10 minutes).

E02/SPEAKING ENGAGEMENT

Workshops

Community workshops differ from presentations in that they are interactive and hands-on. Offering a community workshop is an excellent way to engage with your audience, make community connections, and promote your organization. Don't be afraid to host a workshop that hasn't been done before. Think outside the box. What would draw people in?

Consider hosting the following workshops:

- How to create a memorial scrapbook
- How to create Blessing Bags
- How to honor your loved one's birthday
- How to journal your way through loss
- How to hold the sacred space for someone in mourning (available for ($49.99)
- Laughter Yoga
- Resilience Rx: 10 ways to cope with grief (available for $49.99)

PLAN

1. Determine your workshop focus.
2. Create a catchy marketing title.
3. Select date and time.
4. Secure a venue of appropriate size.
5. Determine whether to charge an entry or registration fee.
6. Advertise the event:
   - press release
   - social media
   - newsletters
   - email blasts
   - website
7. Find volunteers to help manage the workshop. Consider cohosting with one or two other community organizations.
8. Determine a refreshments budget and what refreshments you're going to provide.
9. Secure a display screen, projector, mic, sound system, if needed.
10. Choose a color theme to set the intended mood. Use these colors in your tablecloths, informational material and marketing, refreshment cups, display elements, etc.
11. Determine visual displays and informational material you want to provide. What are the takeaways for your audience?
12. Determine the materials you need to purchase for the participants to use.

PREPARE

1. Set up an entry/registration table. Cover it with a tablecloth in one of your theme colors. Solid colored tablecloths work best (patterns compete for visual attention, drawing the eye away from more important tabletop items).
2. Display informational and marketing material (use separate table if needed).
3. Make the entry table warm and welcoming. Consider adding a seasonal floral or holiday display.
4. Pens, dish of hard candies or chocolate kisses, free marketing gadgets
5. Set up refreshments table using matching tablecloth.
6. Set up A/V or other needed equipment.

LEAD

- Begin on time. Pass out needed supplies prior to introduction.
- Introduce yourself (5 minutes).
- Share your story (10 minutes).
- Begin workshop. Instruct participants on each step.
- Upon conclusion, allow participants to take home anything they made in the workshop.
- Promote your organization (5 minutes).

E04/COMMUNITY WORKSHOPS

Holiday HUGS Program

Pumpkin spice lattes. Steaming hot cocoa. Storefronts dressed in holiday style. 'Tis the holiday season, a season filled with gaiety and Hallmark moments—unless you're missing someone you love.

Many grievers say there is no harder time than the holidays, leaving specialists with a prime opportunity for community outreach through HUGS—Holiday Understanding Grief Support.

WHAT IS HUGS?

HUGS was created over 10 years ago by aftercare specialist Linda Findlay in response to organizations who wanted to do something for grieving families but didn't have the staff or tools. Today, HUGS has partnered with hundreds of organizations to provide a private label program that's helped thousands of families during a difficult time of year.

A successful interactive program that provides comfort and support to your families during one of the hardest times of the year, HUGS is a workshop, sharing circle, and candle-light ceremony all rolled into one special event.

Program includes:

- Workshop to help cope with the holidays
- Sharing circle
- Candlelighting ceremony including candles and music

Organization benefits:

- A positive community impression
- Builds relationships
- Creates referrals
- Your organization receives the recognition while families get the support they need

Use the following instructions and corresponding templates on the following pages. You can download the templates from the specialist portal using the credentials listed at the beginning of this manual.

PLAN

1. Assign lead coordinator and refreshment coordinator.
2. Choose dates, time and location.
    a. Plan one year in advance.
    b. Schedule event one week before Thanksgiving or first week in December.
    c. Ensure a location with ample parking that is well lit, easy to find, and accessible.
    d. Provide directions and sandwich board signage.
3. Create program. See sample.
4. Select program readers.
5. Select music accompaniments or performers.
6. Decide on refreshments. Recommend bottled water, coffee, tea.

PREPARE

7. Create program flyer. See sample.
8. Purchase:
    a. Clear glass ornaments/mementos
    b. Paint pens
    c. Small gift bags for ornaments
    d. Holiday display tree
    e. Refreshments/food
9. Prepare, print and send out invites.
    a. Send to all families — By November 1
    b. Notify local newspapers — By November 1
    c. Notify local radio stations — By November 1
    d. Notify local TV stations — By November 1
    e. Post posters and/or flyers — By November 1
10. Reconfirm location, program and music participants
11. Prepare ornaments by writing loved one's names, then rebox for easy transfer.

LEAD

12. One day prior to event, set up display tree with ornaments.
13. Arrive 60 minutes prior to event.
14. Set up room and display programs.
    a. Side table for sign-in, programs, handouts
    b. Set up refreshments
    c. Adjust room lighting. Keep it sufficiently light but not bright.
15. Greet participants. Have guests sign in.
16. Start on time.

17. Welcome.
    a. Introduce coordinators.
    b. Share housekeeping information.
    c. Workshop program: Offer tips and strategies for coping with the holidays. Refer to the Resilience Rx™ Coping with the Holidays PDF for ideas.
    d. Sharing circle: Conduct a 60-minute sharing circle to help participants share their holiday struggles.
    e. Candlelight ceremony: Refer to Community Vigil instructions in this manual for how to conduct a candlelight ceremony, and modify as needed.
    f. At the end, have someone read each one of the loved one's names while handing out ornaments.
    g. Close.
    h. Proceed to refreshment area.

SAMPLE

HOLIDAY FLYER TEMPLATE

COMMUNITY OUTREACH

HUGS

HOLIDAY PROGRAM

JOIN US

F06/HOLIDAY HUGS FLYER

iCare Café

iCare Café is a monthly social gathering that provides the space for and encourages discussion of afterloss and how to adapt to the transitions that come with loss.

It differs from other social gatherings in that the discussion is not about death. Rather, iCare Café is about life after loss.

GOAL

1. To provide the social space for gatherings focused on life after loss.
2. To facilitate an inclusive discussion in a neutral social setting about how to adapt to the transitions and changes commonly experienced after losing a loved one.
3. To problem-solve common challenges as a group, such as how to address a loved one's belongings. No answer is right or wrong, yet the group discussion can inspire those who are struggling with the task.
4. To establish yourself or your organization as the community expert on death, loss, and grief.

PLAN

1. Identify a schedule. Consider once monthly, such as the first Thursday of each month. Once every two months (six times a year) is another option.
2. Identify a neutral location away from the funeral setting. Ensure adequate well-lit parking and use of public restroom facilities. Consider:
    a. Coffee houses
    b. Library conference rooms
    c. University, college, or high school conference rooms
    d. Community rooms
3. Consider topics you want to cover. Invite others to speak and facilitate the discussion. Topic suggestions:
    a. Healing modalities
    b. Aftercare challenges
    c. Consider featuring authors of newly released grief-related books
4. Identify a refreshment budget. Consider adopting some sort of signature dish that people can count on to enjoy while attending (Death Café features cake). People like food, and will associate iCare Café meetings and discussions with something pleasant. Are you going to provide refreshments, or choose a where people can buy their own?
5. Encourage families to attend, as death affects everyone, but let them know that this is a social gathering and childcare is not provided.

PREPARE

1. Set the location and topic schedule 6 months in advance. Confirm locations.
2. Invite and confirm guest speakers to facilitate.
    a. Ensure that the speaker knows the entire evening isn't a one-way presentation. If a speaker chooses to give a short presentation at the beginning to kick off the discussion, limit it to 10 minutes. People came for a discussion, not a workshop.
    b. The speaker introduces the topic, share some statistics or information, and then invite the audience to engage and participate in a discussion about that topic.
3. Notify the community of the topics and calendar dates via iCare Café newsletters, emails, social media postings, etc.
4. Purchase refreshments, if needed.

LEAD

1. On the appointed night, introduce the topic and facilitator/speaker. If you have no speaker for the night, you act as facilitator.
2. Lay the ground rules.
    a. This is a social discussion, not a support group. The facilitator's role is to keep the dialogue on topic, engaging and interesting.
    b. Make sure one person doesn't dominate the discussion.
    c. Encourage inclusion. As loss is a universal experience, people from all walks of life are welcome.
    d. Ask questions to encourage participation.
    e. Invite people to share their experience or viewpoint on the topic.
    f. If the topic becomes a heated debate, remind them that this is a discussion only.
3. Make support group information and other resources available to those who want it.
4. Lay out fliers about next month's topic, and include meeting location, date and time.

Reunion Service

Families are increasingly memorializing their loved one through reunion services held one year after death. It offers a time of reflection and helps the family continue toward reconciliation. Consider hosting a butterfly, balloon, dove or lantern release as a symbol of letting go and promoting the healing process, or a potluck memorial dinner for all clients who lost a family member in the past year. Consider inviting them to wear their loved one's favorite color, and plant a community tree after the potluck. The possibilities for hosting a reunion service are limited only by your imagination.

Community crisis gathering

A community crisis gathering is a rapid response to any tragedy that deeply affects the community. It addresses peoples questions and provides on-site support and reassurance. Designed for rapid coordination, it is best done within the first 2 days when emotions are high. It can be done on the afternoon prior to an evening candlelight vigil.

The difference between a community crisis gathering and a candlelight vigil is that the gathering invites people to ask questions and release some of the emotional steam, whereas a community vigil provides the place for the community to unite in their mourning.

PURPOSE

- Serve your families and community in times of need
- Provide an opportunity for people to unite
- Helps release emotional steam
- Answers questions
- Provides on-site support

PLAN

1. Secure a community space. A school gym or auditorium works well, especially if the victim(s) are school age. Call the principal and explain that you intend to provide resources and information, and give people an opportunity to ask questions. Also share that other support professionals will be invited to participate. You can also secure public meeting space through the Chamber of Commerce.
2. If the victim(s) were students, ask the school to notify students and invite families. Everyone is welcome, even if they're not a student.

PREPARE

1. Notify local radio and TV stations of the date, time, and location of the event, and ask them to share it.
2. Secure use of 3 mics and speakers or sound system.
3. Prepare a list of local and national support resources including national hotlines, organizations and counseling professionals, etc. Make copies of the list distribute it to people during the gathering.

INVITE SUPPORT PROFESSIONALS TO JOIN YOU

Support comes in all shapes and sizes. Inviting other professionals to join you will strengthen the pipeline of hope for those affected by the loss. Consider inviting the following:

- ❑ Therapy dogs
- ❑ School counselors
- ❑ Crisis teams
- ❑ Local grief professionals
- ❑ Support group chapter leaders
- ❑ Clergy

LEAD

1. Welcome the crowd. Tell them you're glad they came so you can all grieve together. Explain that in a moment, you'll open the floor for people to ask questions and share what's on their heart. Allow the therapy dogs and their handlers to walk among the crowd as you talk.
2. Have two volunteers roam the audience with mics, so people can use them when you open the floor.
3. Invite a local clergy to say an opening prayer.
4. Talk about the grieving process and what to expect.
   a. Explain that emotions will run high for a while but eventually the rawness they feel will soften.
   b. Explain that although you're all grieving for the same person(s), everyone will grieve differently. Encourage them not to judge or compare reactions.
   c. Encourage people to reach out to one another and check in with each other over the coming weeks.
5. Encourage use of local resources and national helplines.
6. Invite the audience to use one of the roaming mics to ask a question or share what they're feeling. Make sure one person doesn't dominate the floor.
7. Share informational resources and encourage use of them.
8. Provide your contact information should anyone have follow-up questions. Be ready to point them in the direction of appropriate resources.
9. Thank them for attending.

Candlelight vigils

Community candlelight vigils offer people an opportunity to come together after loss, especially when it's a high-profile loss or mass casualty event. It gives them a safe place to express sadness, support one another, create a united setting, and take the first steps forward together.

An effective vigil is coordinated in a fashion that makes it memorable for all the right reasons. While informal or impromptu vigils are often held by well-meaning people, one coordinated by a Certified iCare Specialist™ will provide a higher level of community representation and result in a more powerful ritual of remembrance.

In general, it includes speakers, music, some sort of symbolic release such as a balloon or sky lantern release, and a candlelight vigil. It's helpful to create a team of coordinators to oversee important elements and volunteers. Use the following instructions and templates to coordinate a vigil for your community, and modify as needed.

PLAN

1. Determine who will serve as the overall facilitator and act as the main contact person.
2. Set vigil date, time and location. Make sure it's easy for people to find and has adequate parking, bathroom facilities, garbage receptacles, etc. Consider a well-lit public square or waterfront park, or any well-lit public place with plenty of free parking and bathrooms.
3. Send vigil details to local radio and TV stations, and ask them to share.
4. Notify local officials that you're coordinating a vigil. Provide the date, time and location. Invite and confirm 5 of the officials to speak at the vigil. Each speaker can decide what they want to say (short speech, words of comfort, read a poem, etc).
   - ❑ City mayor
   - ❑ Police chief
   - ❑ Fire chief
   - ❑ School superintendent
   - ❑ School principal
   - ❑ Family representative
   - ❑ Community pastor
5. Identify and confirm volunteers to serve as team leads. See duties on following page.
   - ❑ Community facilitator
   - ❑ Balloon team lead
   - ❑ Candle team lead
   - ❑ Music team lead
6. Invite and confirm choir or singers.
7. Invite and confirm one individual who is willing to light the first candle when the time comes. Ask them to come with two lighters in case one doesn't work.
8. Once the schedule and speakers are set, distribute schedule (see suggested schedule below) to each speaker, team leads, choir/singer(s).
9. If using sky lanterns, secure permit from fire department.

PREPARE

1. Purchase or find donated helium balloons, sky lanterns or butterflies.
2. Purchase of find donated candles with wax catchers (ask a church).
3. Secure use of mic and speakers.
4. Purchase or find donated cookies and bottled water to serve to community.
5. Secure 5-gallon buckets of water for people to drop candles in after candlelighting.

CANDLE LEAD DUTIES:

- Find volunteers to serve on the candle team.
- Coordinate donation of candles and wax catchers from store or church. If donors aren't available, they can be purchased from religious stores and arts & craft stores.
- Have volunteers assemble candles inside wax catchers prior to vigil.
- At the appropriate time in the schedule, have volunteers quietly distribute candles among crowd prior to the candlelighting. Another option is to hand them out as people arrive.

MUSIC LEAD DUTIES:

- Find choir or singer(s) to perform during vigil.
- Coordinate one symbolic song to sing during balloon release.
- Coordinate one symbolic song to sing during candle lighting.
- Ensure that choir and/or singer(s) are prepared to perform enough songs to accommodate length of time needed to light all the candles.
- Song suggestions:
  a. Somewhere Over the Rainbow (good for balloon releasing)
  b. I Will Always Love You, by Whitney Houston (good for candle lighting)
  c. Amazing Grace
  d. To Where You Are, by Josh Groban
  e. Wind Beneath my Wings, by Bette Midler
  f. Go Light Your World, by C. Rice

BALLOON LEAD DUTIES: (MODIFY AS NEEDED IF USING SKY LANTERNS OR BUTTERFLIES)

- Find volunteers and multiple vehicles to deliver balloons from store to vigil.
- If donor can't inflate balloons, find a party store who can. Do not inflate balloons at vigil as it's too distracting and it's difficult to keep people from taking balloons.
- Have volunteers secure balloons at vigil so wind doesn't blow them away. Consider tying groups of 10 balloons at a time to chairs or railings. Make sure they're easy to release from chairs when it's time to distribute among the vigil crowd.
- Have volunteers distribute balloons among crowd at the appropriate time in the schedule. Tell volunteers to instruct people to hold their balloon until everybody can release them at the same time when the time comes.

SUGGESTED SCHEDULE

PART 1: COMMENTS

8. Opening comments by community facilitator (3-5 minutes):
   a. Welcomes community
   b. Recognizes donors and volunteers
   c. Mentions and encourages use of local grief resources and/or suicide hot line
   d. Introduces each speaker as they take the mic
9. Opening prayer by pastor (2-3 minutes)
10. School principal speaks (2-3 minutes)
11. School superintendent speaks (2-3 minutes)
12. City mayor or city official speaks (2-3 minutes)
13. Police chief, fire chief, or family representative speaks (2-3 minutes)

PART 2: CANDLE LIGHTING

14. Choir or singers perform in the background while all 5 speakers assemble on a raised platform or benches so they can be seen by everyone (see diagram on following page). Speakers should be close enough together so they can safely dip their candlewick into the flame of the speaker next to them.

15. Once the speakers are in position and choir/singers are performing, begin candle lighting as follows.
    a. City mayor or other prominent community leader stands center (position #1) and is the first candle to be lit. Make sure the person who lights the mayor's candle has 2 cigarette/campfire lighters on hand in case one doesn't work. Once the mayor's candle has been lit, s/he holds the lit candle.
    b. Speakers in positions #2 and #3 dip their candles simultaneously into the flame of the mayor's candle and then hold their candles.
    c. Speaker in position #4 dips his/her candle into the flame of speaker #2 at the same time speaker in position #5 dips his/her candle into the flame of #3.

9. Once all 5 candles have been lit, speakers should momentarily raise their candles in solidarity, pause briefly, and then lower and hold the candles so surrounding people can use the flames to light their own candle. They then offer their flame to those around them, creating a wave of candlelighting (and preventing people from mobbing the 5 speakers). People continue lighting one another's candles until all are lit. Choir continues to sing until all candles are lit.

10. After all candles are lit, allow singers to finish current song, and then ask for a moment of silence.

PART 3: BALLOON RELEASE

12. At the end of the candlelighting, during the moment of silence, balloon team quietly distribute balloons among crowd.

13. After moment of silence, one speaker reads a poem or two (see recommended poems on following pages). If needed, read second poem until everyone has a balloon.

14. Once everyone has a balloon, choir/singers perform one song such as Somewhere Over the Rainbow. When song begins, all 5 speakers simultaneously raise their balloons, pause for a moment and then release their balloons. The community will follow the gesture as the choir sings Somewhere Over the Rainbow.

15. If desired, closing prayer by Pastor (2-3 minutes).

DIAGRAM OF SUGGESTED LAYOUT

SPEAKERS

SUGGESTED POEMS TO BE READ DURING BALLOON RELEASE

POEM #1

As the strings slip through my hand
I think of the beauty you brought to this land
I watch as the balloons float away
Just like when you left me that day

They float into the beautiful clouds
I hear you laughing out loud
Up to the heavens above
Carrying a note from me with love

The life you lived celebrated this day
That is what the balloons are meant to say
Receive the balloons with gentle care
They symbolize the love that will
always be there

Balloons, I release you to float away
Make sure you get up to our loved ones this day
We release you into the sky
We watch you float, we watch you fly

Loved ones, catch these balloons
on this bittersweet day
Read the notes and then go play
Keep us in your hearts
You may be gone but we shall not part

So flat in the heavens and play in the clouds
Releasing the balloons from
our hearts so proud.

POEM #2

by Vicki Hansen

Floating freely in the air,
is a special balloon with all my care,
That I have released to the skies above.
It's really important, it carries my love.

So please be watching for it to come by;
this special balloon, I released to the sky.
Sent to my Angel in heavenly flight,
to let my Angel know I am alright.

I don't really like to be without you.
And many a day, I have been blue!
I know you're in Heaven
and that gives me peace.
So it's with all my love,
this balloon I release.

SUGGESTED POEMS FOR CANDLE LIGHTING

FIVE CANDLES

unknown author

The first candle represents our grief.
The pain of losing you is intense.
It reminds us of the depth of our love for you.

This second candle represents our courage.
To confront our sorrow,
To comfort each other,
To change our lives.

This third candle we light in your memory.
For the times we laughed,
The times we cried,
The times we were angry with each other,
The silly things you did,
The caring and joy you gave us.

This fourth candle we light for our love.
We light this candle that your light will always shine.
As we enter this season and share this night of remembrance
with our family and friends.
We cherish the special place in our hearts
that will always be reserved for you.

This fifth candle we light to thank you for the gift
your living brought to each of us.

We love you.

We remember you.

E03/COMMUNITY VIGIL

TIME WILL EASE THE HURT

by Bruce B. Wilmer

The sadness of the present days
is locked and set in time.
And moving to the future
is a slow and painful climb.

But all the feelings that
are now so vivid and real
can't hold their fresh intensity
as time begins to heal.

No wound so deep will
ever go entirely away,
yet every hurt becomes
a little less each day.

Nothing can erase the painful
imprints on your mind.
But there are softer memories
that time will let you find.

Though your heart won't let
the sadness simply slide away,
the echoes will diminish
even though the memories stay.

CHAPTER 11

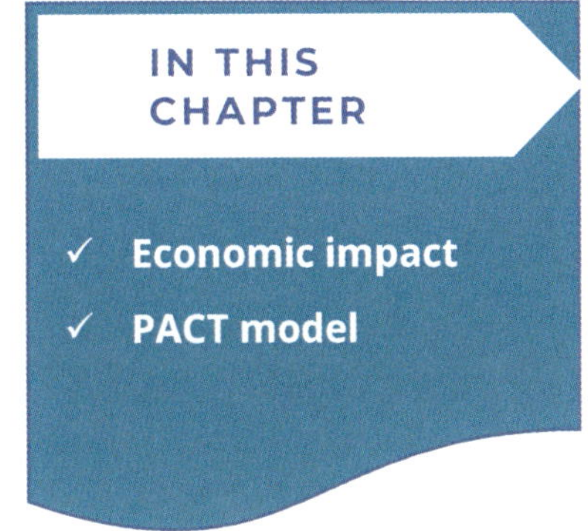

GRIEF IN THE WORKPLACE

The wealth of a company is built on the health of its employees.

INTERNATIONAL GRIEF INSTITUTE

Economic Impact

Employee grief in the workplace costs employers up to $500 billion in lost productivity every year (Medina, 2012). Bereaved employees often describe how the toughest part of returning to work is the inability to focus, make profitable decisions, and talk openly about their loss. Coworkers frequently feel uncomfortable, unsure how to behave yet on average, only 5% of employees use employee assistance programs.

When not proactively managed, dealing with grief in the workplace can take a toll on both employers and employees. Corporate policies vary, but paid leave that grants bereaved employees time to process their loss is largely limited, and the U.S. Department of Labor leaves this up to the employer. Many employers do extend some sort of benefit, usually three to five days, which provides enough time to plan and attend a funeral. Although emotional health is severely impacted by loss of a loved one, there is no statutory protection from grief discrimination in the workplace.

Employers who create a sustainable culture of support translates to happier employees, increased productivity, and reduced turnover. Educating and training employers how to support bereaved employees is largely based upon creating a sustainable culture of support that highlights benefits to the employer. Studies show a return on investment of $7.09 for every $1 spent.

Stats

An unhappy culture leads to:

1. Workers who are less productive cost U.S. employers up to $500 billion every year
2. $4,000 loss per employee per year
3. 48% more turnover
4. Unhappy workers are 10% less productive
5. Less than 5% of employees utilize EAPs

A sustainable culture of support benefits employers through:

1. Attract better employees
   - 40% select employers based on how much the employer values employee health and wellness
   - 85% of job seekers expect employers to support them in balancing work with life
2. Increased productivity
3. Retained talent more than 3x
4. Reduced turnover
5. Supported workers are 12% more productive than the average worker
6. Companies with happy employees outperform their competition by 20%
7. ROI $7.09:$1

SOURCES: Medina (2012), Comparably (2017), Mental Health America (2017) Flexjobs (2017), World Services Group (2018) Edmans (2011), Fast Company (2013) Parnassus Workplace Fund

Importance of supporting employees

Supporting an employee's resilience during a critical time in their life will have a long-term ROI for your company by way of employee recruitment, retention, and performance.

CORPORATE GOALS & OBJECTIVES

- Support all involved including employees and employers
- Minimize workflow disruption
- Maximize production
- Ensure employee safety
- Preserve or improve corporate culture
- Support or improve corporate branding
- Balance corporate needs with employee needs

CORPORATE RESULTS

- Minimized impact and grievances
- Improved performance/ROI
- Increased office confidence
- Improved reputation
- Less turnover

To retain the loyalty of those who are present, be loyal to those who are absent.
-STEPHEN R. COVEY

Grief 101 Refresher

- Grief is a normal reaction to a traumatic event including death of a loved one.
- Grief is unique to each individual.
- There are many stages to grief.
- Grief changes our sense of self.
- Grief doesn't stay in the cubicle.
- Grief is highly distracting and reduces emotional bandwidth.
- Avoid avoidance. Dodge and escape create an elephant in the room atmosphere.
- Avoid trying to distract the employee from pain by keeping him or her busy. This can lead to feeling overwhelmed and reduce good decision-making and/or safety.
- Refrain from giving advice out of respect for different cultures and filters.
- Avoid judgment. Grief timelines are unique to each individual.
- Avoid trying to rationalize fears. Fears are a normal part of the process.
- Grief is unique. Different backgrounds mean we view things differently. Avoid judgment of what you think your coworker should or shouldn't do.
- Grief is unpredictable. Avoid using a calendar to gauge how long it's appropriate for the bereaved to be less productive.

- Grief is complex. Don't try to match losses. Comparing journeys may inflame emotions and reactions, and reduce office morale.
- Trust that the bereaved employee will eventually make steps toward healing. If not, trust that management will handle it.
- During the acute stage of grief, people are actively processing what happened. Reconciliation begins in subsequent stages rather than right away.

PACT Model

PACT stands for Prevention, Action, Communication, and Transition.

It defines a two-pronged strategic approach designed to proactively manage bereavement leave. The 15 PACT strategies outlined in this manual are today's best practices for managing grief in the workplace, and should be used as tools to help modernize existing leave policies and procedures.

The PACT Model is divided into two phases.

A. **Phase A** is the immediate—acute—corporate response to when an employee notifies the employer that a loved one has died. The 5 strategies outlined in the acute phase (Phase A) allow the employer to proactively manage the initial impact within the workplace. It addresses the chain of command, tone of support, exchange of information, and delegation of duties in the immediate aftermath.

B. **Phase B** is the transition response to when the bereaved employee returns to work. Phase B employs 10 strategies designed to proactively manage the transition by addressing expectations, monitoring for predatory employees, managing triggers, respecting customs, warning signs to watch for, pairing of a Bereavement Buddy, and ensuring safety.

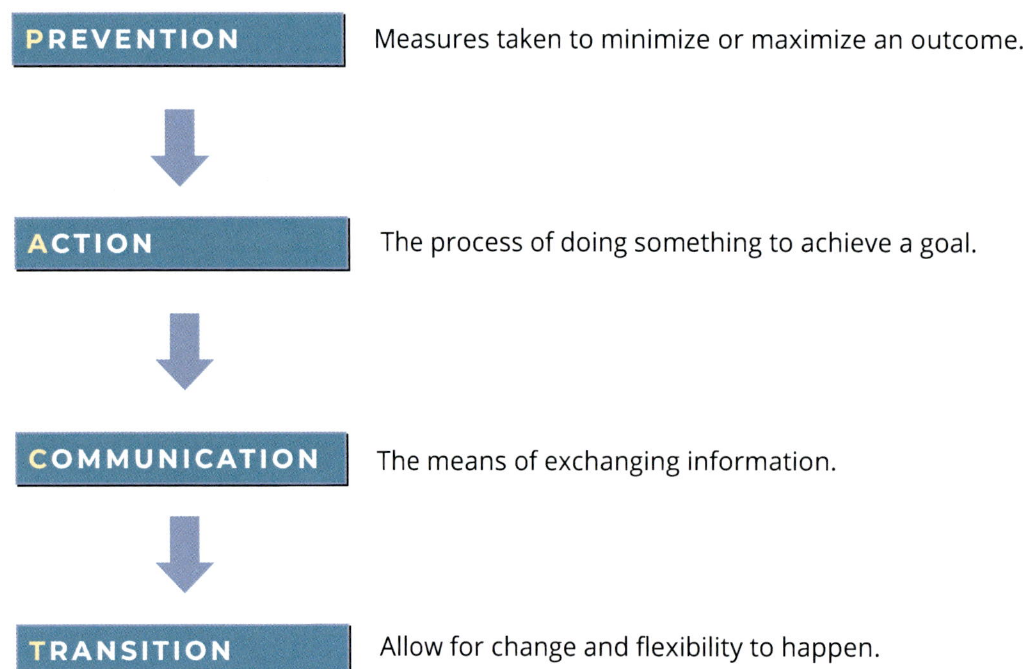

SCENARIO:

- Grieving Gracie notifies her office that her husband just died in a car accident.
- Office notifies Human Resources.
- Bereavement policy details are communicated to Grieving Gracie, including how much paid, unpaid, and vacation leave is granted.
- Grieving Gracie clarifies which information can be made public to staff, etc.
- Within 24 hours, manager calls for 5-minute briefing to share news with staff.
- Staff is notified as to whether they are invited/allowed to attend funeral, and whether personal time or paid time will be granted for same.

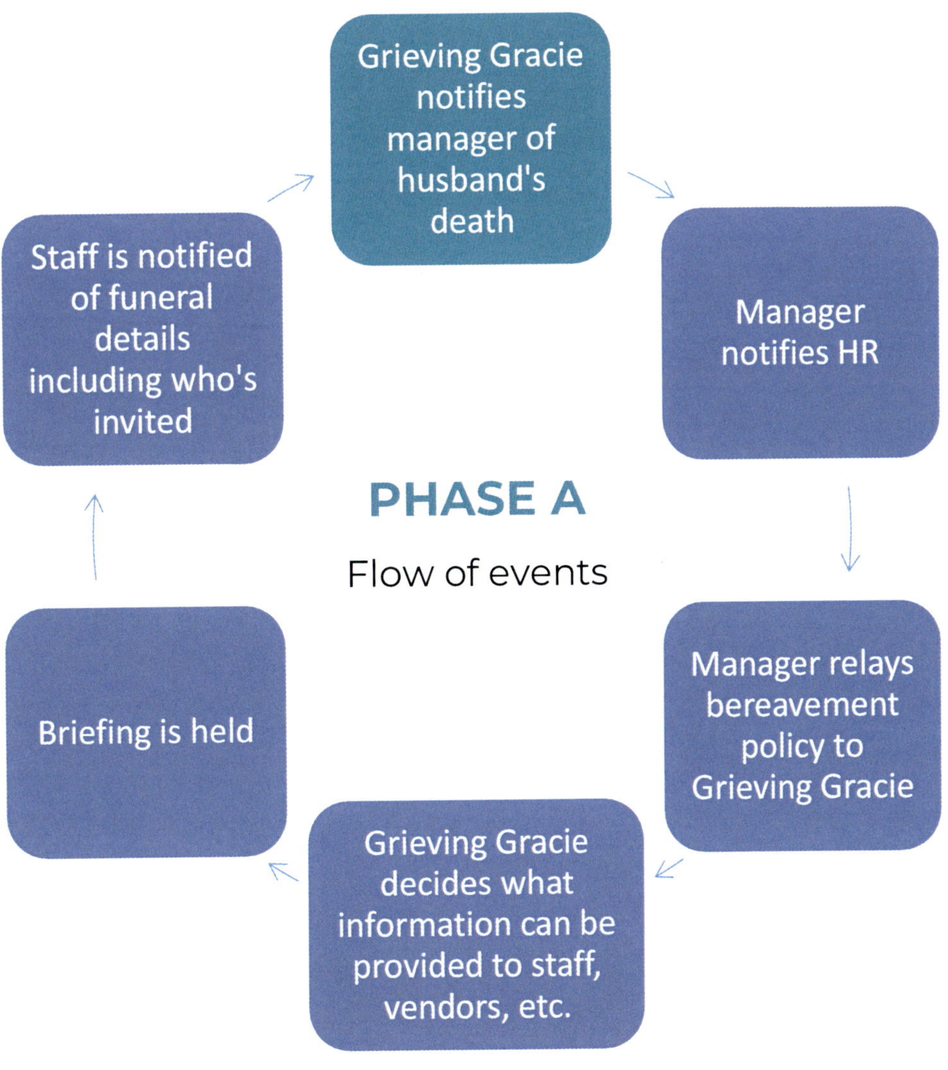

Phase A—Acute strategies

5 ACUTE PHASE STRATEGIES

1. Be prepared
2. Set the tone
3. Provide briefing
4. Conduct debriefing
5. Implement arrangements

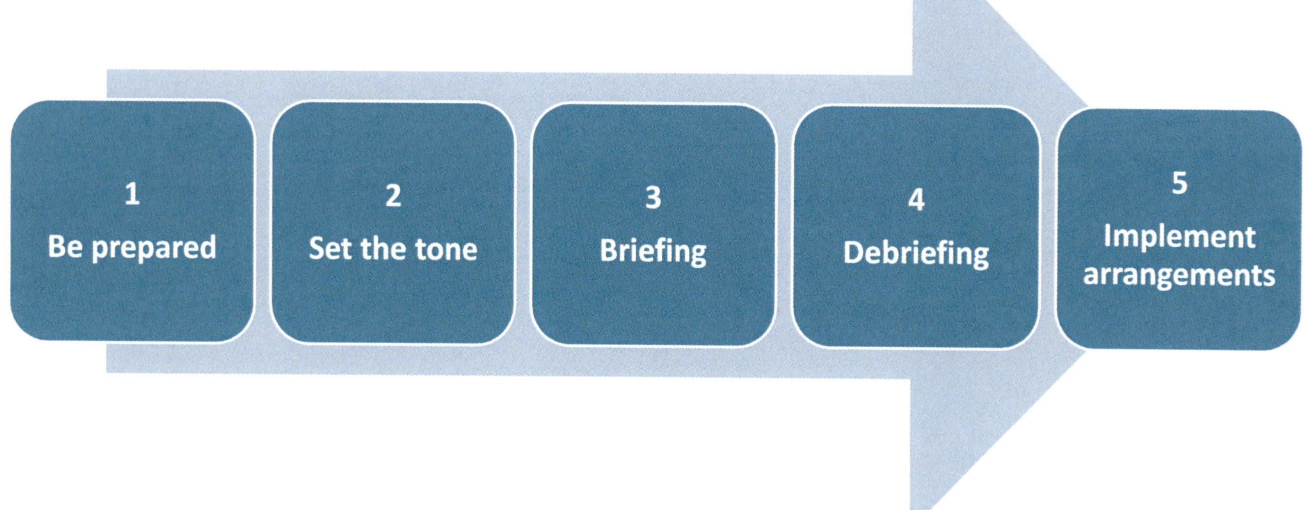

POLICY CONSIDERATIONS:

- Who notifies Human Resources if Grieving Gracie calls closest coworker instead of manager?
- Who calls for briefing? Grieving Gracie's direct manager or Human Resources?
- What information is covered in briefing?
- Who, when, how, and where did s/he die?
- How long will Grieving Gracie be on leave?
- Who will cover Grieving Gracie's work while she's gone?
- Are coworkers allowed to call or visit Grieving Gracie while she's on leave?
- Who will notify Grieving Gracie's customers and vendors that she's out of the office? How much information will be shared with customers and vendors?
- Who's invited to the funeral? Will employees desiring to attend funeral be expected to use personal unpaid time or be granted paid time to attend?

PACT 1: BE PREPARED.

The first strategy of being prepared is designed to ensure that supervisors either know what their policy is, or know where to find it.

Workplace policies establish expectations and provide guidelines for decision-making in certain work situations. They represent clear communication to employees as to what is expected, contribute to the overall culture of the workplace by instilling norms and values, and provide common understanding and agreement between employers and employees.

When it comes to employee bereavement, many supervisors are unfamiliar with their organization's actual policies, and/or those policies may be outdated. By familiarizing themselves with the policy, they prevent confusion and disruption in the heat of the moment for both themselves and their staff.

QUOTE

There is no magic formula for great company culture. The key is to treat your staff how you would like to be treated.
– SIR RICHARD BRANSON

PACT 1: BE PREPARED

PREVENT

Prevent disruption and confusion by having clear expectations and guidelines for bereavement leave. If needed, review and update your bereavement leave policies to align with corporate culture.

ACT

Managers should know and understand the organization's bereavement policies and be prepared to implement it to avoid complaints and misunderstandings.

COMMUNICATE

Supervisors and managers should be ready to explain policy to bereaved employees and coworkers. When flexibility is granted, clear rationales should be offered to substantiate decisions and avoid favoritism.

TRANSITION

Grief responses are unique as a fingerprint. Supervisors and managers should be prepared to be flexible when needed.

PACT 2: SET THE TONE

The second strategy is designed to set the tone from the top down that bereavement leave is to be respected, and staff will be taken care of.

> **QUOTE**
>
> Your culture is your brand. – TONY HSIEH, Zappos founder

The wealth of a company depends upon the health of its employees, and a supportive atmosphere lays the groundwork for a strong, unified company. Organization leaders play the most significant role in setting the tone of a workplace, and employees take their cue from leaders who demonstrate the company's values.

PACT 2: SET THE TONE

PREVENT	ACT
Prevent absenteeism. An employee who feels supported will be more likely to return to full duties sooner.	Handling employee grief starts at the top, and sets the tone that pulling together is a team effort that benefits the whole company.
COMMUNICATE	**TRANSITION**
Make it clear from the beginning and to everyone that loss is a significant event in one's life.	Listen to and provide opportunities for employees to be heard.

PACT 3: PROVIDE BRIEFING

The third strategy is designed to provide information to staff.

An antidote to chaos and confusion is information and structure. Briefing is the process of informing a group of people of the facts via one-way communication. It brings employers face-to-face with employees, customers, and vendors so information can be delivered in a personalized fashion. A team briefing is an excellent way to provide critical information and foster transparency within an organization. It offers a quick overview and important updates.

PACT 3: PROVIDE BRIEFING

PREVENT

Prevent violation of confidential information while maintaining transparency by controlling what information is being communicated both internally and externally.

ACT

Briefing informs the team about any sudden changes in the workflow, and provides an important clarity of facts so everyone hears the same details in the same moment. This helps them mentally prepare for the days ahead.

COMMUNICATE

Make it clear from the beginning and to everyone that loss is a significant event in one's life.

TRANSITION

Listen to and provide opportunities for employees to be heard.

EXAMPLE – IN PERSON BRIEFING:

My name is Jim Barnes and I'm the accounting manager here at Corporate XYZ. This is a briefing regarding accounting program coordinator Grieving Gracie. Yesterday at 5:15 pm, Grieving Gracie's husband Jim was on his way home from work when his vehicle was struck by a cement truck at the intersection of Main Street and First Avenue. Jim died at the scene.

Grieving Gracie has requested no visitors at this time but meals for her children are welcome. Funeral details will be forthcoming, and all those in Grieving Gracie's department will be offered 4 hours of paid leave to attend the funeral. As she will be out of the office for the next 10 days, her work obligations will be managed by Evelyn Peterson on the second floor.

Our employees are part of our work family, and this tragedy is upsetting to everyone. A mandatory debriefing will be held for those in the accounting department to provide Grieving Gracie's coworkers an opportunity to process this as a team. Details regarding that debriefing will be available by the end of the day tomorrow. We are greatly saddened by Grieving Gracie's loss, and will provide support as she faces a difficult time ahead. In the meantime, please direct all questions to either myself or Human Resources.

PACT 4: PROVIDE DEBRIEFING.

The fourth strategy is to provide an emotional release valve for staff.

Grief doesn't stay in the cubicle. When grief happens to one employee, it affects everyone who interacts with that employee and can impact the workplace.

> **KEYNOTE**
>
> Debriefing is not a replacement for professional therapy.

Debriefing is an organized, confidential discussion in group format that provides a secure environment for employees to process emotions, express fears and concerns, ask questions, and share interpretations about an upsetting event.

PACT 4: PROVIDE DEBRIEFING

PREVENT	ACT
Debriefing prevents an atmosphere of passing the buck by outsourcing employee concerns to EAP.	Humans need to talk. Providing a safe and confidential opportunity for coworkers to process the situation will give everyone time to deal with the incident as a team, reduce office anxiety, and minimize gossip.
COMMUNICATE	**TRANSITION**
Offer formal debriefing by grief-trained facilitators who can create a safe place for employees to ask questions and share concerns. This sets the tone that pulling together is a team effort that benefits everyone, including the company.	If formal debriefing isn't available or possible, offer informal debriefing so employees can share concerns without fear of judgement or retaliation.

PACT 5: IMPLEMENT ARRANGEMENTS

The fifth strategy is designed to minimize disruption to the workload.

Successfully delegating workload distribution in an emergency is best managed when arrangements have been included in corporate policies and procedures ahead of time. Play to the strength of your employees within the affected department, delegate fairly by evenly distributing the workflow, and set a timeline.

Making good use of unique skillsets and personalities will result in overall efficiency and minimize need to micromanage. Some tasks won't align themselves as conveniently, but the principle remains the same. If the policy isn't clear, present the tasks to the department as a group and invite a brainstorming session that empowers them to find solutions.

PACT 5: IMPLEMENT ARRANGEMENTS

PREVENT	ACT
Arranging distribution of workload will preserve department efficiency, protect office morale, minimize disruption in the workflow, and maximize productivity.	Delegate and distribute workload arrangements according to corporate policy. Reward employees for their ability to manage unexpected obligations in an emergency.
COMMUNICATE	**TRANSITION**
Communicate corporate policy in writing so staff know how to cover the workload of the bereaved employee during his or her absence.	Don't expect the bereaved employee to find his or her own replacement.

Phase B—Transition strategies

10 TRANSITION PHASE STRATEGIES

Phase B is the transition response to when the bereaved employee returns to work. Phase B employs 10 strategies designed to proactively manage the transition by addressing expectations, monitoring for predatory employees, managing triggers, respecting customs, warning signs to watch for, pairing with a Bereavement Buddy, and ensuring safety. Proactive management reduces the need for more costly reactive management.

1. Reasonable expectations
2. Stay alert
3. Create a safe room
4. Minimize office gossip
5. Bereavement Buddy
6. Plan for triggers
7. Respect customs
8. Warning signs
9. Be proactive
10. Ensure safety

6. Reasonable expectations
7. Stay alert
8. Create a safe room
9. Minimize office gossip
10. Bereavement Buddy
11. Plan for triggers
12. Respect customs
13. Warning signs
14. Be proactive
15. Ensure safety

PACT 6: REASONABLE EXPECTATIONS

The sixth strategy is designed to minimize costly mistakes.

Bereaved people experience distracting thoughts and make mistakes. Practicing reasonable expectations that work within the employee's emotional bandwidth will create a tone of understanding, and help the employee feel secure in his or her job. Employing light cognitive duty will help minimize costly mistakes by giving the employee simple action-oriented tasks that fulfill short-term goals.

STATS

- 85% of managers reported fair to very poor decision-making abilities for months after loss.
- Up to 90% felt at risk of an on-the-job injury due to distraction.

SOURCE: Grief Study Index, 2003

PACT 6: REASONABLE EXPECTATIONS

PREVENT

Being patient and having reasonable expectations creates a safe environment for employees, and reduces predatory opportunities.

ACT

Consider placing the employee on light cognitive duty, and adjust the workload to include simple action-oriented tasks that fulfill short-term goals in lieu of decision-making and complex detail-oriented tasks.

COMMUNICATE

Mistakes that come to a supervisor's attention should be handled with care to prevent predatory employees from using mistakes to their advantage.

TRANSITION

Flexibility and communication are key. Set reasonable expectations to avoid mistakes and poor quality outcome.

PACT 7: STAY ALERT

The seventh strategy is designed to mitigate employee resentment.

> **KEYNOTE**
>
> Your number one customer are your employees.

Conflict can occur within any organization, but especially poses a risk in situations where emotions run high. A disgruntled employee who feels resentful, discontent, and frustrated about picking up the slack can express it through passive and/or aggressive insults, noncooperation, bullying and anger. Stay alert to disgruntled employees who are upset about picking up the slack. Handle mistakes with care to prevent predatory employees from using bereaved employee's mistakes to their advantage for personal or professional gain. A safe environment equals productive environment.

PACT 7: STAY ALERT

PREVENT	ACT
A disgruntled employee can escalate into a bullying situation if not kept in check. A zero-tolerance bullying policy should be clearly indicated in employee handbook.	Address interoffice conflicts as quickly as possible. Follow procedures identified in policy manual. Employees feel supported and safe when expectations are clear from the beginning.
COMMUNICATE	**TRANSITION**
Engage disgruntle employee in a private discussion to address the root of his or her resentment or frustration. This will help to deescalate the situation and help him or her feel valued too.	Be aware of interoffice personalities and practice flexibility when needed.

PACT 8: CREATE A SAFE ROOM

The eighth strategy employs a safe room for bereaved employees to release emotional energy and regain composure out of view.

> **KEYNOTE**
>
> If not addressed, emotional turbulence can result in agitation that reduces the bereaved employee's ability to focus and be productive.

Emotional pain overwhelms thinking and clouds judgment. Creating a safe place for the bereaved to naturally release emotional buildup through crying is vital to good physical, mental, and spiritual health. Studies show that suppressed emotions can compound emotional toxicity later, resulting in insomnia, physical ailments, anger, anxiety, and more. Providing a private place within the office for bereaved employees to cry will support healing and promote a faster return to full productivity. Clearly communicate parameters of the safe room, such as frequency and time limit, if any.

PACT 8: CREATE A SAFE ROOM

PREVENT	ACT
Emotional releases in a contained environment prevents escalations, and helps the employee clear his or her thinking and judgment.	Create a safe room within the office where the bereaved employee can release his or her emotional buildup in private.
COMMUNICATE	**TRANSITION**
When the employee returns to work, explain that the safe room is designed for him or her to escape to when his or her emotional bandwidth has reached its threshold.	Be flexible. A safe room need not be fancy to serve its purpose.

PACT 9: CONTROL THE NARRATIVE

The ninth strategy is designed to manage office gossip.

It's human nature for people to be curious, and it's natural to satiate their curiosity through gossip and sharing. People want to know what's going on in their workplace. When employees feel that they lack information, they make up information to fill in the blanks. When information is proactively guided, it prevents partial truths from becoming speculation.

QUOTE

I have a zero-tolerance-plus-one policy for gossip. I will teach you once, and then I will fire you.
-DAVE RAMSEY

PACT 9: CONTROL THE NARRATIVE

PREVENT

Prevent gossip from disrupting the workplace and the business of the work.

ACT

It's natural for people to gossip and share. It's better to proactively guide the discussion. Not everyone needs to know everything, and violation of privacy can damage employee morale.

COMMUNICATE

Proactively share the basics without details. Assure employees, customers, and vendors that they will be cared for through this process.

TRANSITION

Consider whether you're sharing enough information. Reduce the need to speculate. Make a list and think it through in advance. Be willing to modify as you learn more.

PACT 10: BEREAVEMENT BUDDY

The tenth strategy is designed to smooth the transition via a support officer.

A Bereavement Buddy employs a buddy system arrangement in which the bereaved employee is paired with a coworker trained in trauma or grief support.

Every office should have at least one trained staff member who serves as a support officer for the bereaved employee, while also serving as a liaison for management by monitoring for signs of distress before it escalates.

PACT 10: BEREAVEMENT BUDDY

PREVENT	ACT
Bereavement Buddy™ acts as a liaison and helps management stay ahead of potential issues before they escalate.	Pair the employee with a trained, tactful and supportive coworker who is willing to check in with the bereaved and act as a liaison when needed.
COMMUNICATE	**TRANSITION**
Communicate the purpose of a Bereavement Buddy, and his or her role in the employee's transition back to work. Ensure that the bereaved employee doesn't see the Bereavement Buddy as a watchdog.	Every office should have at least one staff member trained as a Bereavement Buddy.

PACT 11: PLAN FOR TRIGGERS

The eleventh strategy is designed to minimize disruption by managing grief triggers.

> **KEYNOTE**
>
> Ignoring grief triggers can backfire by escalating the situation.

Part of every healing process, a grief trigger is anything that unexpectedly elicits a memory of the loved one and educes an involuntary flood of emotions.

Cyclical triggers, like birthdays and holidays, become easy to anticipate and give the bereaved employee time to prepare for and cope with the heightened emotions. Unexpected triggers associated with a sight, sound, song, smell, place, or mannerism spark an emotional reaction that can derail the employee from what he or she was doing.

The intensity, extent, and frequency of these events vary immensely among individuals depending on the circumstances surrounding the death of your loved one, the emotional investment in the person, belief systems, etc.

PACT 11: PLAN FOR TRIGGERS

PREVENT	ACT
Understanding and managing triggers in the workplace will minimize disruption and early shift releases.	Identify and agree on a plan so the bereaved employee knows and understands expectations ahead of time. Encourage use of the safe room and, when needed, a Bereavement Buddy.
COMMUNICATE	**TRANSITION**
Inform and educate coworkers about grief triggers and explain how the bereaved employee will cope when triggers happen. This will help reduce fear and reassure staff that a plan is in place.	Unique triggers will require flexibility in expectations and arrangements. Some of these may be unknown, so be open for change.

PACT 12: RESPECT MOURNING CUSTOMS

The twelfth strategy is designed to preserve corporate culture and minimize litigation risk by honoring differences.

The act of mourning dates back to the beginning of mankind, yet nearly every culture and religion has its own traditions for observing death and grief. For some, death represents the end of life while others believe it is only a rest stop on the soul's journey.

Are photos of the deceased allowed to be on the employee's desk? Are lit candles allowed in cubicles? Will traditional mourning attire be allowed to replace a uniform and, if so, for how long?

With the backbone of Corporate America built on a multitude of diversity, the unfamiliarity of different grief rituals can be used as an enrichment and team-building opportunity. Including a reference section in corporate policies about different grief customs will provide an efficient means of conveying cultural information quickly with minimal effort.

PACT 12: RESPECT MOURNING CUSTOMS

PREVENT	ACT
Respecting bereavement customs will help minimize litigation risks.	Set the tone that cultures around the world honor loss in unique ways, and grief customs will be respected in the workplace.
COMMUNICATE	**TRANSITION**
Signal that your organization embraces office diversity by encouraging staff to use this time to learn the bereaved employee's culture.	Be flexible in what's allowed. Cultural practices and rituals help promote healing and a quicker return to normal duties.

PACT 13: WARNING SIGNS

The thirteenth strategy is designed to protect employee asset.

Grief can easily be one of life's most traumatic events. Any person who has experienced a traumatic event is at risk of suffering psychological stress that stretches beyond the limits of their inner resilience. Lack of support in personal and/or professional circles, lack of resources to access support, lack of life experience or emotional intelligence can all play a role in whether an employee is at risk of grief's danger zone.

QUOTE

The greatest achievement of the human spirit is to live up to one's opportunities and make the most of one's resources.

-LUC DE CLAPIERS

As warning signs aren't always obvious, and can vary between people, employ the Bereavement Buddy strategy, and invite coworkers who work closely with the bereaved to report questionable comments and/or behavior.

Cautious observation for potential warning signs and quick reaction are prudent to ensure a good outcome and prevent tragedy.

PACT 13: WARNING SIGNS

PREVENT

Getting a bereaved employee the help s/he needs will minimize workflow disruption, and is an investment in your organization's culture and the employee's future.

ACT

Identify a plan of action that includes professional help outside the office. Ensure that corporate policy clearly indicates when and where to access resources and intervention.

COMMUNICATE

Assign a Bereavement Buddy when the bereaved employee returns to work. Warning signs can indicate need for professional intervention. If a Bereavement Buddy isn't available, refer to a higher level of care, or call 911.

TRANSITION

Be flexible with the schedule to allow the bereaved employee to attend medical or therapy appointments.

PACT 14: ENSURE SAFETY

The fourteenth strategy is designed to minimize workplace accidents and injuries.

Grief is a neurocognitive pain that causes a significant disruption in the brain's cognitive processes resulting in impaired concentration, memory, decision-making, and low mental energy and bandwidth.

When the brain is focused on pain, it is less focused on safety and fails to see hazards. During the acute stage of grief, when an employee is actively processing what happened rather than healing, assigning the employee to light cognitive duty will help prevent on-the-job accidents. As the individual's coping skills strengthen, they begin to recover, and so does the brain.

KEYNOTE

Minimize injuries by putting the employee in an environment that works within his/her current emotional bandwidth.

PACT 14: ENSURE SAFETY

PREVENT

When an injury occurs, time and production are lost. A positive attitude toward workplace safety and accident prevention are key.

ACT

Consider assigning light cognitive duty for up to six months. This allows the bereaved employee to adjust without pressure.

COMMUNICATE

Communicate that safety is a much a priority as production schedules. Avoid pressuring the bereaved to immediately resume full cognitive duties or putting him/her in a position to make critical decisions after returning to work.

TRANSITION

Bereaved employees are focused on pain and fail to see hazards. Be flexible in the length of time granted for light cognitive duty.

PACT 15: BE PROACTIVE

The fifteenth strategy is designed to minimize cost by encouraging proactive management instead of a more costly reactive approach.

Proactive management is dealing with expected difficulties in advance by taking necessary precautions to mitigate risk. Clear policies and procedures create a sense of security in times of crisis.

> **KEYNOTE**
>
> Proactive management will prevent reactive management.

A proactive approach to managing grief in the workplace removes uncertainty, reduces risk, minimizes disruption and maximizes productivity. Employing PACT strategies—prevention, action, communication, and transition—will create a sustainable culture of support by fostering employee compassion, empowerment and collaboration. By investing in proactive strategies, the return is substantial for both employee health and corporate wealth.

PACT 15: BE PROACTIVE

PREVENT	ACT
Proactively managing grief in the workplace will reduce risk, improve corporate brand and culture, preserve employee wellness, and maximize productivity.	Proactively update bereavement policy by incorporating PACT strategies. rather than reactively managing bereaved employees on an individual basis.
COMMUNICATE	**TRANSITION**
Clearly communicate policies and procedures to create a sense of security in times of crisis. Employees don't need to memorize the new policy, but need to know where to find the information and trust that their best interest will be a priority should crisis strike.	Consider inviting employee feedback and input when updating corporate bereavement policy.

CORPORATE GOALS & OBJECTIVES

- Support all involved including employees and employers
- Minimize workflow disruption
- Maximize production
- Ensure employee safety
- Preserve or improve corporate culture
- Support or improve corporate branding
- Balance corporate needs with employee needs

SUPPORT

Support all employees and coworkers.

MINIMIZE

Minimize workflow disruption.

MAXIMIZE

Maximize office production and safety.

CORPORATE RESULTS

- Minimized impact and grievances
- Improved performance/ROI
- Increased office confidence
- Improved reputation
- Less turnover

NOTES:

CHAPTER 12

DEBRIEFING 101

Whatever life throws at us, our individual responses will be all the stronger for working together and sharing the load.

QUEEN ELIZABETH II

IN THIS CHAPTER

- ✓ Control keys
- ✓ Agenda
- ✓ Ground rules
- ✓ Script

Debriefing is a type of interactive support session held within 72 hours for homogenous groups who all experience the same traumatic event. A structured group discussion, it is designed to mitigate stress by serving as a vent for intense emotions after a particularly traumatic and/or gruesome event, provide stress management education, and identify external coping skills moving forward.

Originally developed to support first responders following a traumatic incident, debriefing has evolved into different models for helping groups address their reactions and emotions to what they experienced. The end goal is to help the group destress, "take the edge off" the experience and facilitate resilience.

The word "homogenous" is used to identify those who experienced the same level of exposure to the event itself. For example, staff who all witnessed the same traumatic death of an employee from a forklift accident. If this happened on school grounds, students who witnessed the same event would undergo a separate debriefing.

DEBRIEFING PURPOSE

The purpose of debriefing is to hold a group discussion of a traumatic event to help participants understand that they are not alone in their physical and emotional reaction, and help is available.

DEBRIEFING GOALS

- Mitigate crisis stress and lower tension
- Facilitate normalization; set expectations that the group will eventually return to normal
- Serve as a forum for stress management education
- Identify external coping resources

REFRESHER

A **traumatic event** is any incident that overwhelms one's ability to cope, and results in distress, impairment or dysfunction.

DEBRIEFING FACILITATORS

Facilitators can be peer support specialists or any other specialist trained in debriefing. Clergy and a mental health clinician are welcomed additions to the team, when available.

KEYNOTE

Defusing and debriefing are not a cure nor a substitute for psychotherapy.

DEFUSING VS DEBRIEFING

Defusing is another technique designed to soothe or neutralize high emotions when guards are down and needs are high, yet is not the same as debriefing. The goals of defusing are to stabilize the trauma in that moment before people go home, as studies show that defusing has no effect after the initial twelve hours after the event. Defusing is limited to thirty minutes, and participants don't go into detail, whereas debriefing is two to three hours, and participants are invited to go into detail so they can externalize their thoughts and emotions. This chapter is about debriefing.

Plan

Debriefing is a controlled session facilitated by two trained debriefers. On the following pages are the control keys, agenda, ground rules, and scripts. Given the intense emotions, it is strongly recommended you work in tandem with another debriefing facilitator. Inviting a mental health clinician and/or clergy to sit in is recommended though not required.

Groups should be no more than 15 people. If needed, conduct debriefings in shifts. For instance, if the event happened in a 24-hour facility, conduct a debriefing for those who were on the afternoon shift, and then again for those who were on the evening shift.

All personnel who witnessed the event firsthand should be included. If needed, ensure that each participant is relieved of his/her duties during the debriefing to minimize disruption. Debriefing lasts between two to three hours. Given the intensity of emotions, breaks are intentionally left out so as not to interrupt the flow.

This is not a free-for-all setting where people are invited to speak any time they wish. There are two ways to conduct the debriefing: Go around the circle, or in chronological order of who arrived on the scene first, who came second, etc.

ORDER OF EVENTS:

1. Introduction and ground rules
2. Brief review of the event
3. First impressions
4. Event de-stress
5. Signs of distress and stress management information
6. Summary

CONTROL KEYS

- Debriefing should be held 24-72 hours after the event to give personnel time to gather themselves.
- Plan for 2 to 3 hours from beginning to end.
- Participation should be mandatory. Hold debriefings in shifts and in groups of 10 to 15 if needed.
- Employee rank is not recognized. Within a debriefing, everyone is treated the same.
- Offer circle seating when possible to increase communication and decrease authority.
- During the debriefing, you'll go around the circle each time you ask a question.
- What is said during the debriefing should be treated with complete confidentiality.
- No critiquing. Conflict must be minimized; we're there to listen and observe without judgment.
- Everyone is given the opportunity to speak, and are encouraged but not required to do so.

KEYNOTE

Complete confidentiality is crucial. People need to know it's safe to express themselves without fear of reprisal later on.

Prepare

Preparation is key to success. Review agenda, ground rules, and don't hesitate to use index cards to help you stay on track. Participants do not receive the agenda. It is for your use only.

AGENDA:

- Introduction. Welcome everyone and establish ground rules (see next page). This will help to lower anxiety and make everyone more comfortable.
- Thank everyone for attending. Remind them that debriefing is a time to validate individual emotions.
- Brief review of the event. Give each person an opportunity to briefly describe the event they experienced. Details are not necessary here.
- First impressions: Give each person an opportunity to share the thoughts and/or feelings they experienced. Keep on task here.
- Event de-stress: Give each person an opportunity to share what most distressed them about the event.
- Sum up signs of distress and triggers they might experience. Discuss where to find further resources.
- Thank participants for attending.
- Debrief with key management after meeting, if available, but remember confidentiality of debriefing process.

TIPS

1. **Listen.**
2. **Scan the room.**
3. **Look at body language.**
4. **Check understanding; make no assumptions.**
5. **Restate what you hear.**
6. **Keep time.**
7. **No hogging of the floor.**

GROUND RULES:

- Please silence all cellphones.
- Confidentiality is 100%. Anything shared here stays here.
- Please do not leave the room. If you do, a team member will follow to ensure your welfare.
- Everyone will have a chance to speak but nobody is required to speak.
- Speak only for yourself. Do not speak for others.
- Do not monopolize the conversation nor interrupt others.
- Respect different beliefs and circumstances, and do not judge another's feelings, story, or experience. Everyone has a right to express what they feel.
- Do not give advice. Share only your experience and emotions.
- No notes or recordings are allowed during the debriefing.
- No reports shall be passed on to managers, supervisors or administration. Information and suggestions given to the group to assist with their emotions may be shared with administration.
- Debriefing is not an investigative tool nor a critique of what went wrong. It focuses on the human experience, and its sole purpose is to provide support and information.

IMPORTANT

If a participant leaves the room, one facilitator should follow to check on his/her welfare.

Lead

EXAMPLE OF A DEBRIEFING SCRIPT:

Hi, my name is Facilitator Fred and this is Facilitator Felicity. We are here today to help you process the loss of _____________.

This process is designed to lessen the overall impact of what you experienced. Some of you feel as though you can handle this on your own. While that's probably true, experience demonstrates that people who try to handle it alone take longer to do so. Those who talk about it tend to have less disruption to their home life.

The main part of this meeting is a discussion of the event's impact on you. The purpose of this is to give you an opportunity for support, understanding and learning. Our objective is to help you validate your emotions and ventilate some of the intense reactions and thoughts you are experiencing.

Although this is not a therapy session, loss can be tough for everyone. Your participation here will help your fellow staff feel not so alone with their own emotions. Even if you don't think you need help, others here may need help, and your presence is comforting.

People often differ in their responses to such a loss. You do not have to be experiencing any particular difficulty to benefit from this debriefing. Some of you might feel more like talking than others. There are no specific expectations for you aside from the ground rules.

Before we begin, please allow me to share the ground rules.

- This debriefing focuses on the human experience, and the sole purpose is to provide support and information.
- There is no rank during this discussion. Everyone in this circle is seen as equal human beings.
- Please silence all phones, radios, and electronic devices.
- Sharing is encouraged but voluntary. You do not need to share if you do not want to.
- One person at a time speaks. Speak only for yourself.
- Do not interrupt others, monopolize the conversation, or give advice. Share only your experience.
- This is not an investigation nor a critique of the event. Please refrain from judgmental comments, even if recollections and thoughts differ from your own.
- This is confidential. Please do not discuss what was expressed here today once you leave this room.
- Please do not leave the room during the debriefing. If you do, a team member will follow to ensure your welfare.
- No notes or recordings are allowed during the debriefing.
- No reports shall be passed on to administration. Information and stress reduction suggestions given to the group may be shared with administration.

We'll begin by going around the circle. [Ask one question, and allow each participant to answer before moving onto the next question.]

1. Please state your name and give us a brief description of what happened.
2. What was the first or most prominent thought that entered your mind?
3. What was the worst or hardest part of this event? What's most painful?
4. What physical or behavioral changes have you experienced since this happened?
5. What has life been like since this event? What emotions do you find hardest to deal with?

[Explain stress reactions and offer guidelines for managing stress.]

[Identify external resources.]

Are there any questions? [Answer questions.]

Thank you for your participation. Please remember to keep what you heard confidential, and do not repeat anything other than information you learned about stress management.

If you have additional questions after the debriefing, please notify one of us and we will arrange for follow-up and/or referral when necessary or requested.

[Hand out]

NORMAL STRESS REACTIONS

COGNITIVE

- ✓ Difficulty with concentration
- ✓ Sleep disruption
- ✓ Triggering of addiction
- ✓ Trouble with decision making, confusion

EMOTIONAL

- ✓ Anger
- ✓ Irritability
- ✓ Anxiety
- ✓ Depression

PHYSICAL

- ✓ Headache
- ✓ Stomach ache
- ✓ Muscle tension
- ✓ Elevated blood pressure
- ✓ Sweaty palms
- ✓ Rapid pulse
- ✓ Jaw clenching

RED FLAGS

If you experience any of the following, please seek immediate help or call 911.

- Delusions
- Hallucinations
- Disabling guilt
- Paranoid ideation
- Suicidal ideation
- Homicidal ideation
- Panic attacks
- Infantile emotions
- Immobilizing depression
- PTSD
- Violence/abuse
- Antisocial behavior
- Poor hygiene
- Self medication
- Immobility

RESOURCES

- ❑ **Emergency: 911**
- ❑ **National Suicide Prevention Lifeline:**
- ❑ **1-800-273-TALK (8255)**
- ❑ **Crisis Text Line:**
- ❑ **text TALK to 741741**

HELPFUL TIPS

Following are tips to help with emotional aftershocks and to help ease or moderate some stress reactions (International Critical Incident Stress Foundation, 2015).

- Periods of appropriate physical exercise alternating with relaxation will help alleviate some of the physical reactions to stress.
- Structure time. Maintain as normal a schedule as possible but pace yourself. Wearing yourself out will reduce your emotional threshold and ability to cope.
- Spend time with people who support you, and talk to them. Talk is the most healing medicine.
- Be aware of numbing the pain with excessive use of drugs, alcohol, or risk taking.
- Give permission to feel rotten.
- Write in a journal through sleepless hours.
- Do things that feel good to you.
- Don't make any big life changes.
- Do make as many daily decisions as possible that will give you a feeling of control over your life.
- Don't fight recurring thoughts or flashbacks. They are normal and will become less painful with time.

A RELAXATION EXERCISE

One basic mechanism for stress reduction involves deep breathing. The following exercise may be a valuable tool for reducing excessive arousal quickly and effectively during upsetting moments (adapted from the book by G.S. Everly, Jr. *A Clinical Guide to the Treatment of the Human Stress Response*, 1989).

- Assume a comfortable position. Rest your left hand (palm down) on top of your navel. Now place your right hand so that it comfortably rests on your left. Your eyes should remain open.
- Imagine a hollow pouch lying internally beneath your hands. Begin to inhale, imagine that the air is entering through your nose and descending to fill that internal pouch. Your hands will rise as you fill the pouch with air. As you continue to inhale, imagine the pouch being filled to the top. Your ribcage and upper chest will continue the wavelike rise that was begun at your navel. The total length of your inhalation should be 3 seconds for the first week or so, then lengthen to 4 to 5 seconds as you progress in skill development.
- Slowly begin to exhale to empty the pouch. As you do, repeat the phrase, "My body is calm." As you exhale, you will feel your raised abdomen and chest recede.

Repeat this exercise two times in succession. Should you begin to feel lightheaded or should you experience any discomfort, stop. You may wish to shorten the length of the inhalation to avoid lightheadedness.

If you have any health concerns, consult your physician prior to using this exercise. NEVER use this exercise while driving.

NOTES

CHAPTER 13

COMPASSION FATIGUE

A desperate helper can't help a desperate client.

BABETTE ROTHSCHILD

IN THIS CHAPTER

- ✓ Role of resilience
- ✓ Trauma input
- ✓ Debriefing
- ✓ Relationships
- ✓ Active optimism
- ✓ Exercise
- ✓ Nutrition
- ✓ Rest

Compassion fatigue is a disorder that develops from doing your best work. Also known as vicarious trauma, it is secondary traumatic stress absorbed by repeat exposure to indirect trauma that results in cumulative physical, emotional and psychological effects.

When professionals are unable to refuel and recharge, the emotional residue of secondary traumatic stress erodes their own mental, emotional, and physical health, making it critical for professionals in caregiving fields to take steps to guard against it.

Your organization has an invested interest in you taking care of both yourself and their clients. You can't pour from an empty cup, nor would they want you to. If you feel an emotional burnout, it's important to share this with your staff. The longer you let it go, the harder it can be to recover from.

PROFESSIONALS AT RISK

- Grief specialists
- Funeral professionals
- Human service workers
- Healthcare workers
- First responders
- Therapists & clinicians

Role of Hormones

The body uses hormones to help us respond, manage, and adjust to different situations. They are a lifesaving part of our body, but too much or prolonged secretion of a hormone throws our body and brain out of balance.

POSITIVE HORMONES:

- Oxytocin (love)
- Dopamine (pleasure)
- Serotonin (happy)

STRESS HORMONES:

- Adrenaline (energy surge)
- Cortisol (stress)
- Norepinephrine (arousal)The goal

Compassion fatigue is emotional burnout attributed to the cost of caring for others. It occurs when we help others without recharging our own batteries. Below are common signs and management tips for dealing with compassion fatigue. More tips are available in *Compassion Fatigue in the Funeral Profession*.

COMPASSION FATIGUE SIGNS

- Emotional exhaustion & irritability
- Physical exhaustion
- Mental exhaustion
- Difficulty concentrating & clinical errors
- Lapse in judgment with client boundaries
- Reduced sense of meaning in work
- Decreased interactions with others
- Inability to complete assignments and tasks
- Lack of flexibility
- Negativism that contributes to toxic work environment

MANAGEMENT

- Understand how stress affects you
- Engage in activities that trigger the brain to secrete positive hormones
- Stay hydrated
- Set emotional boundaries
- Practice good sleep hygiene
- Maintain a healthy work-life balance

Role of resilience

Resilience is the ability to resist, recover from, or adapt to difficulties. Building and strengthening resilience through strategies that support the brain, body and emotions can help prevent or mitigate compassion fatigue.

When faced with a challenge, there are three possible outcomes:

1. Full recovery and ability to function.
2. Partial recovery and stunted ability to function.
3. No recovery and halted function (burnout).

"One of the critical ways to mitigate compassion fatigue is to take care of yourself."

AMERICAN PSYCHOLOGICAL ASSOCIATION

GOAL

To build resilience, foster emotional recovery and a return to full function before the secondary traumatic stress affects your well-being.

RESILIENCE STRENGTHENING

Step 1: Learn to understand stress and how it affects you.

Step 2: Take good care of yourself. We can't always predict stress and the outcome, but we are in control of how we care of ourselves mentally, physically, emotionally, and spiritually.

Step 3: Use evidence-based therapies that trigger the brain to release positive hormones to offset stress hormones.

Trauma Input

It's important to recognize the amount of trauma information that we unconsciously absorb throughout the day. Take an honest look at the amount of traumatic news you are exposed to through television, radio, and conversations and take steps to minimize that exposure by changing the channel.

- ❑ Does your day begin with the morning news? How many disturbing images, difficult stories, actual images of dead or maimed people you come across?
- ❑ At work, how many difficult stories do you hear outside your own client work?
- ❑ After work, do you listen to the news on the way home or watch it on TV at night?
- ❑ If you have a spouse who is also in the helping field, do you talk shop?

CREATE A TRAUMA FILTER

Our brain is hardwired to be empathetic. When listening, we often create mental images to help us follow the story line. You can be attentive and sympathetic without injecting yourself into your client's story. To understand it, it isn't necessary to picture it.

A trauma filter helps our brain maintain control over empathy by filtering incoming data from the story.

- ✓ **Listen to client's story without visualizing it.** Imagine the trauma happening on a movie screen to distance yourself from the emotional impact.
- ✓ **Maintain a calm sense of detachment.** By sitting close to your client, mirroring his or her gestures and facial expressions, you come to feel nearly what your client is feeling. To be of any help, one person, however sympathetic to the plight of the other, needs to maintain a sense of calm detachment.
- ✓ **Put a physical barrier between you and your client** such as a stack of books, a desk, or a short floral bouquet.
- ✓ **Do you have your own shadow ACE** (adverse childhood experience) or that of someone you love that might be a hidden emotional impact? If so, resolve to seek therapy to reconciliate it. This will prevent it from looming again in your work.

TIP

When working with a client, maintain awareness of your body's sensations and expressions. Check yourself:

- ❑ **Are you taking shallow breaths?**
- ❑ **Is your pulse rapid?**
- ❑ **Are you leaning into your client's bubble?**

Debriefing

Debriefing is an organized, confidential group discussion for those who experience a traumatic event or an emotionally charged situation such as preparing a funeral for a child or the victim of a sensationalized crime.

Originating in the military years earlier, the first psychological debriefing model was officially developed in 1974 to provide quick intervention for those responding to psychological trauma. Now used around the world, debriefings provide a safe and secure environment for both professional and lay staff to process emotions associated with the event, and provide a supportive atmosphere.

Because the wealth of a company is built on the health of its employees, debriefings invite staff to release emotional steam and help set the tone that pulling together is a team effort that benefits everyone.

DEBRIEFING GOALS

- Mitigate emotional stress
- Reduce the impact of an upsetting event
- Facilitate normalization of work
- Serve as a forum for stress education
- Identify external coping resources

Studies show that staff who undergo debriefing in the workplace within a 72-hour period experience less short- and long-term psychological trauma. (Mitchell, 1988; Young, 1994).

TIP

If your organization isn't familiar with how to facilitate a debriefing, call International Grief Institute for assistance or consider becoming a Certified Debriefing Specialist™.

Relationships

Nourishment is life sustaining. We eat nutritious foods to fuel our bodies. We engage in activities to nourish the soul. We volunteer time and resources to nourish those around us. Yet we often neglect to develop nourishing relationships—an essential element of happy lives.

It's important to find friends with whom we can share stories and express ourselves freely without judgement. Seek those who settle for less than perfection and make allowance for human weaknesses. Those types of friendships are fulfilling and rewarding for everyone, and can last for life.

Because loving bonds come in a variety of flavors, look for healthy friendships in a variety of places.

TIPS TO GOOD RELATIONSHIPS:

- Be authentic. Honesty is a cornerstone.
- Be one another's cheerleader. Inspire.
- Listen. Avoid starting any sentence with "You should . . . "
- Cultivate joyful memories together.
- Give without expectations.
- Protect confidentiality.
- Love yourself first.

In today's busy world, it might feel challenging—stressful even—to find time to truly prioritize a good relationship. Many of us have a group of people in our lives who we value deeply.

Nurturing those relationships don't take immense effort, time or planning. In reality, it's the little things that count.

NURTURE A RELATIONSHIP YOU VALUE

- Confide in your friend something your struggling with.
- Text a warm memory to make him or her laugh.
- Plan an outing together.
- Send a "just because" card.
- Send a care package.
- Share something new in your life.
- Be a good listener – the best gift of all.

BOUNDARY EXERCISE

(for the difficult people in your life)

1. **Close your eyes. Envision yourself on a stage.**
2. **Where are you on that stage? Left, right, front or back?**
3. **Now envision someone in your life who drains the energy from you. Pluck him or her from thin air and place them on your stage. Where do they land in relation to you? How does your body react?**
4. **Notice what s/he is doing. Laughing? Talking? Criticizing you?**
5. **Envision a glass dome going down around that person, keeping their energy contained.**
6. **How do you feel now?**

Active optimism

> **KEYNOTE**
>
> Active optimism is the backbone of resilience.

The backbone of resilience, optimism is the tendency to take the most positive view and expect the best outcome. The ability to persevere during difficult times makes optimists naturally more resilient than pessimists.

Active optimism is a set of simple skills that train an optimist lens through challenging times.

Passive optimists hope things will turn out well and believe that they will. But those who merely hope and believe are surrendering control of their circumstances to someone or something else. Active optimists, on the other hand, act in a way that increases the likelihood that things will indeed turn out well.

ACTIVE OPTIMISM	PASSIVE OPTIMISM
♦ Takes most positive view	♦ Hopes things will turn out well
♦ Expects best outcome	♦ Surrenders control to something else
♦ Acts in a way that increases the likelihood of a positive outcome	♦ Can see problems as chronic rather than short-lived
♦ More likely to persevere	♦ Can see problems as malignant
♦ Believes they can make a difference	♦ Tries to control things outside their control (like other people)
♦ Believes problems are short-lived	
♦ Believes problems are non-malignant	
♦ Can successfully differentiate between what they can and can't control	
♦ Focus their energy on things they can control	

Because the brain is built with a greater sensitivity to unpleasant news, a protective mechanism to make sure you don't miss potential threats, it's been estimated that 80% of people are born with a bias for negativity. The good news is that you can retrain your brain—neuroplasticity is key.

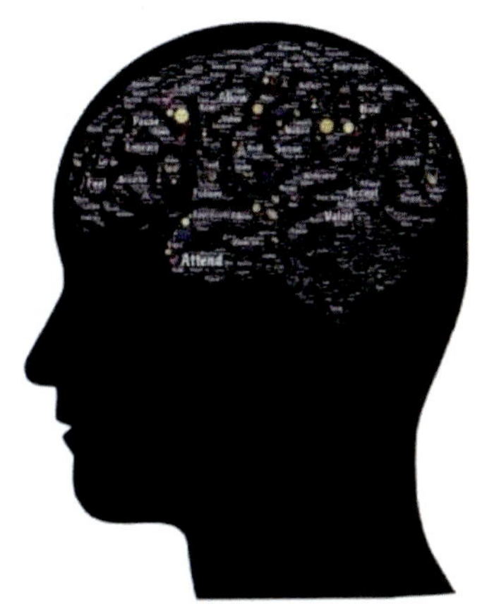

NEUROPLASTICITY

Neuroplasticity is the brain's ability to rewire. Because the brain is like a muscle, repetition is key to changing your brain via neuroplasticity. Not only can the brain rewire following a traumatic brain injury, with practice, it is possible to change dysfunctional thinking patterns and develop new mindsets.

The more you do something, the more the pattern is hardwired into the neurofabric of the brain. The brain can't differentiate between negative and positive. The more you worry, the better you become at worrying. The more you think optimistically, the more optimistic you become.

KEYNOTE

The human brain is like a muscle. It grows stronger with use, stronger yet with challenge, and weaker from inactivity.

COGNITIVE REAPPRAISAL

Because the brain is malleable until about age 70, the brain can be trained to be more positive. Cognitive reappraisal trains the person to focus on the positive rather than the negative.

Consider this—we hinder ourselves by believing adverse events cause us to be stressed or anxious. A traffic jam doesn't have to cause you to be stressed or fearful, rather it is your belief. What you say to yourself greatly affects the ultimate consequence.

An example of reinterpretation is the empty Reese's cardboard. "This is not an empty package. It's a reminder to get more."

We try sometimes to control things that are outside our control and risk our happiness on the outside events going on in the world around us. How disabling could that be? Very!

We cannot control everything in the world but we can control how we react to those events. Dispute negative beliefs, and replace them with positive, constructive interpretations. Failing isn't the end of the story, just the end of a chapter. As one chapter closes, the next one opens. Sometimes, failing allows us to focus on things we might not have noticed before.

This is a classic example of cognitive reinterpretation. There is a self-fulfilling prophecy that says, "If people define situations as real, they are real in their consequences."

Thus, expectations matter. If you believe you will fail at something, the chances of your failure are enhanced. If you think you will succeed, the chances improve dramatically because you dismiss failure, you try harder. You're using tenacity to be successful.

Self-efficacy is the belief that one will be successful at things to which they apply themselves. If you think you won't make a sports team, you won't try out for it, and it becomes a self-fulfilling prophecy.

KEYNOTE

Are your thought patterns self-hindering or self-aiding?

TIPS

- Tenacity is an important predictor of success.
- Observing others who are successful builds confidence vicariously.
- When facing very large challenges, break them down into "swiss cheese." Bite-size challenges.
- Self-control influences self-efficacy. Learning to control impulses and emotions, especially under stress, can convey a confidence that translates into proactive resilience.

Physical Exercise

The wisdom of the body dictates that physical exercise is a physical release of emotional stress. It is the most effective way of ventilating stress in a health-promoting manner. One study showed that after four months, exercise reduced depression more effectively than Zoloft (Archives of Internal Medicine, 1999). The failure to exercise after stressful experiences can lead to a wide variety of anxiety or stress-related diseases, called hypokinetic diseases (Kraus and Raab, 1961).

HOW IT HELPS

- Exercise increases cognition and neuroplasticity.
- Exercise increases steroid reserves to counter stress.
- Exercise reduces anxiety, improves learning through increased neuroplasticity, and improves sense of self-efficacy and self-control.
- Without exercising, caloric restriction ranges from 50 to 70% efficiency. Adding exercise increases dietary efficiency to 95% efficiency.

Nutrition

Where exercise strengthens resilience, nutrition fuels resilience. "You are what you eat." Certain foods can assist with resilience.

GOOD FOODS:

- Food such as chocolate, peanut butter, and red wine may have health promoting effects because of the antioxidants that stabilize free radicals that can damage cells.
- Plant-based foods such as fruits, nuts and berries contain 5x to 35x more antioxidant content that animal-based food. Herbs, coffee, tea and chocolate also have particularly high antioxidant content.
- Red wine is a good source of polyphenol antioxidants, but studies show no increased effectiveness beyond 1 glass per day.
- Good liquids for the body are water, tomato juice (contains lycopene), cranberry juice (possible anti-bacterial properties), chamomile tea can reduce anxiety, orange juice (antioxidant).
- One drink more than any other may protect nerve cells: green tea, which contains catechins, an anti-oxidant that prevents neurons from dying when exposed to amyloid, a toxicprotein.

DANGER FOODS:

- Energy drinks typically increase neurotransmitters of adrenaline, which can potentially increase post-traumatic stress.
- Caffeine consumption in excess of 300 mg/day can cause anxiety, panic and rebound fatigue.
- Sugar can cause rebound fatigue from uneven glucose.

KEYNOTE

The half-life of caffeine is 5 hours. A coffee at noon means that 50% of that caffeine is still in your system at 5 pm, and 50% of that is still in your system at 10 pm.

Rest & Relaxation

According to the American Academy of Sleep Medicine (2010), adults require 7 hours of sleep per night. During sleep, the brain cleanses itself of waste products. If you miss sleep, the cleansing process is incomplete. The risk of errors and accidents increase by 13% for 10-hour shifts and 28% for 12-hour shifts (NIOSH, 2014).

OPTIONS TO MAKE UP FOR LOST SLEEP:

- Power naps: The brain is wired to nap in the afternoon. Twenty to thirty minutes can provide 2-3 hours of further productivity. KEY: Do not enter REM state (dream state).
- Relax: Fifteen to twenty minutes a day of mindfulness, meditation, prayer, yoga, muscle relaxation, imagery, or biofeedback (hypometabolic state) can be restorative, and may instill a form of immunity to stress (Harvard Medical School, 1975) by creating a buffering effect at the neuron level.

KEYNOTE

When measured against cognitive metrics—how well one thinks and solves problems—sleep deprivation is as impairing as alcohol intoxication.

- **17 hours** without sleep is equivalent to 0.08% blood alcohol level.
- **24 hours** without sleep is equivalent to 0.10% blood alcohol level.

MINDFULNESS

Mindfulness encompasses two key ingredients: awareness and acceptance. Awareness is the knowledge and ability to focus attention on one's inner processes and experiences, such as the experience of the present moment. Acceptance is the ability to observe and accept—rather than judge or avoid—those streams of thought.

A person's experience of time tends to be subjective and heavily influenced by their emotional state. Fears and insecurities about the past and the future can make it difficult to fully appreciate the present. The key is learning how to pay attention.

Mindfulness can take place through meditation sessions or smaller moments throughout the day. To cultivate a state of mindfulness, you can begin by sitting down and taking deep breaths. Focus on each breath and the sensations of the moment, such as sounds, scents, the temperature, and the feeling of air passing in and out of the body. Shift your attention, then, to the thoughts and emotions that you're experiencing. Allow each thought to exist without judging it or ascribing negativity to it. Sit with those thoughts. The experience may evoke a strong emotional reaction. Exploring that response can be an opportunity to address or resolve underlying challenges.

To cultivate awareness, observe your thoughts and emotions and explore why those specific ideas might be surfacing. To cultivate acceptance, avoid judging or pushing away unpleasant thoughts. Emotions are natural and everyone has them—acknowledging them can help you understand yourself better and move forward.

Mindfulness is frequently used in meditation and certain kinds of therapy. Its benefits include lowering stress levels, reducing harmful ruminating, and protecting against depression and anxiety.

Review studies suggest that mindfulness-based interventions can help reduce anxiety, depression, and pain. Mindfulness encompasses awareness and acceptance, which can help people understand and cope with uncomfortable emotions, allowing them to gain control and relief.

To cultivate these skills:

- Concentrate on breathing to lengthen and deepen your breaths.
- Foster an awareness of the five senses.
- Notice your thoughts and feelings, and practice curiosity and self-compassion.

RESTORE & RECHARGE

- ❑ **Exercise 30 minutes a day 3x per week**
- ❑ **Don't increase caffeine to increase energy**
- ❑ **Sleep at least 7 hours per night**
- ❑ **Take a power nap when tired, but not within 4 hours of sleep**
- ❑ **Don't use alcohol to help fall asleep**
- ❑ **Practice relaxation 10 minutes a day 4x per week**

Summary

Charles Darwin said, "The single best predictor of resilience in the wake of adversity is the support of others." So while the best protection against compassion fatigue is strengthening and fueling inner resilience, our resilience also comes from being connected to those around us as well as the connection we foster with our own mind, body and heart.

When finding yourself struggling with symptoms of compassion fatigue, use the suggestions in this chapter coupled with the Resilience Rx handouts to strengthen and protect against compassion fatigue and career burnout. Most important, reach out to those around you for support. They have an invested interest in YOU.

You can't pour from an empty cup, nor would they want you to.

QUOTE

If you don't heal what hurts you, you'll bleed on the people who didn't cut you.

-MATT OMYANCIC, SWAT

We live in a time when science is validating what humans have known throughout the ages: that compassion is not a luxury; it is a necessity for our well-being, resilience, and survival.

-JOAN HALIFAX

SECTION THREE
Resources

iCare Aftercare™ offers a suite of quality turnkey solutions including easy online solutions, mailing programs, email programs, prepackaged workshops and more, all designed to help you build relationships and stay engaged with your families and communities.

Build a new aftercare program or augment your existing one using the iCare™ advantage of cost-effective solutions. Each product is available on the iCare Aftercare™ website at www.iCareGriefSupport.com.

NATIONAL RESOURCES

INTERNATIONAL GRIEF INSTITUTE

A collection of courses, certifications, turnkey products, resources, and more.
www.Internationalgriefinstitute.com

ICARE GRIEF SUPPORT

Full circle programs for the funeral and bereavement industry.
www.icaregriefsupport.com

GRIEF DIARIES

A vast collection of stories about surviving loss.
griefdiaries.com

WHEN YOU LOSE SOMEONE

A healing connection for all.
www.whenyoulosesomeone.com

ELLIES WAY

A nonprofit organization serving bereaved parents, grandparents and siblings.
www.elliesway.org

OUTSIDE WALLS

Resources and a ministry blog by Rev. Roland H. Johnson III.
www.outsidewalls.org

WIDOWLUTION

An organization dedicated to supporting widows.
widowlution.com

THE WIDOWERS SUPPORT NETWORK

An organization dedicated to helping widowers heal.
widowerssupportnetwork.com

OPEN TO HOPE

A nonprofit organization dedicated to helping people find hope after loss.
www.OpentoHope.com

NATIONAL ALLIANCE FOR GRIEVING CHILDREN

A nonprofit organization dedicated to serving bereaved children.
childrengrieve.org

TAPS

A nonprofit organization dedicated to helping families who lost a military member.
www.taps.org

MISS FOUNDATION

An organization dedicated to supporting people after loss.
missfoundation.org

SOARING SPIRITS INTERNATIONAL

An organization dedicated to supporting widows.
www.soaringspirits.org

LITERATURE & BOOKS

RESILIENCE RX™ – ONE SHEETS

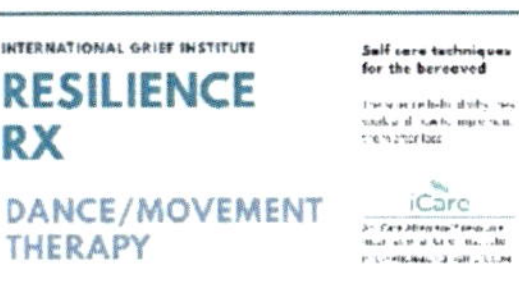

Resilience Rx™ promotes evidence-based self-help techniques and positive coping strategies that support mourners through loss. Each one-sheet is a snapshot of the science behind the technique and how to implement it after loss.

Sold in packs of 10. Size 8.5x11"

1. Chromotherapy
2. Dance/Movement Therapy
3. Forest Therapy
4. Hug Therapy
5. Laugh Therapy
6. Sensorial Therapy
7. Holiday Tips
8. Insomnia after loss

P07 | $15/10-PACK | ICAREGRIEFSUPPORT.COM/RESILIENCE

ICARE PLANNING GUIDE

Filled with helpful prompts, the iCare™ Planning Guide is an easy-to-do form-based guide that helps clients decide and document their own funeral wishes. Measures 8.5 x 11, 22 pages. Sold in packs of 10.

$49/PACK | ICAREGRIEFSUPPORT.COM/PLANNING

COMMUNITY-BASED ICARE SUPPORT GROUP

Everything you need to start and lead a community-based grief support group. Leader Manual is designed for repeat use. Chapter Workbooks are for participants to keep and use.

INTERNATIONALGRIEFINSTITUTE.COM/CHAPTERS

CHRIST-BASED ICARE SUPPORT GROUP

For church or communities, everything you need to start and lead a Christ-based grief support group. Facilitator Manual is designed for repeat use. Participant Workbooks are for participants to keep and use.

INTERNATIONALGRIEFINSTITUTE.COM/CHAPTERS

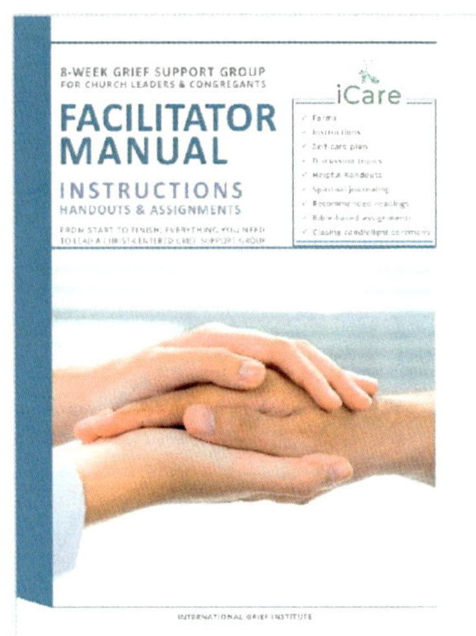

ONLINE SOLUTIONS

ICARE™ LIBRARY

A comprehensive collection of over 150 topics, articles and evidence-based grief support resources available to your families 24/7. Seamless integration with your website.

$99 MONTHLY SUBSCRIPTION | ICARELIBRARY.COM/DEMO

ICARE™ GRIEF SUPPORT WEB PORTAL

Provide your families with the iCare™ suite of aftercare resources available 24/7 through our easy iCare™ grief support web portal. Includes books, printables, videos and more.

D01 | $49 MONTHLY SUBSCRIPTION | ICAREGRIEFSUPPORT.COM/ICAREDEMO

CUSTOM GRIEF SUPPORT WEB PORTAL

Hotlink the iCare™ suite of aftercare resources with a custom URL right to your website for your community to access 24/7. Maintained by iCare.

D02 | $69 MONTHLY SUBSCRIPTION | ICAREGRIEFSUPPORT.COM/DEMO

ICARE™ KEYCARDS

Include an iCare™ keycard in your family's at time of need packet to give your families unlimited access to all the iCare™ grief support resources they'll find helpful that first year and beyond.

P01 | $10 EACH | ICAREGRIEFSUPPORT.COM/ICAREKEYS

CUSTOM KEYCARDS

Include a keycard branded with your logo in your family's at time of need packet to give your families unlimited access to all the iCare™ grief support resources through your custom URL.

P02 | $15 EACH | ICAREGRIEFSUPPORT.COM/CUSTOMKEYS

VIRTUAL SUPPORT GROUPS

Support groups are important, but many organizations don't have the time or staff to host them. iCare™ can help through our 6-week virtual support groups just for your families. Hosted by you, facilitated by IGI.

D03 | $540 PER 6-WEEK PROGRAM | ICAREGRIEFSUPPORT.COM/GROUPS

MAILING PROGRAMS

RESILIENCE RX™ MAILING PROGRAM

The Resilience Rx™ mailing program sends 7 easy-to-read handouts of evidence-based healing modalities to your families at appropriate intervals throughout the year. Fulfilled by iCare via private label with your return address.

P06 | $20 PER SET | ICAREGRIEFSUPPORT.COM/RXMAILING

ICARE BOOKLETS MAILING PROGRAM

The iCare Series offers easy reading and helpful support through the first year. The books are designed to be read at 1, 3, 6 and 11 months during the first year of grief, yet are helpful any time. Fulfilled by iCare via private label with your return address.

P05 | $24 PER SET | ICAREGRIEFSUPPORT.COM/BOOKLETS

REMEMBRANCE CARDS MAILING PROGRAM

The iCare remembrance cards consist of 4 cards that are sent at appropriate intervals during the first year of grief. Fulfilled by iCare via private label with your return address.

P03 | $20 PER SET | ICAREGRIEFSUPPORT.COM/CARDS

PRENEED MAILING PROGRAM

The iCare preneed mailing program consists of 6 mailings in total, including 3 letters, an anniversary card, a family care survey, and a holiday card. Fulfilled by iCare via private label with your return address.

P04 | $15 | ICAREGRIEFSUPPORT.COM/PRENEEDMAILING

ICARE NEWSLETTER EMAIL PROGRAM

Have the monthly iCare newsletter sent via email to your families. Each newsletter features helpful tips and information to support them as they adjust to life after loss including preplanning information. Price includes unlimited number of emails. Fulfilled by iCare.

D04 | $29/MONTHLY SUBSCRIPTION | ICAREGRIEFSUPPORT.COM/NEWSLETTER01

CUSTOM NEWSLETTER EMAIL PROGRAM

Have a custom monthly newsletter sent via email to your families. Each newsletter branded with your organization features helpful tips and information to support them as the adjust to life after loss including preplanning information. Fulfilled by iCare.

D05 | $39/MONTHLY SUBSCRIPTION | icaregriefsupport.com/newsletter2

WORKSHOPS

RESILIENCE RX™

AN INTERACTIVE PRESENTATION

One of the biggest challenges of coping with grief stress is taking care of yourself. Resiliency Rx™ explains 10 self-care techniques, the evidence-based science behind why they work, and how to implement them in everyday life. Audiences will learn experiential exercises that relieve stress, process emotions, and cope with adversity by keeping their mind and body healthy. Price includes PowerPoint presentation and teacher's manual PDF. Student manuals sold separately, $5/ea, sold in sets of 10.

AUDIENCES LEARN:

- The complementary roles of self-care and resilience
- Evidence-based science that supports self-care and wellness
- Experiential exercises that relieve stress and help process emotions

D07 | $99 | ICAREGRIEFSUPPORT.COM/WORKSHOPS

HOLDING THE SACRED SPACE

AN INFORMATIVE PRESENTATION FOR FAMILY & FRIENDS OF THE BEREAVED

Holding the Sacred Space is a 90-minute presentation for family and friends who want to support someone in mourning. The presentation explains the "grief dance," and offers tools to help everyone survive the turbulence. Audiences will learn how to meet the bereaved on their level, caregiving pitfalls to avoid, the power of loving actions, and what to expect along the way. Handouts included. Price includes PowerPoint presentation and teacher's manual PDF. Student manuals sold separately, $5/ea, sold in sets of 10.

AUDIENCES LEARN:

- Different types of grief
- How to meet the griever on their level
- The role of sympathy and empathy
- To understand and handle triggers
- Potential red flags
- Caregiving pitfalls to avoid
- The importance of self care
- What to expect along the way

D06 | $99 | ICAREGRIEFSUPPORT.COM/WORKSHOPS

HOLIDAY HUGS PROGRAM

The HUGS program—Holiday Understanding Grief Support—is a successful interactive program that provides comfort and support during one of the hardest times of the year. Hosted by you, facilitated by IGI.

- Workshop to help cope with the holidays
- Sharing circle
- Candlelighting ceremony including candles and music

D08 | $1,200 + TRAVEL | INTERNATIONALGRIEFINSTITUTE.COM/HUGS

EVENTS

THE GRIEF CRUISES

www.TheGriefCruises.com

Join us for the trip of a lifetime and leave with a lifetime of hope.

A grief cruise is more than sharing tears and precious memories. It's filled with special moments, inspirational workshops, and new friendships that will last for life.

Seven days of respite, healing and hope, now in its fourth year of sailing, **The Grief Cruise** is a journey aboard an award-winning Royal Caribbean cruise ship.

Offering all the amenities of a 5-star cruise, The Grief Cruise features presenters, workshops, a memorial walk, creative activities and an optional burial at sea. Go for the trip of a lifetime and leave with a lifetime of hope.

"So much compassion, overall one of the greatest and most helpful 7 days I have ever experienced in my entire life."
-Anna

"You gave me my first week of peace in 7 years."
–Jane

"I lost my 17-year-old daughter to suicide 2 years ago. The cruise has been very healing."
–Lisa

"What a great way to heal. The trip was fabulous and the seminars were small enough to connect and share experiences. The presenters were so sweet and gave excellent advice."
-Melanie

GRIEF DIARIES AWARD-WINNING ANTHOLOGY SERIES

GRIEF DIARIES: SURVIVING LOSS OF A CHILD

Surviving Loss of a Child shares the poignant journeys of 22 women as they search for healing and hope after losing a child. Exploring how each mother faced a journey they couldn't fathom, **Surviving Loss of a Child** offers comfort and hope and is a reminder to others who find themselves facing the same journey that they can survive. Foreword by Grieving Men's R. Glenn Kelly.

$16.95 | ISBN: 978-1944328009
shop.alybluemedia.com

GRIEF DIARIES: THROUGH THE EYES OF A WIDOW

Through the Eyes of a Widow is a collection of tender stories by widows as they learned to adapt after losing her husband. Each shares the challenges, where she found the most help, and the hope she found along the way.

$16.95 | ISBN: 978-1944328641
shop.alybluemedia.com

GRIEF DIARIES: SURVIVING LOSS OF A SPOUSE

Surviving Loss of a Spouse features the poignant journeys of 15 men and women as they move through the aftermath of losing a husband or wife. Each narration offers a firsthand account of how each widow and widower faced the funeral, handled his or her spousal belongings, navigated the year of firsts, and how each fought to find hope in the aftermath. Foreword by award-winning playwright Carol Scibelli, author of Poor Widow Me.

MSRP $14.95 | ISBN: 978-1944328016
shop.alybluemedia.com

GRIEF DIARIES: SURVIVING LOSS OF A PARENT

Whether one loses a parent in the natural order of life or it occurs much earlier than expected, the emotional aftermath can challenge our fears, familial relations, and even our sense of self. **Surviving Loss of a Parent** offers 17 firsthand accounts that yields a powerful look at how such losses can influence every aspect of our life. Foreword by radio host and author Christine Duminiak.

$14.95 | ISBN: 978-1944328078
shop.alybluemedia.com

GRIEF DIARIES: SURVIVING LOSS OF A SIBLING

Losing a sibling is a heartbreak that leaves a hole in the fabric of every family. Facing a challenging journey that's often ignored cast into the shadows behind the bereaved parents, struggling through such emotions can be devastating lonely, **Surviving Loss of a Sibling** features the stories of 13 sisters and brothers as they fight to find the meaning of life without a sister or brother. Foreword by Benjamin Scott Allen.

$14.95 | ISBN: 978-1944328023

shop.alybluemedia.com

GRIEF DIARIES: THROUGH THE EYES OF MEN

Breaking the man code and offering readers an inside look into the hidden world of male grief, Through the Eyes of Men features the stories of 14 men of different ages who tackle the tender subject of male bereavement from the very moment their lives changed with a loved one's death. Foreword by Glen Lord, past president of the national board of directors of The Compassionate Friends.

$15.95 | ISBN: 978-1944328481
shop.alybluemedia.com

GRIEF DIARIES: SURVIVING LOSS BY SUICIDE

Three-time medalist, **Surviving Loss by Suicide** examines the aftermath of losing a loved one to suicide from the perspective of 12 different people. Voicing their thoughts and emotions through the funeral and beyond, each writer offers a candid look at a taboo journey. Foreword by award-winning author and suicide prevention advocate Emily Barnhardt.

$15.95 | ISBN: 978-1944328030
shop.alybluemedia.com

GRIEF DIARIES: SURVIVING LOSS BY OVERDOSE

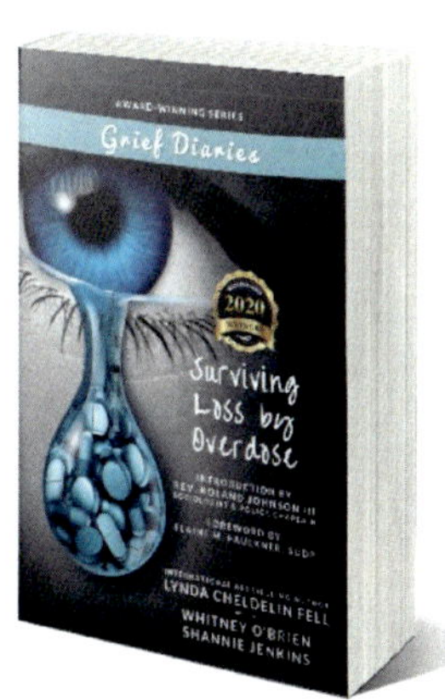

Book Excellence Awards Winner 2020, **Surviving Loss by Overdose** is a compilation of stories by 12 people who answered 18 questions about losing a loved one to overdose in hopes of raising awareness, educating, and inviting society to offer survivors the compassion that's often denied in a stigmatized death. Forward by Elaine M. Faulkner, SUDP.

$16.95 | ISBN: 978-1950712076
shop.alybluemedia.com

GRIEF DIARIES: SURVIVING SUDDEN LOSS

Surviving Sudden Loss is a collection of 14 stories by parents, spouses, siblings, children, and grandparents who share their own personal insight into the hidden and often unspoken challenges of unexpectedly losing a loved one, including the emotional, mental, physical and social shifts they're forced to reckon with in the aftermath. With poignant narration, each writer shares the truth of their loss, where they found the most support, and how they rebuilt their lives in the aftermath. Coauthored by Maryann Mueller.

MSRP $18.95 | CHURCH PRICE $9.00/ea | ISBN: 978-1944328894
shop.alybluemedia.com

GRIEF DIARIES: SURVIVING LOSS BY CANCER

Surviving Loss by Cancer offers inspiring true stories about caring for a loved one with cancer all the way through to their final breath, and beyond. Filled with compassion and understanding, the collection of stories serve as a life raft in the storm of emotions, and offer readers hope, strength, courage after losing a loved one to cancer. Foreword by hospice director Dana Brothers.

$15.95 | ISBN: 978-1944328818
shop.alybluemedia.com

GRIEF DIARIES: SURVIVING LOSS BY IMPAIRED DRIVING

A silver medalist in the 2016 USA Best Book Awards, **Loss by Impaired Driving** examines the journeys of 17 men and women who lost one or more loved ones to a drunk, drugged or impaired driver. A must read for young, new drivers and for AA groups. Foreword by Candace Lightner, founder of MADD.

$15.95 | ISBN: 978-1944328269
shop.alybluemedia.com

GRIEF DIARIES: SURVIVING LOSS BY HOMICIDE

Surviving Loss by Homicide shares personal accounts of coping with a violent tragedy, and sheds insight into the strength needed to stay afloat in the aftermath of intense heartache and rollercoaster of emotions ranging from shock, anger, sadness and disbelief to healing and hope. Foreword by radio host Lady Justice.

$15.95 | ISBN: 978-1944328146
shop.alybluemedia.com

For a full listing of Grief Diaries titles, visit www.AlyBlueMedia.com.

ACKNOWLEDGEMENTS

She who heals others heals herself.

LYNDA CHELDELIN FELL

LYNDA CHELDELIN FELL is founding partner of the International Grief Institute and international bestselling author of over 35 books including the award winning Grief Diaries series. A former firefighter/EMT and a bereaved mother since 2009, Cheldelin Fell has a background in trauma, grief, and is certified in critical incident stress management. A popular keynote speaker and educator, she is a member of the continuing education faculty at Whatcom Community College where she teaches classes on resilience, managing grief in the workplace, and compassion fatigue. To research grief's impact on society, she has interviewed people around the world including societal figures such as Martin Luther King's daughter, and Heaven is For Real's Pastor Todd Burpo. She has earned seven national literary awards and six national advocacy award nominations for her work.

lynda@internationalgriefinstitute.com

LINDA FINDLAY has worked with grieving families for over 30 years. After losing her daughter in 1989, she started a resource and referral service for grieving families. Soon after she began providing personalized aftercare solutions for hundreds of funeral homes across the nation. Linda is now an aftercare specialist who has created, facilitated, and coordinated hundreds of workshops, services, and support groups. A Christian lay counselor, Linda's highest honor is to enter people's lives and help make a difference. To date, Lin has supported over 158,000 people on behalf of funeral homes across North America.

linda@internationalgriefinstitute.com

PUBLISHED BY ALYBLUE MEDIA
www.AlyBlueMedia.com

Made in the USA
Columbia, SC
14 November 2021